DOWNSIZING

How to get big gains from smaller computer systems

DOWNSIZING

How to get big gains from smaller computer systems

Richard H. Baker

McGraw-Hill, Inc.

New York   St. Louis   San Francisco   Auckland   Bogotá   Caracas
Lisbon   London   Madrid   Mexico City   Milan   Montreal   New Delhi
Paris   San Juan   São Paulo   Singapore   Sydney   Tokyo   Toronto

FIRST EDITION
FIRST PRINTING

© 1992 by **McGraw-Hill, Inc.**

Library of Congress Cataloging-in-Publication Data

Baker, Richard H.
    Downsizing : how to get big gains from smaller computer systems /
by Richard H. Baker.
        p. cm.
    Includes index.
    ISBN 0-07-004563-1 (H)   ISBN 0-07-004564-X (P)
    1. Microcomputers.   I. Title.
QA76.5.B24   1992
651.8′416—dc20   92-2701
                                                                      CIP

For information about other McGraw-Hill materials, call
1-800-2-MCGRAW in the U.S. In other countries call your nearest
McGraw-Hill office.

Sponsoring Editor: Jerry Papke
Book Editor: William Schwartz
Managing Editor: Sandra L. Johnson
Director of Production: Katherine G. Brown
Series Design: Jaclyn J. Boone
Cover and Photo Credit: Jeheber & Peace, Inc.   WT2

Contents

Introduction

The personal computer revolution has been underway for more than a decade now. Desktop devices have been claiming more and more territory from the larger systems. Until recently, this process has been more or less unplanned, a type of guerrilla warfare typical of most revolutions in their early stages. The PCs simply moved in on the strength of their innate ability to serve their individual users.

Increasingly, though, the change is becoming deliberate, and the PCs are looking more and more like a regular army. Growing numbers of corporate uses are making the decision to downsize. Instead of running everything off a big-iron mainframe, these organizations are beginning to look at putting applications on PC-based platforms. Usually, though not always, they are moving to local area network (LAN) systems that incorporate PC LANs and client/server databases.

These companies see two main advantages to downsizing:

- Cost. The mathematics are deceptively simple. It's been well established that the most powerful PC-based systems can match some of their larger brethren in capacity and performance, at but a fraction of the cost.
- Flexibility. Users, the people who need information to play their roles in running the business, can gain immediate access to that information. Once they have it, a host of PC-based analysis, writing, and graphics tools can help them evaluate, report, and illustrate it. Not only can the users gain better access to the data they need, but they can make better use of it.

The typical company has a host of candidates for productive downsizing. Corporate mainframes continue to process many limited-use applications because when they were written many years ago, there were no personal computers on which to run them. These applications make ideal downsizing candidates. They can run on cheaper resources and leave mainframe resources for the larger-scale work that they do best. Also, many applications are rigid and unresponsive to their users' needs. These applications can profit from the friendlier interface of a PC.

Some drawbacks

If it sounds too good to be true, it is. Downsizing is not nearly as simple as just replacing an expensive old computer with inexpensive new ones. When it comes to downsizing, Murphy's Law is in full force and effect. If anything can go wrong, it will—particularly true of the worst-possible-moment proviso.

Until recently, in fact, conventional wisdom said that you should never entrust critical or high-volume applications to a PC network. The first LANs just didn't have the horsepower to handle complex applications. Even when networked into LANs, PCs were still personal computers. They made their users more productive in word processing or spreadsheets, as well as being a big help in supporting decisions. Still, you didn't quite want to risk the business on them.

Things are changing rapidly. The newest LANs and servers have industrial-strength capacity, with further increases in size and performance expected. Reliability and security, major LAN bugaboos, are rapidly being brought up to more-than-acceptable levels. These developments will make downsizing increasingly attractive.

Still, some of the old worries remain, along with some new considerations. Downsizing is not a plug-and-play application, any more than is any other form of business computing. As consultant Cheryl Currid puts it, "Nobody has come up with an easy-to-install, shrink-wrapped downsizing pack. Since all corporate shops are a little different, nobody has figured out how to develop a one-size-fits-all model. That makes it as much a creative process as a technical one."

Individual downsizers have to create their own systems. Along the way, such problems as these must be confronted:

- Hidden cost. The hardware to support a downsized application costs only a fraction of the same capacity in a larger system. Mass-market PC software is much less expensive as well. Even so, conversion costs can eat up much of the savings. In particular, nearly everyone, from systems programmers to data entry clerks, will probably have to be retrained. The technology and the tools are different. That means people need new kinds of knowledge and expertise.
- "Child support." As another consultant, Susan Spiner, puts it, "While most LAN technology has barely reached puberty, the manufacturers of LAN products have sold the customers on the idea that the products are mature, stable technology." As a result, customers require a high degree of support that they often don't get. Consider-

ations of security and reliability (main concerns of large-systems people) still work against downsizing. These considerations are particularly important because the term *mission critical* appears so often in discussions of what applications to downsize.

• Human factors. The most serious obstacles to successful downsizing are not technical. They involve the people who must live with the new system, including those who must give up the old. If yours is a typical downsizing experience, the human problems might be more troublesome than the technical ones.

What this means is that downsizing can save significant amounts of money while giving employees better, more productive access to corporate data. The downsizing project must be well planned, however, to keep from stumbling over the many obstacles that litter the path to success.

The purpose of this book is to help you achieve success while avoiding the pitfalls. It discusses such major topics as:

• Why downsize? What objectives to set, and how to reach them.

• Networks and other resources. A primer on networking for downsized environments.

• Database design and implementation. A guide to planning and implementing database applications, which are among the most common downsizing projects.

• Planning and implementing a downsizing project. How to maximize your chances for success.

• Dealing with human problems. Often, the most difficult problems are with people, not systems.

The object of this book is to help anyone, with or without technical expertise, who is considering the possibilities of downsizing. If you decide to take the downsizing plunge, this book does what it can to make the difference between a cannonball and a well-executed jackknife.

DOWNSIZING

How to get big gains from smaller computer systems

1
CHAPTER

Downsizing
What and why

Corporate America is using uncounted thousands of computer applications that have limited usefulness.

It's not that they're bad applications. On the contrary, many are vital to the organizations that use them. The problem is that many applications have fallen behind the expectations of modern users, the needs of modern organizations, and the potential of modern computing equipment. Some of these applications are the wrong size. Most were developed years ago, when personal computers, local area networks (LANs), and client/server databases had hardly been conceived, let alone made available on desktops throughout the organization. Thus, many applications were written for mainframes or minicomputers. And the choices were limited: You wrote these applications for large systems, or you didn't write them at all.

Many of these applications are now prime candidates for downsizing. By porting them over to smaller systems, particularly PCs and networks, organizations can make productive use of lower-cost computing power. Some organizations can give up their mainframes and minicomputers entirely. Others can save costly large-system capacity for applications that really need it. At the same time, downsizers can take advantage of the PC's friendlier and more efficient interfaces. User-friendliness is not the only issue. Ease of use makes employees more productive. Also, the people who need data in performing their jobs should not have to contend with the primitive interfaces characterizing large-system applications or penetrate elaborate security systems to use even noncritical applications.

What downsizing is

Downsizing is based on transfer of large-system applications to cheaper, more flexible networks. With downsizing a recent phenomenon, its full dimensions aren't always clear. The original definition still makes sense: *Downsizing* is the process of converting strategic applications to a distributed environment, using personal computers and local area networks.

This definition isn't the only possible one. Some people, particularly large-system professionals, point out that *any* move to a smaller system can be called downsizing. There need not be a PC or a LAN anywhere in sight. Midsized computers make excellent servers for many applications. Specialized users in fields like publishing or engineering may find graphic workstations better than PCs for their purposes.

To some extent, this definition reflects continuing skirmishes in the sad and costly class warfare between large-system and PC users. More importantly, the argument makes a key point: Successful downsizing does not require that you use, or avoid, any particular type of system, large or small.

It is more productive to think of downsizing in terms of the purposes it is intended to serve. As this chapter discusses later, organizations that downsize their systems have two main objectives: to save money and to give users better access to corporate information. A PC-based server usually meets the cost objective much better than a midsized or mainframe system. A PC is usually the best choice for access and flexibility—usually, but not always.

Though this book often discusses downsizing in terms of PCs and LANs, it is done only because they are the most likely choices, not the only possibilities.

Other perspectives

Sometimes downsizing actually is upgrading. Some 486-class PCs are now more powerful than the larger systems they replace. The company that installs a high-powered PC network often can upgrade its computing power.

You can also think if downsizing as *streamlining for competition.* The process makes the organization more flexible and responsive. In today's competitive market, flexibility and responsiveness could be more important than the lower cost and greater usability downsized applications can offer.

Second generation

Downsizing has also been described as an advanced application of computing's second generation. The first generation was characterized by traditional large systems and dumb terminals. The second generation uses distributed resources based on the microprocessors of PCs. The PC is at the center of this type of system. Everything else functions as an extension.

In this configuration, the PC network has reversed the traditional economies of scale. Conventional wisdom holds that a larger, centralized system ought to be more efficient. However, the LAN is usually much *less* expensive per unit of capacity than a large system.

This difference does not mean that either large systems or the people who run them will inevitably be replaced by PCs and networks. In a sense, downsizing should really be called *rightsizing*. That's not an evasive euphemism like the same term used to describe a personnel downsizing. The key to successful computer system downsizing really is to match the size of the system to the size of the job. For some applications, a large system is still the right size. But for others, PCs are adequate. In that case, putting these applications on larger systems is a waste of valuable resources.

The trend is down

Early in 1991, a survey sponsored by *PC Week* found that 57% of the nation's largest PC sites had done one of two things: Either they had shifted applications from mainframes or minis to LANs within the previous 18 months, or they planned to do so within the next 18 months. The survey covered more than 200 corporations, institutions, and government agencies, each having at least 250 PCs.

These figures don't mean the larger systems are being abandoned, with the move to PC LANs being accomplished at the expense of the mainframes and their support staffs. Rather, numerous firms keep running older applications on mainframes or minis while building more flexible, user-friendly applications on PC LANs. Also, some firms are setting up a front-end network of PCs as clients of a database server that continues to run on a large system.

Other survey results bear this out. Out of the 84 sites that had moved applications to smaller platforms, the reasons cited most often were easier access to data and greater flexibility in developing or modifying applications. Short-term cost cutting was important, but it wasn't the main incentive for moving to the LANs.

Parallel trends

Downsizing works in parallel with several other trends. Columnist William F. Zachmann has identified a related phenomenon he calls *upsizing*. This term refers to the widespread and growing trend to use personal computers for larger and more sophisticated applications. Upsizers are usually smaller organizations, or small departments, for whom the cost of computerization was previously out of sight. Now, relatively inexpensive PC technology lets them automate critical operational or decision-making tasks for the first time.

PARALLEL TRENDS

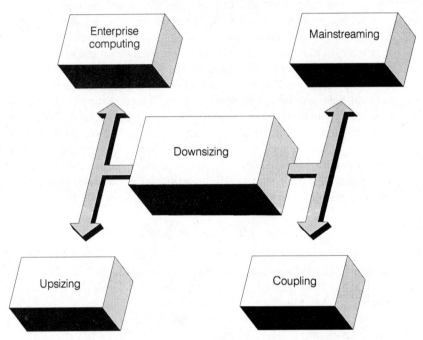

Downsizing is one of several related trends that is bringing computing onto the desktop and into closer relationships with both individuals and organizations.

Another trend is the closely-related phenomenon of *enterprise computing*. This term generally refers to the networking of individual PCs into more and larger networks, and even the networking of networks, with the object of sharing data throughout an entire organization. This development has been described as closing a gap between communication and data processing. Other commentators go further. What really is involved, they say, is a new definition of a computer system. The network itself is the system, and even a connected mainframe is only a subsystem.

Yet another development is the *mainstreaming* of information systems. This process has caused a lot of stress among systems professionals. Some people have resisted the fast-spreading idea that their value should be based on their contribution to the organization as a whole, not just their mastery of technology. They are used to a model in which the data processing organization was isolated—with its own career paths, its own issues and concerns, and often its own building. With the help of PCs, the data processing function now must become a central part of the organization's strategy.

A parallel development has been a closer relationship between people and information systems. At one time, computers primarily processed numerical data. Now, they respond to their desktop users by presenting the same kinds of information in words and pictures.

These movements differ in their starting points, but all are moving in the common direction of networked PCs serving entire organizations in new, more efficient ways.

Why downsize

Reduced cost is only one of several reasons to downsize. For many organizations, it might not be the best or most important reason. It is hardly unimportant, though, and it does have a place among the three best reasons to downsize:

- Reduce costs.
- Increase sales.
- Increase access to information.

WHY DOWNSIZE?

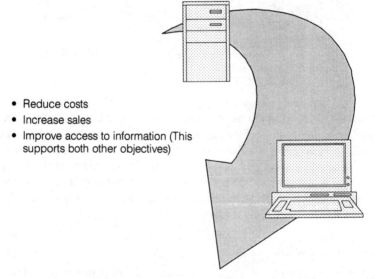

- Reduce costs
- Increase sales
- Improve access to information (This supports both other objectives)

There are three main reasons to downsize, but better access to information helps meet both the other objectives.

Cost reduction

The potential cost savings from downsizing come in two major areas:

- The costs of acquiring and maintaining equipment.
- Reduced personnel costs.

SOURCES OF COST SAVINGS

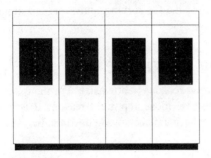

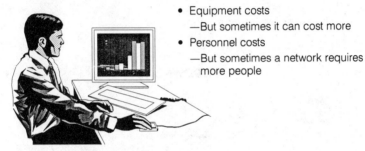

- Equipment costs
  —But sometimes it can cost more
- Personnel costs
  —But sometimes a network requires
  more people

Normally, downsizing reduces both equipment and personnel costs. Nevertheless, there are important exceptions.

In either case, unexpected expenses can cut sharply into the savings. Some PC/LAN installations cost only a fraction as much as the same processing capacity in a larger system. Even so, the cost of acquiring a new PC-based system can be substantial, particularly if you need a custom configuration or special equipment not available at mass market prices.

By the same token, smaller systems do not automatically require fewer people: Some actually require more. In any event, a distributed system always has significant management and maintenance costs.

Improving sales

For many organizations, improving sales is the best reason to downsize. One of the greatest values of a downsized system is that it can provide information *before the sale*. The typical sales management system is a historical record. It records what happened *after* the sale has been made or lost. It records the results, but it does nothing to help make the sale in the first place.

On the other hand, a sales representative who has immediate access to information can use it to help make more sales. For example, a customer might want a certain style or design. Is that in the current catalog, and is it available? A salesperson with immediate access to this information via a

- It supports the sales effort (By providing data in advance)
- It doesn't just record the sale

A readily accessible sales management system can provide useful information when it's needed to help make the sale.

desktop PC can immediately tell the customer what is available. If you can't meet the customer's specifications, perhaps the system can help search for alternatives. Without a PC, or some equally flexible means of access, a mainframe-based inventory and catalog system is rarely that readily available.

Better access

The previous example shows how better access to information can help improve sales. Employees have better access to data because you don't have to put everything in a large database. You can use a sales management program as a front end.

The improved access can also save system costs because the data can also be spread around less expensive PC memory. The lower system costs are offset to some extent by the increased costs of managing a distributed system.

Better access can have another healthy effect, too. As a business responds to the improved availability of information, it can streamline its organization, cultivate its ability to respond to changing business conditions, make better use of its resources, and respond more quickly to changes in the competitive situation.

Candidates for downsizing

When most organizations think of downsizing, they think first of database applications. These are often excellent candidates. Modern PC front ends and servers can match larger systems in performance, the SQL standard has become common to systems of all sizes, and PCs can give users new opportunities for interactive, creative use of the data. Even those bulky, transaction-oriented databases that properly should remain on large systems could benefit from better access via PC networks.

Databases are leading candidates for two main reasons. Usually, databases can readily be moved to downsized systems, and they often have a high degree of interactive use. Downsizing can not only save money, but the friendlier PC interface can promote more creative and productive uses of the data.

Among the database applications for which downsizing is often fruitful:

- Billing and invoicing.
- Maintaining customer lists, particularly in direct mail.
- Inventory and sales records.

Consider office systems

Office systems offer opportunities that are similar but less well recognized. Office systems tasks that once ran on minicomputers and other larger systems are being run on less expensive PC-based hardware. Existing systems are being downsized; new installations are being networked from the beginning.

Although office systems typically are designed to improve the productivity of individuals or small groups, many are centrally based and run on large host computers. A giant round of office automation preceded the PC revolution by a few years, fueled primarily by minicomputer-based word processing systems. Those systems and their close relatives are still in service. Knowledge workers and support staff members still use dumb terminals to connect with older applications. These systems are ripe for both downsizing and modernization. Typical office system conversions have included:

- Storing and tracking legal documents.
- Developing group documents.
- Filing and retrieving business records.

Why downsize office systems

The three main reasons to downsize an office system are:

- Improved control over the system.
- Cost savings for the organization.
- The creation of a distributed, cooperative, computing platform.

Many organizations have found that office systems that operate on smaller platforms allow greater control. In most applications, for instance, a PC has a quicker response time than a host computer. Fewer users are affected by other users' activity or by system maintenance operations. Operating from a smaller platform enables IS departments to provide better service to their users.

There is also the time-honored motive of saving money. As personal computers become increasingly more affordable, their power and capabilities increase as well. LAN technology lets users share expensive hardware and resources. Initially, the acquisition of PC workstations and network hardware and software usually requires a significant outlay of capital. However, after this outlay, adding new users simply means adding new workstations, a relatively inexpensive process.

When an office system is running in a downsized environment, cooperative processing can provide additional benefits to the long-term strategy of your organization. With cooperative processing, the PC becomes a front-end processor for the end-users' computing. PC software is designed to handle the user interface and data entry. The PCs' responsiveness and ease of use make these natural functions. When necessary, the PC still can extract data from a large-system server. The file server efficiently processes the data and passes the results back to the local processor. The processing on the server is reduced, as well as the communications traffic on the network.

Application development

This is a familiar exercise to many: Application development may qualify as the first widely used example of downsizing. Programmers, using PC versions of large-system languages, are able to write and test applications more quickly than if they waited on old-style batch processes. In its modern form, PC-based application development involves networks and databases as well.

A case in point is the CGI Group, a major Canadian consulting firm, which has been developing a suite of major database applications such as revenue accounting and labor distribution for a government agency. The agency ultimately will run these applications using a mainframe database from Computer Associates International (Garden City, NY). For prototyping, development, and testing, however CGI uses a PC version of the mainframe database, running on a 386-class database server. This server is the heart of a network that includes 19 PC workstations and a separate network server. A multi-user gateway ties this network to the client's mainframe.

This system lets the consulting firm develop and run applications on the PC network that, when finished, they can transfer to the client's large system. The PCs allow higher rates of productivity, including less time to compile and edit programs. Another advantage: The use of this network helps large-system programmers make the transition to a PC environment.

Making downsizing decisions

Downsizing has become a fashionable buzzword. Any organization considering downsizing must decide whether the organization would truly benefit from it. The alternative is simply to write off downsizing as a computerized fad, in the same league with the pet rock and the hula hoop. After that, come more decisions:

- What applications do you downsize?
- Onto what platforms do you downsize them?

THE BASIC DOWNSIZING QUESTIONS

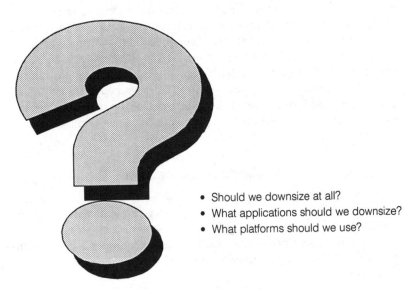

- Should we downsize at all?
- What applications should we downsize?
- What platforms should we use?

It all boils down to essentials like whether, what, and where.

Deciding whether it's for you

First, there is the basic question of whether to downsize at all. Often, an organization will reach this question when it finds its large system reaching the limits of its capacity. It appears feasible to invest in a PC network as an alternative to a much larger investment in the large system. But then what? Do you downsize everything and simply give up on the large system? Or, as many organizations have learned to do, do you try to gain capacity by offloading selected applications? Which applications, then, are downsized, which remain, and which are split between the large and networked systems?

The questions sprawl across the line that separates a healthy variety from a confusing overkill. Most downsizing decisions start with the general idea of moving an application from a large system to a PC network. Such a transfer isn't the only available hardware route. Alternatives include the Macintosh, Unix workstations—and even keeping the application on its present platform, using personal computers as workstations. Only one type of hardware is absolutely ruled out: the dumb terminal. Unlike a networked PC, such a terminal is merely an input/output device; it cannot process information.

The modern mainframe

Advocates of downsizing have sometimes preached that large systems are dinosaurs, soon to become extinct, as high-capacity, PC-based network servers take over—just what opponents of downsizing have often feared.

The mainframe is not dead, but is apparently evolving into a new role within a downsized environment. Though the best network servers can match larger systems in many measures of performance and capacity, they lack the sustained data throughput capabilities of even the smaller mainframes. Some large, heavily used mainframe programs could quickly overwhelm the data-handling capabilities of many LAN servers.

The real issue is how to incorporate the mainframe's processing capacity into an overall enterprise strategy centered on downsizing. A key role for the mainframe will be as a corporate data repository, consolidating all the information generated and used by the millions of PCs sitting on corporate desktops. Mainframes are evolving into that role. The ideal system for that type of service does not yet exist, but the newest designs are offering such network-sensitive features as these:

- Increased power. Network service places new demands on large systems, and manufacturers are expanding the capacities of their products. "The inventory of large systems in terms of power is still growing in excess of 30% per year," says a statement from IBM. This trend, expected to continue, means today's mainframes may soon be too small to meet the demands of tomorrow's downsized environment.
- Communication. The network-conscious mainframe can play a key role here. Ideally, it should create a seamless link between the desktop PC and the organization's large-system data repositories.
- Database management. If the mainframe is to evolve to serve as the data repository, it will need the ability to store increasing amounts of data and to provide more rapid access to it. Some recently developed systems feature new machine instructions designed to greatly speed up database manipulation.
- Security. The mainframe excels over the LAN in its ability to provide both physical and technical security, and is still the place for vital data you must absolutely protect from theft or corruption. New systems have been programmed to automatically monitor incoming data streams for viruses.
- Network management. The management of some networks will be a mainframe-sized task, particularly as local networks are connected with each other, and wide area networks become global.

REPORTS OF ITS DEATH:
Greatly exaggerated

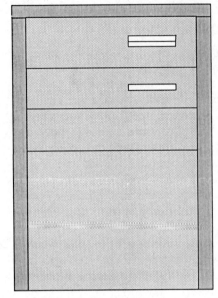

Adapted to network service, large systems still have valuable functions:

- Computing power
- Communication service
- Database management
- Security
- Network management

Downsizing often is less a matter of replacing larger systems than of putting them to newer, more efficient use.

Money isn't the only thing

There's no doubt that a downsized system is initially much less expensive than its larger counterpart—particularly true when you measure the cost in dollars per millions of instructions per second (MIPS). Based on its study of costs and trends, the Diebold Group has projected that soon a PC station will cost $100 per MIPS. Comparable performance on a mainframe will cost $15,000.

Nevertheless, the cost advantage is not as great as it might seem at first, and cost is not the only issue in a downsizing decision. There are many other questions to consider: reliability, flexibility, manageability, ease of integration, the retraining of users and IS professionals.

Downsizing and business strategy

There's another issue, too, that many don't recognize until they encounter it head-on. Downsizing may, and should, have a substantial effect on business strategy. Remember, downsizing is not just a cost-saving measure, but a way to improve an organization's competitive posture.

The best and most effective downsizing plan will, in effect, take the organization along with it. Uncounted numbers of companies have demonstrated that a well-planned downsizing program can help revamp the organization, realign responsibilities, and allow scarce resources to be devoted to other valuable purposes.

However, not every organization, or every application, is a candidate for downsizing. It would be folly to entrust a bank's account records or an airline's reservations to a small system. These mainframes process constant streams of transactions and maintain huge databases. Such big jobs call for big systems.

COST ISN'T THE ONLY FACTOR

Other things to consider:

- Reliability
- Flexibility
- Management
- Integration
- Training

Most of all, the effect on business strategy

Many downsizing projects start with the idea of saving money. In practice, other advantages often become more important.

There are many applications, though, in which downsizing can lower costs while improving the organization's efficiency and its ability to respond. This new efficiency can come from several factors:

- Integrating the business and its systems. One enduring characteristic of a large system is its remoteness from the people who require its services. The data you need just doesn't seem to be there precisely when you need it. Input is by carefully prescribed data entry screen. Output is by cartloads of striped paper.

    Downsize this application, and chances are it will become more responsive to the organization's needs. A downsized system can close the generation gap between today's business needs and traditional mainframe applications. The time needed to complete a project will then be measured in days instead of months. The increased productivity has advantages beyond the obvious: You now have the chance to try such new kinds of technology as image processing.

- Better engineering. The downsizing process provides a chance to reevaluate and redesign existing information systems, a process called reengineering. Determine how well they continue to support the organization in the pursuit of its goals. Look for ways to reshape the existing systems and make them work better, even when the reshaping doesn't involve downsizing.
- More options. Downsizing creates an open environment in which you can integrate the systems for a variety of vendors. A new vendor might turn out to be someone with an exciting new opportunity. A little competition between vendors is usually a good thing for the customer.
- Streamlined responsibilities. In downsized a environment, there are fewer specialists. The responsibility for the application is shared by programmers, analysts, managers, and users. In particular, it's easier to bring users into the process and, often for the first time, give them significant input into the design of the technology with which they work. Modern application development tools make it increasingly easier for users not only to express their own ideas, but to execute them.

THE STRATEGY OF DOWNSIZING

How new systems can boost efficiency:

- Getting the system closer to the organization
- Re-engineering existing systems
- Providing options and spurring competition
- Spreading responsibilities

Downsized systems can improve an organization's efficiency and responsiveness in ways that go beyond questions of first cost.

Downsizing as a management decision

There is one unavoidable caveat: Any downsizing project must have the support of senior management. That, of course, is a familiar litany for nearly any worthwhile organizational effort. When a major project is being undertaken, the people who run the company should know and approve.

More to the point where downsizing is concerned: Downsizing can have a significant effect on the organization's structure. The transition from a large-system environment to a PC network has a significant and immediate impact on the ways in which the organization does business—its form, methods, and competitive position, involving a host of management processes:

- Strategy. A more useful and flexible information system can vastly expand an organization's internal information processing ability. It often has such a great impact that management must reevaluate its business objectives and strategies to match. Better information also can both enable and require such changes as better service, delivery, and product quality, and even allow the organization to look into new markets.

- Finance. Even though PCs are much less expensive than large-system resources, an investment in downsizing is still going to be considerable—just how substantial depending on the organization's needs and operations. Senior management must be willing to stand behind the project financially, providing enough money not only to pay for the downsizing but to maximize its impact. A selling point: Not only can the organization expect to recoup its investment in a year or two, it will also enjoy reduced maintenance and development costs.

- Operations. The leading candidates for downsizing, particularly in the early stages, are applications with few users, but that consume large amounts of system resources. Be careful, though, not to confuse size with importance. Downsizing an unimportant application takes just as much money and effort as downsizing a critical one, and it will have a smaller payoff. A management perspective is needed to distinguish between applications important enough to justify downsizing, and those that might seem to be good candidates, but really are not worth the effort.

MANAGEMENT CONSIDERATIONS

- Capitalizing on new opportunities
- Reducing cost
- Improving operations

Downsizing is not just a technical operation. It has important consequences in the way the organization is managed.

Getting support

Because downsizing is still a new idea to many managers, it's easy for them to be unsure about some aspects of its performance. Managers will also naturally be concerned with such issues as responsiveness and security—the two being inherently contradictory. It's important to educate all levels of management about what downsizing can accomplish, and it's equally important to be realistic about its limitations.

Discussions with management should not present downsizing as a predominantly technical issue, but as a matter of business strategy. Show how the technical change can help the business perform better, and how it can open new competitive opportunities.

Don't stop talking when management finally approves the project. Keep the lines of communication open. Give management regular updates on the progress of the project. Be honest about the problems that you will encounter.

HOW TO GET MANAGEMENT SUPPORT

- Talk about opportunities
  —Not technology
- Address major concerns
  —Security
  —Responsiveness
- Don't stop talking
  —Keep the lines open

To get management's support, talk about the things management wants to hear.

Beware, however, of too many formal committees that must make too many formal reports to too many levels of management. Committees like these are the places where good ideas go to die. Use task forces when necessary to plan, communicate, and involve the affected employees. The basic rhythm of the project, however, should be based on time schedules and goals that you can use to measure your project.

Don't ignore the human factor, to which we devote an entire chapter. While IS professionals will no doubt play major roles in developing and implementing the plan, representatives of management and the using departments must be well represented as well. They are the experts on what they need in a downsized application, and on what they can accomplish with it.

The consultant's role

A consultant can be a valuable ally in this process. One of the consultant's great assets is that he or she can work without the pressures and distractions of running the organization. A consultant is also more free to stand back and examine those two important cliches, the long range and the big picture. In particular, a consultant can help you in these areas:

- Evaluating the need. That also includes recommending a solution. A consultant's fresh, outside perspective can help an organization make a thorough, objective evaluation of its situation and determine the project's goals—including assessment of the organization's needs for communication, support, and processing. The consultant's function also involves evaluating such criteria as response time, security, interaction with users, timeliness of data, access restrictions, and the organization's ability to support the system.

- Selecting the system components. A consultant can cut through the confusion of multiple platforms, networking systems, and other elements. One thing to watch: Be sure the consultant bases these decisions on what you need, not on what he or she may be in the business of selling.

- Overseeing a smooth transition. Downsizing presents an organization with many things to do at once. A consultant can help you keep things straight and juggle the many responsibilities, including those of technology, training, and keeping peace within the organization.

- Managing the process. While the downsizing process is going on, members of the organization will have more than their share of distractions. They will, after all, be trying to run a business. More fundamentally, managers distracted by their day-to-day responsibilities may neither see nor take advantage of the opportunities that technology has to offer. A consultant can help overcome distractions and inertia by educating managers on new approaches they can take and on how the downsized system can improve their competitive position.

- Shooting troubles. The move to a smaller hardware platform is not problem-free. For example, training users on the new products that run on the smaller computing platform can be harder than expected. The users must learn how to use PCs and LANs, and they usually must also learn to use new kinds of word processing software. Many organizations initially underestimate the enormous training requirements involved in the move.

WHAT A CONSULTANT CAN DO

- Evaluate the need and recommend solutions
- Select systems
- Oversee the transition
- Manage the process
- Offer a fresh perspective

Whoever performs these tasks, they are some of the most important in the process.

Downsizing as a financial decision

When most people think of downsizing, they think first of cost reduction. After looking at the cost of owning and maintaining their large systems, they scan the mail-order advertisements and see even high-powered PCs at a fraction of the cost. Downsizing can save money all right. It's obvious, of course, that you will not save the full price difference between the large system and the PC. There will naturally be many other costs. What is not obvious is that some of these costs are significant and well hidden.

The most deceptive part of any cost analysis has been the recent low cost of PCs. It's easy to set up a PC and a reasonable supply of software for well under $3,000. When you amortize this cost over several years, as most corporations do, the cost looks very affordable, particularly in comparison with the many-times-higher costs of large systems.

Even the per-unit cost is deceptive. The accompanying chart pegs the average per-station purchase price at $4,000. To be sure, the individual workstations are inexpensive. But for a downsized application, you probably will need at least one high-powered server that will not be nearly as inexpensive.

Your figures will vary, but for the sake of discussion the example given allows $80,000 for basic systems and software. That sum will cover 20 sta-

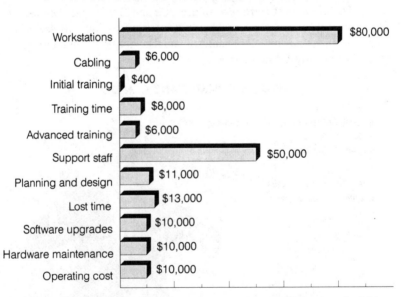

THE REAL COST OF A PC NETWORK
How 20 "low-cost" PCs can cost $10,220 each

Workstations	$80,000
Cabling	$6,000
Initial training	$400
Training time	$8,000
Advanced training	$6,000
Support staff	$50,000
Planning and design	$11,000
Lost time	$13,000
Software upgrades	$10,000
Hardware maintenance	$10,000
Operating cost	$10,000

PC networks are less costly than large systems, but not by as much as it might seem. This typical 20-node network could cost a total of $204,400.

tions at $3,000 each, plus an allowance of $20,000 for servers and other units whose cost exceeds the minimum, plus such vital accessories as printers.

What this buys is a bunch of stuff in boxes. It still must be installed before it can become a network. This example allows $300 per station, a typical expense for a DOS network. That additional sum includes the cost of the cable and installation, plus such often-hidden costs as planning and documentation. The installed wiring will cost a total of $6,000.

Training users

The 20 people who use the 20 computers will have to know how to use them. That means they will require training. Even users who are basically familiar with their PCs will require some orientation in how to use the newly installed network. If an instructor charges $25 an hour to conduct a two-day class, that's a total of $400, or $20 per station.

That's not the total cost. The operators will necessarily be absent from their jobs to attend this 20-hour course. Someone has figured out that it costs $25 per hour to pay the average employee, provide benefits, set up desk space, and so on. At 16 hours per employee, this is $400 per station, for a cost of $8,000. This is part of the cost of training.

Those same 20 operators will not be there every day. They will quit, get sick, and take vacations. Substitutes and replacements will also have to be trained. New software, as well as new versions of familiar software, will constantly appear, necessitating continued training for even highly skilled employees. Figure $300 per employee per year for both instruction and training time. That's $6,000 for the 20 workstations in this example.

Professional help

You will need someone to administer the network and support the users. For an average DOS network, this will amount to one full-time employee. There might be some variation, such as using two employees, each working half-time. Still, the basic support requirement usually boils down to a full-time administrator or the equivalent. The kind of professional you need for this job will command a salary of about $50,000 a year. This breaks down to $2,500 per station.

More professional help will be needed at the outset to help with planning and design. Five weeks at $55 per hour, a typical consultant's rate, will cost a total of $11,000, or $550 per station.

Figuring the fiddle factor

Computers give employees new ways to be more productive, offset by many new ways to be nonproductive. PC use always involves a certain amount of human downtime. Instead of doing productive work, people find themselves unjamming printers, reading junk E-mail, searching for lost files, or even playing games. Each employee spends at least half an hour a week on this kind of thing. At $25 per hour, that amounts to $650 per employee every year, or a grand total of $13,000 simply for messing around with the computers.

Figure $10,000 a year for software upgrades. It can cost another $10,000 to maintain your equipment and install new items like video cards and added memory. Count on yet another $10,000 in operating costs, such as communication charges. It all adds up to a whopping $204,400. Those "inexpensive" PC workstations cost $10,200 each to own and operate.

Other costs

There are still other costs that haven't been included in this analysis. If you do your own application development, the programming, testing, and training costs will be additional. These costs vary even more widely than some of those listed in the analysis.

There are also intangibles like opportunity cost. If the time a manager spends establishing and maintaining a network could have profitably been spent doing something else, you suffer the cost of that lost opportunity.

Still costs less

On the other hand, even with its hidden costs, a PC network usually costs much less than a large system. Economies of scale are not great within a PC network, but the per-station cost does diminish somewhat as the network grows. One hypothetical analysis of a 40-station network produced a cost estimate of about $7,000 per PC. The per-terminal cost of a large system can run at least twice that.

Another cost consideration: It often is possible to staff the downsized network with people cut loose from duties on the larger system.

The network still has a substantial cost advantage. It's important, though, not to jump to premature conclusions about all the money you'll save.

Paying for less

"You get what you pay for," despite this expression's overuse, has a lot of truth to it. If you pay less for a downsized system, do you also get less?

In some respects, the answer is yes. Furthermore, the typical LAN falls short of the typical mainframe in some particularly important respects: the reliability of the system, and the integrity and security of the organization's data.

"The system is down"

Earlier, it was suggested that a computer system is now actually a network, not a single box. Consider that idea in conjunction with the familiar announcement, "The system is down."

Many applications being transferred to PC networks qualify for the increasingly familiar designation, "mission-critical." A manufacturer's order entry system is an example. Should the system go down, critical transactions could go with it. Modern mainframes have been made increasingly fault-tolerant just to protect such vital data.

A network that is properly designed and installed can also be reliable. The question is whether it can be reliable enough for a truly mission-critical application. Networks can be tricky, and they do go down. Even if you don't lose vital data, the cost of excessive downtime, compared with more reliable mainframes, can be significant.

That can be an important consideration for the organization that has critical data or handles high transaction volumes on a mainframe system. Such applications are not strong candidates for downsizing all the way to a PC LAN.

Still, such an application may be a good candidate for partial downsizing: Leave the application on the mainframe as a back-end server, but grant front-end access by way of the network. There are probably many other applications that could be fully transferred to PCs, especially in the case of smaller organizations that have not yet invested in larger systems. Their ability to run on a network may mean they never have to make a heavier investment.

Then, there's security

There are many computer security experts who believe that moving critical data to networks opens whole new occupational specialities for disgruntled employees and industrial spies who want to steal, damage, or destroy this information. Though there are others who take a less dire view of the future, those security-conscious experts should be taken seriously.

In fact, many LANs have little or no effective security. There are many places on a network that can be attacked, and many ways to do it. Dial-in connections are always a vulnerable spot. Wires can be tapped, though this is less serious a threat than casual uses might believe. The ease with which disks and even backup tapes can be slipped in or out of an office is a two-way threat. Not only can data check out, but viruses can check in.

One electronics manufacturer developed a new circuit board, then was shocked to see a leading competitor introduce a nearly identical product at nearly the same time. The competitor had penetrated its network and stolen the design. A computer vendor discovered that its communications were being tapped. The intelligence service of a European nation was stealing secrets and passing them to its own country's vendors.

In spite of stories like these, a network need not be wide open to abuse. A coming chapter discusses network security in detail. For now, the main point is this: Security is primarily a human problem, not a technical one. With these human factors at work, neither PCs nor mainframes have a monopoly on safety or vulnerability.

2
CHAPTER

Issues in downsizing

Conventional wisdom holds that a PC network is not as reliable as a mainframe or minicomputer. The large system acts as a central point of contact for dumb terminals. It achieves hard-wired levels of reliability, backup, and fault tolerance a LAN cannot approach.

An application of Murphy's Law suggests that a LAN offers many new places for things to go wrong. One of the most serious issues in downsizing is the fear that LANs will prove to be less reliable than the larger systems they are to replace.

Downsizing for reliability

The *Washington Post* defied conventional wisdom, then, when it replaced its minicomputer-based editorial system with a LAN—and did it for the sake of greater reliability.

The decision was the result of a bad experience. In 1988, on an election night no less, the computer system used by editors and reporters went down for two hours. No one could accomplish anything, and the newspaper resolved not to repeat that experience. Other factors intruded, too. The system was a proprietary installation that ran a one-of-a-kind operating system, 10 years old, and many editorial staff employees had been urging the newspaper to install a more modern PC-based system.

The *Post* installed 700 PC workstations and servers running OS/2 and LAN Manager. They are connected via token ring networks to a Tandem Nonstop TXP computer. Each hardware component—the main processor, gateways, bridges, servers, and the network itself—has a twin for backup. Each of several interconnected networks has PC workstations and a pair of servers.

BEFORE DOWNSIZING:

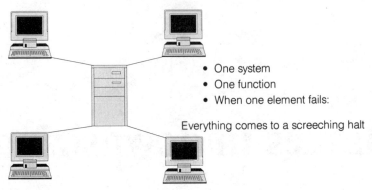

- One system
- One function
- When one element fails:

Everything comes to a screeching halt

A large system has many built-in reliability features, but when something fails, everything fails.

The PC terminals run application software for writing, editing, messaging, and related functions between the Tandem host, the network servers, and the individual workstations. The Tandem host connects to bridges in the seventh-floor computer center. Active news stories are processed on the workstations. Periodically, the local servers take snapshots of stories in progress. Should the Tandem go down, which does happen about twice a year, reporters and editors can continue working locally. Archived and inactive stories reside on the Tandem.

The new system is designed to serve new functions as well. Reporters can dial into commercial news and information services, and they can tap into a special server that runs commercial spreadsheet, database, and graphics software. They can download information and graphics from these sources for use in their stories. Reporters at the *Post*'s 17 U.S. news bureaus are still able to dial up and go online or work locally on their PCs.

Plans also call for a system that can scan incoming wire-service stories for key words. It then can route stories to reporters and editors based on interest profiles they have supplied earlier.

Keys to success

This installation illustrates several key points:

- A large system is not exempt from trouble. Murphy's Law applies here, too: it happened at the worst possible moment.
- There are ways to enhance the reliability of a downsized system. At the *Post*, the emphasis is on redundancy. If one part of the system fails, people still can get their work done.
- A downsized system can add valuable new functions that older systems can't provide.

AFTER DOWNSIZING:

- Multiple systems
- Expanded functions
- When one element fails:

The rest keep on going

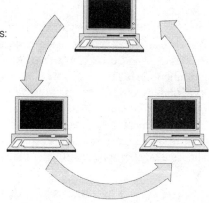

A networked system can open new opportunities—along with space-program redundancy.

KEY RELIABILITY POINTS

- Large systems can fail
- Small systems can be improved
- You may gain valuable new functions

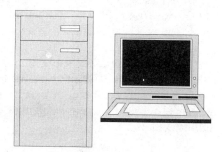

A small system can be as reliable as a larger one. It just has to be made that way.

Smaller systems often work better

Many MIS managers who have investigated downsized systems have come away convinced that a LAN actually can be more secure and reliable than a larger system.

Generally, available networking technology should not be a problem, says consultant Cheryl Currid. "Desktop computers, client/server databases, and the networks that connect everything together are powerful and cost-effective alternatives to mainframes. Some of the technology might not be rock-solid yet, but the risk/reward relationship is too compelling to ignore."

The Keystone Group, a Boston-based mutual funds company, has used a downsized system to provide for longer-lasting backup of its data. Under a mainframe system, the backup files were stored on magnetic tapes. Tapes can degrade over time.

The PC-based system stores the backups on optical disks. While these don't last forever either, they do have a much longer life span than tape.

Not all happy campers

Not everyone is happy with their downsized applications. The city traffic department in Long Beach, CA, moved its towing records application from a mainframe to PCs at five remote sites, connected by a network, a move that gave employees quicker access to data supplied by the state's Department of Motor Vehicles.

The department got its faster access, but the system also became a headache to its administrators. It is estimated that technicians spend four to eight hours a week troubleshooting at the remote sites.

The rules are different here

"In many ways," says Currid, "the challenge is to recreate some safeguards of the mainframe world. Unfortunately, it isn't as easy as porting things down intact. LANs speak a different language, and some things defy precise translation. The technology is different, the tool set is different, and the expertise needed is different. Reprogramming is required for both people and procedures, and that takes a little time.

"Unfortunately, nobody has come up with an easy-to-install, shrink-wrapped downsizing pack," she continues. "Since all corporate shops are a little different, nobody has figured out how to develop a one-size-fits-all model. That makes it as much a creative process as a technical one. In the meantime, pioneers in downsizing will have to contend with less-than-a well-marked path."

**THE CHALLENGE:
BUILD YOUR OWN SAFEGUARDS**

There are some problems

- Translation isn't easy
- Technology is different
- Tools are different
- People need different skills

Moving large-system reliability to a network isn't easy, but it can—and should—be done.

These things can help

The solutions to problems of LAN reliability are generally simple. Among them:

- Maintain a central help desk, and give users full-time access.
- Obtain and use the best network management tools. Use them to diagnose network problems, in many cases before they become severe.
- Make sure all connecting links remain in good condition.
- Back up data frequently, particularly on file servers. Keep at least one copy of the backup data off-site.
- Back up the system as well as the software. Provide alternate facilities and routes.
- Install uninterruptible power supplies, particularly for network servers.
- Install fault-tolerant features such as mirrored servers or disk drives. Some network operating systems can detect the failure of one drive and automatically switch to its duplicate. Future systems may do the same for entire servers.

TO KEEP THE GEARS TURNING

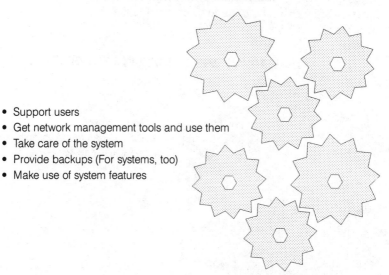

- Support users
- Get network management tools and use them
- Take care of the system
- Provide backups (For systems, too)
- Make use of system features

Taking care of simple tasks will help keep the network up and running.

Reliability built in

Downsizers can make use, too, of the reliability and security features found in network-oriented hardware and software. For example, on the software side, DOS and OS/2 database management systems (DBMS) are taking on tasks that once required a minicomputer or mainframe. Large companies such as Aetna Insurance, K-Mart, and Merrill Lynch are all using PC-based DBMS systems to perform online transaction processing (OLTP), a demanding, high-activity type of application. These OLTP applications formerly ran on minicomputers or mainframes.

LAN-based database servers offer such standard features of large-system DBMSs as rollback and two-stage commit. In case of a power failure or shutdown from some other cause, the rollback feature returns the database to its original condition before any uncompleted transactions could begin. This keeps the database from being corrupted by data from partly completed transactions. In a single, nondistributed database the transaction might update one or more tables. If the transaction is completed, it ends with the SQL key word COMMIT. If there is an interruption, the system can undo a transaction with the SQL key word ROLLBACK. Otherwise, should the system fail, one table might get changed, but another table might not. If these two changes depend on each other, as in a transfer of money between two bank accounts, a half-completed transaction could leave corrupt data. The process of forcing either both changes or none is called transaction control.

The two-phase commit is a way to provide transaction control across a network, reaching all the tables in a distributed database system. If two tables in different locations are to be changed, either both will be changed or neither.

TAKE ADVANTAGE OF BUILT-IN RELIABILITY

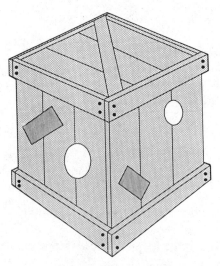

- Access control
- Transaction control
- Disk mirroring and verification
- Transaction tracking

Network systems and applications have many reliability and security features. Use them.

Network help

Network operating systems also duplicate many of the security and reliability features typical of larger systems. For example, Novell's NetWare Version 3 advertises such reliability features as read-after-write verification, disk mirroring, disk duplexing, resource tracking, a transaction tracking system (TTS), and uninterruptible power supply (UPS) monitoring. All are designed to increase network dependability by safeguarding data against failure in critical parts of the network.

For more reliable service

The idea that LANs are unreliable does have some basis in fact. Top-level networking systems are near-matches for the reliability features of mainframes and minis, but there is still the familiar human factor. When networks fail, it is often because their human operators fail to implement or use these data integrity features. You can avoid this problem if you remember these points:

- **Don't try to do it yourself**. Networks are complicated—particularly the kinds of network installations usually needed to handle former large-system applications. Many companies get into trouble when they install their own LANs without sufficient experience or knowledge. Hire a professional trained in network design and installation to do the job, or at least to oversee your work.
- **Be prepared to spend some money**. Users who try to save money on professional help also often try to save money on their systems. The small, peer-to-peer LANs now on the market have attractive prices, typically $99 per node. But these are light-duty units intended mainly for file and printer sharing within small offices. They also tend to be incompatible with larger networking systems. A downsized application will usually need something much huskier.

  Shopping for the cheapest hardware and operating system may ease the initial financial pain, but bargain shopping will cost you in the long run. Make sure you buy from reputable hardware and software vendors committed to supplying adequate support.
- **Check out your dealer**. That includes value-added resellers (VARs) and system integrators as well. Get references from companies that have implemented networks similar to the one you anticipate. Otherwise, you may find that your source will abandon you at the first sign of significant trouble.
- **Plan carefully**. Most networks happen to come together more or less by accident. Then, as they get bigger and take on more critical roles, the lack of planning produces an unmanageable tangle. Decisions about user accounts, directory structures, and who has access

to what kinds of data should be made early. Then you can plan and install the network with an eye toward future growth.

- **Be realistic**. Many organizations expect a network installation to be a quick and easy process. Your network will be neither. That's because no network is quick and easy. Don't expect a quick payoff, either. Downsizing may not favorably affect the bottom line for many fiscal quarters to come.

- **Be prepared for problems**. Even top professional networkers rarely get everything right the first time. Don't move mission-critical applications over too quickly. Expect a shakedown period while all the bugs get worked out.

COMMON NETWORKING MISTAKES

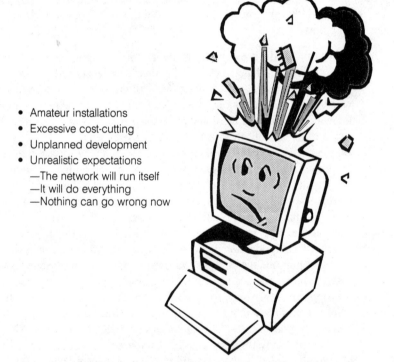

- Amateur installations
- Excessive cost-cutting
- Unplanned development
- Unrealistic expectations
  —The network will run itself
  —It will do everything
  —Nothing can go wrong now

Networking need not be difficult, but many users get in trouble by expecting it to be too easy.

- **Be prepared to work on maintenance**. One of the most serious mistakes a company can make is assuming that anyone can manage the LAN. This is yet another manifestation of the tendency to try the cheapest solution. Every network, regardless of size, requires the ongoing attention of a trained network administrator. Backups, application installation and maintenance, management of user accounts, and hardware and software compatibility are just a few of the issues the network manager will have to deal with almost every day. Make sure you have someone on tap who is up to this responsibility.

- **Invest in training**. Many companies fail to train users to work effectively in a networked environment. Often, the training is superficial. Users are simply issued passwords and shown how to log onto the network. That isn't enough. Users need to be schooled in such subjects as working with shared peripherals and shared applications.

- **Don't forget backup**. This often-joked-about fault among individual users could lead to serious disaster on a large network. Regular backups should be done regularly—daily is ideal. Make full backups as often as possible. Don't forget menus and batch files. They can be harder to replace than nearly any other kind.

- **Have a disaster recovery plan**. Every company should have one. It's particularly important when your business depends on continued operation of the network. Key considerations include the impact of a system failure, the amount of time required to get the network back into service, and designating someone to take charge of implementing the recovery plan.

Networking and security

First Security National Bank and Trust (Lexington, KY) seems willing to bet heavily on the reliability of a newly installed network. The bank has given some serious thought to entrusting its payroll application to a downsized system.

The bank, which has already implemented several other downsized applications, had been running a mainframe-based payroll system. Although using an outside service was at first considered a logical alternative, the bank is now instead leaning heavily toward implementing a PC LAN-based system in the payroll department. As at the *Post*, user demand is a factor in the decision.

The main attraction is the networked system's greater flexibility in accessing, viewing, and analyzing data. Users are finding new ways to get better views of their data.

The PC LAN also compares favorably with the mainframe system in providing the reliability and security required for a payroll system. The payroll LAN is physically isolated from other systems. Unlike the mainframe, it's connected to nothing else. Its data is available only to authorized workers in the payroll department.

More unconventional wisdom

IS professionals like to point out that PC networks lack many of the security and data integrity features of their larger kin. They look at a typical traditional application: a large system with dumb terminals connected. All the processing is done on this one machine. All the screen handling, program logic, referential integrity checks, security checks, and similar functions are done on the mainframe. The terminal simply provides a view into that bigger machine.

Many developments are combining to change that picture. Ease of use has become important, as witness the spread of graphic interfaces. Databases that once resided on large systems are being moved to network servers. There's a movement in the opposite direction, too, as stand-alone PC databases migrate into client/server architecture.

Are LANs more vulnerable?

Confidential information was reasonably well-protected when it resided on a single large system with its multiple built-in protective mechanisms. That information is much harder to protect now that PCs have entered the picture. DOS, the prevailing PC operating system, has virtually none of the technical checks and balances that large systems provide.

Another serious problem is that PCs are physically more accessible than their larger counterparts—that is, DOS lacks *built-in* security measures, which now must be provided by system administrators. You can't sit back and let a downsized system take care of its own security. You must actively provide it. For example, First Security Bank has found ways to physically isolate its payroll processing network from either physical or outside-line intrusion. The bank had to take special steps to replace the built-in security measures of its mainframe, but in the end it had even greater access control.

Are LANs really different?

It's probably true that if you need ironclad protection for truly sensitive data, a LAN may not measure up to a well-protected mainframe. Still, it is possible to achieve a high degree of security, even in the relatively open environment of a network.

For example, Amoco maintains critically sensitive information on a Chicago-based network. That network must be available to dial-in access from employees at other locations. Borrowing from mainframe technology, the company instituted a call-in system. An inbound caller cannot gain access to the full network. The system accepts the caller's log-in information, hangs up, and redials a telephone number associated with that identification.

That kind of active self-protection would be necessary with any kind of system. A network whose managers want to control dial-in access is in much the same position as a large system that requires the same controls.

Physical protection is another common concern for systems of all sizes. Just as large systems are located in secure, dedicated rooms, a LAN can also be physically isolated. Power supplies and bridges can be placed in locked closets; file servers can be located in secure rooms. The networked PC workstations, then, present little more security risk than dumb terminals connected to a mainframe.

Often, a downsizing project moves just the application program to desktop computers. The data itself remains on the larger system. In particular, large corporate databases prevalently remain on the main computers, with access provided by gateways and similar communication links.

This pattern may have little to do with security, however. One small college, for example, is installing an extensive network system, but has left student grade and financial records on its mainframe. The main reason, officials explain, is not security but the mainframe's ability to handle the sheer volume of data.

TOUGH SECURITY FOR A LAN

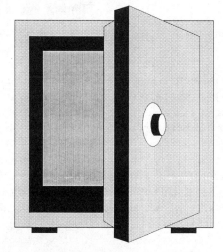

- Physical protection
  —Servers
  —Connections
- Access control
  —Dialbacks
  —Passwords
- Encryption

No system offers ironclad security, but even a network can come close.

System security

Network operating systems and allied utilities are increasingly providing security features not provided by the PC operating systems. In addition to safeguards mentioned earlier in this chapter, there are programs that scan for viruses and utilities that can restrict access to specified directories or files.

Most PC networks, particularly Novell NetWare and Banyan Vines, include account control features that restrict users to particular workstations and particular times. Administrators can use these features to keep people from logging in from home or after hours. For example, you can use an account control feature to permit log-ins to the finance department network only during normal working hours. This helps prevent unauthorized users, whether from inside or outside the company, from looking at the corporate books.

In addition, most network operating systems let administrators set up different levels of access to files and data. While users may, for example, need access to certain types of corporate data, they won't need the ability to change or delete that data. Granting them read-only access to those files protects the data from deliberate or accidental modification.

Unlike DOS, some individual operating systems also have built-in security features. Unix and OS/2 provide access controls and limit the permitted types of use of designated directories and files. OS/2 also has a facility to restrict the number of licensed application programs that can operate on a network—helping to prevent the use of pirated software, a potential security problem as well as a copyright violation.

The human factor

The real security challenge for a LAN administrator is to manage the human factor.

PC users constantly frustrate security professionals with their less-than-careful habits. These are people, for example, who use stick-on notes to post their passwords in plain sight. In particular, those who have come to regard PCs as truly personal tools may not understand that in a networked environment they may become responsible for corporate data that needs more protection.

For that reason, many security experts and PC managers say user education is a critical part of their security policies. Training is a high priority, concentrating on such subjects as how to recognize hazards and observing security procedures. One bank's security training program includes sessions in such subjects as managing change.

The idea behind this: The implementation of a new network is a major change in the way an organization does business. A system is most vulnerable at times of change. It's a time when errors are frequent; a new program disk may contain a virus; access controls may not yet be in place or may not work properly. The training is intended to help managers monitor and educate their employees more closely during this period.

Says one PC manager: "Users need to understand that even transferring a file from a floppy disk to their hard drive constitutes a significant change in their system." That means there is a potential hazard they should be trained to recognize.

This is one area where IS professionals can continue to use their talents in a downsized environment. They can do what they're good at, maintaining the security, validity, and integrity of the data. This lets the users go about their own jobs. It also frees them to find new ways to retrieve and use the organization's data.

The ease of use factor

This division of labor can help overcome another security problem. Maintaining a high degree of security in a networked environment can conflict with a major objective of downsizing: ease of use. PC users, in any event, are accustomed to user-friendly applications. They often aren't receptive to institutional security procedures.

There's more than personal preference involved here. Often, obtrusive security measures can keep people from doing their jobs as effectively as they might, and there's no surer way to build a dissatisfied work force.

One solution is to implement as many of the security measures as possible at the network level rather than at individual workstations; this might include the use of a security-conscious operating system like OS/2, as well as keeping critical components within locked rooms.

Involve the users

Another important measure in downsizing is to involve the users. To resolve conflicts between security and ease of use, many organizations have set up cooperative working arrangements in which users can discuss their needs and problems with security and systems professionals.

This process can break down resistance and build cooperation by helping each side understand the other. It also gives the participants a sense of ownership in the downsizing project. There's no better way to build enthusiasm and support.

Hackers and viruses

The two most heavily publicized types of security problems, hackers and viruses, are also among the least serious threats to most systems. Security experts estimate that the country holds only a handful of hackers of the type who might cause deliberate damage to a system. The number of actual virus infections also does not match the apparent threat.

A protection strategy

People think of crimes as being committed by mysterious strangers: shadowy muggers or scheming hackers. But whether in computers or other areas of life, most crimes are committed by somebody the victim knows. In business, that known party is almost always an employee. The second most likely cause of data loss is the simple accident—the mispunched key at a critical moment or the cup of coffee spilled on a floppy disk.

Even so, when it comes to computer security, many corporations focus on protecting themselves from outsiders rather than insiders. Corporations spend a lot of money on expensive security systems, when their time might be better spent making sure passwords are properly used, educating their employees on the need for security, and ensuring that backups are performed regularly.

The first question

How much security do you really need? That's the first question to ask when planning for network security, and its answer depends on the answer to another question: "What would the damage be if the most sensitive information on my LAN were compromised?" If the answer is "Not much," you need only to warn your workers not to write their passwords on stick-on notes. But if the damage would be severe, you must do more to make sure your network is secure.

What and how much you must do depends on several things: security features in the LAN operating system and applications, physical protection of the server and communication media, and the kinds of threats you face. Many users do not view all these items as a whole. In part, that's because vendors tend to offer piecemeal solutions. Each solution may be able to respond to one security threat easily, but your system probably has holes somewhere else.

IN SECURITY, TEAMWORK COUNTS

All elements must work together

- System features
- Physical security
- Threat analysis
- Training and procedures

Security features must work as a system, not as individual components.

Rate your risks

Developing an effective protection strategy requires that you identify the specific risks you face. Classify your PCs and networks based on how they are used. Their use usually is an index of the security threats they present.

You then can develop a security plan that responds to those risks. This could range from locked rooms for a network carrying a payroll application to regular virus detection on a PC used mainly for word processing.

One company has developed a three-level system for classifying PCs and networks:

- Systems that handle highly confidential data such as client records and information on corporate strategy.
- Mid-level systems handling information whose disclosure would not be a serious threat but whose loss would cause problems.
- Systems that hold only departmental files and personal work.

Once the security classification has been established, the company institutes security measures to match. The top-category systems get a security package that includes passwords, data encryption, and audit trails. These systems are also physically secure and isolated from other networks.

At the mid-level, where loss of data is the greatest threat, the company requires password access to sensitive files and limits transfers of files and programs. Regular backup is also a priority here.

Bottom-level systems are often individual PCs, where the emphasis is on regular virus scanning. Some of these also require password access.

What you can do

Whatever the system, security problems tend to fall into the same few broad categories. Many of the problems of PC network security are just the same as those of mini and mainframe security.

A few preventive measures will take care of a majority of potential security problems. The major challenge is to make administrators and users aware of the potential problems and inform them of the tools available to solve them.

The two best steps an organization can take are to perform regular backups and to implement a system of passwords, say security consultants. Take the time to make sure you have backups that are both available and reasonably safe. In particular, regular backups help with the small, everyday problems of lost files and data.

The password is probably the most important security measure you can take on any system. Says one security consultant: "Your system security is only as good as the password."

But what makes a good password? It should be hard to guess. That creates an immediate source of conflict with users, because they want passwords that are easy to remember. Even so, enforcing good password choice is a big win because most outsiders who get into business systems do so by defeating the password system.

For example, there are programs that will run through a password file comprising the obvious ones. Hackers use such programs to find usable passwords. System administrators should use the same programs to identify easy-to-guess choices within their own systems, and get them changed.

For high-security use, consider a program that forces users to change their passwords frequently. Some of these programs do so at preset intervals and issue new passwords to the users. The passwords, generated at random, are harder to guess.

Depends on people

Whatever the protection plan, it ultimately depends on people, not technology. User education will always be one of the most important elements of any security program.

The most serious threat to your system comes from inside, not outside, and that threat is much more likely to be accidental than deliberate. It can involve acts like accidentally erasing a file—things that are preventable with proper precautions. Proper training can teach and motivate employees to take those precautions.

For example, you can't back up all the files on individual systems from a central location. It's the users who must do that. Consider regular seminars on the personal aspects or computer security. Back up the seminars with a regular newsletter, or with articles in other company publications.

Involve employees

These measures still won't work if they appear to the employees like edicts handed down from the mountain. Individual departments and users are intimately familiar with their operations, including the dimensions of any conflict between security and ease of use. Contrary to some managers' cynical expectations, most employees want to do their jobs effectively and will resent any security measures imposed from above that keep them from doing it.

Involve employees in these discussions. Solicit their ideas for striking a balance. Not only will you have the benefit of their knowledge and understanding, but you will have the enthusiastic cooperation that comes from a sense of participation in the results.

Don't overreact

There is a so-called "newspaper effect" that causes many system administrators to worry most about the most highly publicized external threats, while giving too little attention to basic measures like backups and passwords that can protect them from the much more serious internal threats.

On a percentage basis, however, the threat from viruses is minuscule. While an estimated 80% of all damage is caused internally, the external threat remains real. It can become more serious if a downsizing project

SIMPLE SECURITY

Things everyone can do:

* Make regular backups
* Use passwords to control access
* Educate employees (Security is in their hands)

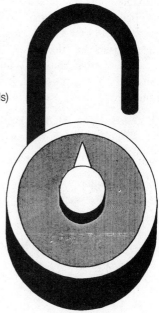

Many security problems respond to simple solutions, no matter what the type of system.

actually involves an upsizing from local area networks to wide area networks (WANs). LANs tend to be closed systems; many have no external gateways at all. Once you go through a gateway outside you LAN, you've multiplied the number of people who can possibly gain access to your data. Most hackers gain their access by discovering or guessing commonly used passwords. Thus, a well-managed password system that avoids such common terms is the best defense.

Carelessness and ignorance by honest employees make up the largest menace to information security. A survey by the Executive Information Network showed that 55% of all computer security losses could be attributed to errors or omissions. Dishonest and disgruntled employees accounted for 25% of losses. External threats such as natural disasters caused 20%, leaving only 5% for all other causes, including invasions by outsiders.

Commonsense protection

Viruses are a case in point. They happen, but only a minority of all PC users have been victims. One generally recommended protective measure is to get software only from reputable vendors, buy it shrink-wrapped, and avoid public domain software and shareware. If you must download bulletin-board programs, try to limit yourself to those whose source code is available. This lets the system administrator examine the code for oddities.

Because even commercial software has been known to conceal viruses, users should run virus-scanning software at least once a month—more often if users are adding software or sharing a PC.

One word of caution: While virus scanning software works well and is constantly being improved, it is not foolproof. Don't rely on this strategy alone.

DON'T BE FOOLED BY PUBLICITY

Major causes of loss:

- Accidents
- Dishonest employees

Minor causes of loss:

- Hackers
- Viruses

For most users, the most highly publicized threats are actually the least serious.

The tradeoffs of downsizing

At Courtaulds Performance Films (Fielddale, VA), a maker of high-tech window films, downsizing has been complete. The company ditched its mainframe and all its applications and switched to a Unix computer.

Officials say they're happy with the results. Information is now consistent throughout the company, there is an integrated application, and users are doing things they couldn't do before. Nevertheless, these benefits have come at some cost. One early discovery was that Unix is not as robust as the proprietary Unisys Corp. operating system it replaced. "You gain a lot, but you also give up some things," one official said.

That experience is typical of the types of tradeoffs downsizing entails. Downsizing can reduce hardware and software costs, decrease application development times, reduce maintenance costs, create more intelligent applications, and allow for greater flexibility. But downsizing also has its costs and potential traps that you should understand before undertaking any major project.

Also, the benefits of downsizing may not be the benefits you expect.

Cost isn't everything

At Hyatt Hotels, a downsized reservation system has resulted in a more than 20% cost saving in leasing fees and maintenance. Even so, the greatest benefit of the new system is the ability to respond quickly to changes in a highly competitive marketplace.

One example is an express reservation and check-in service via a toll-free telephone number. Hyatt had earlier tried and failed to establish such a customer-service feature on the mainframe-based wide area network that supports its reservation system. Now, phone operators at Hyatt's Omaha location field the call and then log onto a specific hotel's computer over the company's transmission control protocol/internet protocol (TCP/IP) network. Once connected with the hotel, the operator can confirm a reservation, down to the room number.

At the Sara Lee Corp., an ongoing downsizing project has produced the expected benefits of reduced maintenance costs and other expenses. That still is not the primary benefit the firm says it has enjoyed from its system.

Distributed, client/server platforms give employees the flexibility to choose the method and tools by which they will gain access to and use the corporation's information resources. The goal has been to enable users to use corporate data, but also to create a variety of reports, data inquiries, and decision-support questions, using such familiar PC-based tools as spreadsheets, databases, word processors, accounting applications, executive information systems, and decision-support software. These systems move the responsibility for gathering and manipulating information away from the MIS staff and into the hands of those who actually require the information to perform their jobs.

Saving personnel costs

The typical downsizing project can also save on personnel costs. It generally takes fewer people to run a PC network than a mainframe-centered information systems (IS) shop. Still, the savings may not be as great as expected. The threat of staff reductions can also be a morale buster, with employees becoming fearful that system downsizing will also mean personnel downsizing. This fear is particularly strong among IS professionals who have not upgraded their skills to keep up with downsized systems—and a downsized labor market.

A 1990 survey by *PC Week* found that only 16% of the firms that had downsized had reduced the size of their IS staffs. Still, several MIS directors said staff reductions remain a real possibility.

Downsizing and outsourcing

Downsizing is also a close companion to outsourcing—farming out IS operations to outside contractors. Few who do this were as brutally frank as an EDP manager for a West Coast bank. When asked if the IS staff had resisted, he snapped, "There was no resistance—we got rid of them." In fact, the bank spun off its 35-person data processing staff into a separate company, which is then sold.

A Cleveland law firm laid off some unexpected people: its PC support specialist, its telecommunications manager, its training services manager, and its help-desk operator. The training and support functions have been contracted to an outside firm; the MIS manager now finds himself handling the help-desk calls.

One possibly fruitful area for outsourcing is application development. One advantage is that outside consultants give specific dollar estimates to develop applications. When you do it in-house, you cannot be as sure how much it's going to cost.

Elusive savings

Even so, many companies that have downsized report this experience: They can save some staffing expenses, but not as much as they had expected. A firm may need fewer network administrators than mainframe communications people, but those administrators may require higher skills and salaries to match.

3
CHAPTER

The downsizing experience

Downsizing is more than the simple transfer of applications from large systems to PCs and networks. Its effects go far beyond reducing costs. Companies that have downsized have learned that downsizing actually constitutes a major modification in the company's business philosophy. It also changes the way a corporation uses the vast amount of information at its disposal.

Downsizing also is not without its problems—and a certain amount of risk. Some downsizing projects have encountered problems, expected and unexpected, solved and unsolved. No one who is considering a downsizing project can afford to ignore these unpleasant experiences.

Technical variety: Sara Lee's downsizing experience

These downsized systems can cover a wide variety of technologies. They include distributed processing, client/server architecture, portable network operating systems, graphical user interfaces (GUIs), computer-aided systems engineering (CASE), and both local and wide area networks.

Sara Lee relies heavily on client/server systems in which the client component is responsible for presenting and manipulating data at the workstation, and where the server portion can be located on mainframes, minis, or LAN-based systems. This approach has allowed the company to take advantage of each platform's strengths.

ADVANTAGES TO A LARGE ORGANIZATION

- Ability to adapt to changes
- Easier access to data (By putting it closer to the users)
- Cost effectiveness
- Flexibility
- Faster application development

Sara Lee's extensive downsizing program has produced multiple benefits.

Products like Channel Computing's Forest and Trees and Lotus's Datalens can be used to retrieve information and give users the ability to make better use of their divisions' information resources. Graphic user interfaces such as Microsoft Windows substantially reduce training requirements. They also make it possible to implement a single GUI front end that can interface with multiple mainframe sessions simultaneously. For example, one division has been working on an interface to six separate customer service systems that reside on various hardware platforms.

Part of the program can run on the host system, while another part resides on the client workstation. These systems make use of protocols such as LU6.2, Novell's transport protocols, or transport tools supplied by database vendors. These allow interprocess communications to be made across the network between the client workstation and the host, be it a mainframe, midrange system, or PC server.

Market orientation

Techniques like these have let Sara Lee and its divisions make transitions from production-oriented large systems to those that are oriented to markets and customer service. The company has found that customer-oriented systems do a better job of reflecting the world in which users serve their customers.

That is only one of several advantages the organization has found. Others include:

- A greater ability to adapt the system to changes.
- Easier access to more data.
- The ability to use more cost-effective systems.
- More flexible choices of methods and tools.
- More efficient application development.

DOWNSIZING SPURS A TRANSITION

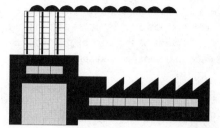

From production-oriented systems . . .

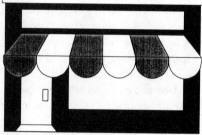

. . . to marketing and customer service

Larger systems are oriented toward getting work out of the system. Networks are oriented to getting work out of the organization.

More adaptable

In the past, more than 70% of the MIS computing budget was devoted to maintaining existing software and hardware. Management had expressed a strong interest in implementing more cost-effective technology, while at the same time expecting accurate, complete, and timely information.

Meanwhile, users grown accustomed to the freedom and flexibility of personal computers had developed growing appetites for access to greater amounts of information. Users want the flexibility to retrieve corporate data using the desktop platform with which they are most familiar.

Cost-effective access

Downsizing to the client/server architecture has improved access to data. At the same time, it has allowed the company to select the most cost-effective hardware platform available for a specific use.

To assess this cost-effectiveness, the company has developed a method that balances user requirements with the requirements of the project. The client/server architecture lets the system components be placed close to the individuals who use them. This decentralization promotes efficient application processing and has reduced network traffic. Distributed processing, combined with the client/server architecture, allows each platform, from mainframes to PCs, to work in unison. Often, the existing mainframe and minis, with their high-speed I/O buses and large disk drives, have become effective networked on-line data depositories.

Of course, the PC's lower cost is a major factor in cost-effectiveness. PCs, particularly when networked, can run powerful business applications and store large amounts of data at a fraction of the cost of mainframes. Downsized systems also usually reduce maintenance and staff costs.

Better tools

Cost is only one reason Sara Lee has continued to pursue its downsizing. Distributed, client/server platforms make departmental employees more efficient by giving them the flexibility to choose the method and tools by which they will retrieve and use the corporation's information resources. These systems move the responsibility for gathering and manipulating information away from the MIS staff and into the hands of those who use the information to do their jobs.

Downsized systems also provide a scalable investment both in hardware and software. This lets the organization start with small-scale, manageable systems and over time, increase their use with no loss of the original investment. Typically, large-scale host platforms must be replaced almost entirely with every upgrade.

Faster development

Yet another benefit of downsizing has been to speed up the traditionally tedious process of application development. Sara Lee, with its long-standing development backlog, was no exception. The networked environment provides a platform for faster and more efficient development.

One reason for this increased efficiency is the wide range of graphic- and object-oriented development tools now available for PCs. These offer a friendly and intuitive programming environment that simplifies the development process, sharply reducing the time, and thus the cost, of getting new applications online. For example, host-platform emulation products, such as Micro Focus Cobol and California Software's Baby/400, allow programmers to develop Cobol and RPG applications on a LAN. Once completed, these can be moved to a host platform for execution or run on the network as a LAN-based application.

But there are some drawbacks

Along with the multiple benefits of downsizing, Sara Lee has discovered this: Downsizing requires that you install hardware and software from a multitude of vendors, and you must properly integrate these systems. Don't assume that the task is simple just because the hardware is less expensive. These systems are complex and require a high level of expertise.

Paul Bandrowski, who as manager of advanced technology at Sara

Lee, has overseen much of the downsizing process, says he strongly encourages system managers to "hire outside expertise to aid in the planning, development, and implementation of a downsizing project. This includes developing a strong relationship with a systems integrator." In many cases, Bandrowski says, "It would have been virtually impossible for us to implement our downsizing projects without the participation of outside consultants.

It is also wise to consider outside help if you have these needs:

- Specialized industry knowledge and skill.
- Strategic or competitive positioning.
- Action within a limited time.
- Transfer of knowledge from outside experts to the existing systems staff.
- A third party perspective.
- Someone to act as a catalyst in implementing change.

WHAT SARA LEE DOESN'T LIKE

- Multiple products from multiple sources
  —Someone must put them all together
- Need for outside experts
  —They're usually the "someone"

Nobody makes downsizing system that lets you just open the box.

Hyatt overcomes reservations

A hotel chain's reservation system would seem to be one of those high-volume, transaction-oriented systems that still belongs on a mainframe. Nevertheless, the Hyatt Hotels Corp. has replaced its mainframe-based reservation system with a relational database management system that runs on multiple processors.

In the process, Hyatt switched from an older, proprietary operating system to Unix. It also switched from customized software to a commercial relational database management system, and moved to a nonproprietary wide-area network.

In its first year, the reservation system produced a cost saving of 20% over the old system; the mainframe had cost more than $7 million a year to lease and maintain. In what has almost become the classic downsizing experience, though, even that amount of money was only part of the downsizing payoff. The new system is more responsive, and it allowed the organization to go forward with a customer service move it had been unable to implement on the larger system. This is the automated check-in system, described in chapter 2. It gave Hyatt a strategic advantage in a highly competitive field.

The reservation system, located in Hyatt's Oak Brook, Illinois, data center, has four AT&T System 7000s. These are reduced instruction set computing (RISC) servers built for AT&T by Pyramid Technology Corp., replacing an IBM 4381 mainframe. Hyatt also moved an older online transaction processing (OLTP) environment to a relational database from Informix Corp.

BENEFITS OF THE HYATT SYSTEM

- Reduced cost
- Better customer service
- Freedom to expand and change

The hotel chain hopes to take advantage of customer service opportunities.

Drawn to scale

One appeal of the downsized system is that expansions and changes can be implemented quickly and easily. It is also scalable. The same basic system will serve any size hotel in the chain. That's the source of another unexpected advantage: A manager transferred to a new location doesn't have to learn a new system.

The system also has added potential in the customer service area in that it provides more specific and up-to-date information on room availability to airline reservation systems. Travel agents use the airline systems to book cars and rooms as well as flights.

Lessons from Experience U.

A few years before the reservation system was installed, Hyatt had installed several AT&T 3B2 servers in its hotels. Those installations provided a learning experience with valuable lessons for downsizing reservations. Hyatt found that its staff was unskilled in maintaining and administering the server systems, and also that AT&T was not accustomed to supporting a 7-day, 24-hour system carrying mission-critical applications.

Getting closer

Those problems had been corrected by the time the reservation system was installed. The experience also prompted Hyatt executives to build closer than usual relationships with its principal vendors, AT&T and Informix. The idea: Work as partners rather than customer and client, so Hyatt would not be in the position of "betting the ranch" on the new reservation system.

Senior executives from the three firms met every six to eight weeks. Within the partnership arrangement, it was still up to Hyatt to state its requirements and specifications; the vendors' role was to see that the system met all expectations. For instance, a test of the reservation system a few months before it was to go online revealed that the typical response time was 15 seconds. Working together, the hardware and software vendors figured out how to improve performance. By the time the system was activated, it could complete 95% of all transactions within 2 seconds.

TURN VENDORS INTO PARTNERS
Work together toward the same goals

Plans work out best when everyone is trying to do the same thing.

Insurance firm copes with success

By its fourth year in business, the Financial Guaranty Insurance Co. was facing a crisis in computer capacity. FGIC is a New York-based firm that insures municipal bonds issued for such purposes as road and school construction. The mainframe-based system that managed its investments was straining under a growing workload and an inflexible design that failed to produce some of the information needed by regulatory agencies and business partners.

To remain competitive, the firm had to find a way to retrieve and process information more quickly and to cope with the job of managing a fast-growing portfolio. Furthermore, to meet the deadlines for required reports, all this had to be done within 18 months.

That was in 1987. FGIC solved its problem by launching one of the nation's earliest downsizing projects. FGIC decided that developing and enhancing its own applications on a LAN was the only way it could close the gap between its applications and its business needs.

The downsized system has accomplished that. Three years after it was installed, the system was processing and reporting on 13 billion separate insurance portfolios and $1.25 billion in assets. It provided the flexibility FGIC needed to operate and enhance its system, meet client's needs and handle information in new business areas. As a bonus, the firm's annual systems budget has been reduced from $10 million to $2 million.

DOWNSIZING CUTS THROUGH PROBLEMS

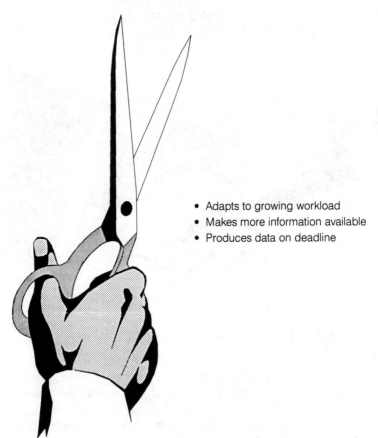

- Adapts to growing workload
- Makes more information available
- Produces data on deadline

Downsizing is usually a response to common problems.

Five key applications

FGIC's business analysts and clerks use five interlinked database applications originally written in FoxBASE. FGIC now uses its FoxPro successor. These applications analyze and track bond insurance policies and monitor the firm's exposure to risk. The applications run on a Compaq Systempro 486/33 on a NetWare 386 Token-Ring LAN. Four other servers provide backup, serve as development platforms, and run other critical applications.

One strong point of the system is that it can be enhanced quickly to provide a new report required by a regulatory agency, or to reflect the latest changes in FGIC's portfolio of outstanding policies. The system also can be quickly adapted to handle insurance in new types of business, such as bonds for health care facilities.

WHAT A FLEXIBLE SYSTEM CAN DO

- Adapt to legal changes
- Produce new kinds of reports
- Respond to business conditions
- Open new business opportunities

The adaptability of downsized systems can be used to good advantage.

Instantly outdated

One reason FGIC turned to the LAN was that the data produced by its mainframe financial reporting system was already outdated. This ancient data was not only creating a danger of missing legal deadlines, it kept the company from closely monitoring its own financial status.

One major goal of the downsizing project, then, was to do credit analyses to such a degree, and far enough in the future, that the firm could be reasonably sure it was not going to incur losses.

To accomplish this, FGIC's business analysts need access to a wide variety of data. For example, before insuring a bond issue for an electric generating plant, FGIC analysts want to analyze economic forecasts to determine how many customers the utility can expect in the future.

Another group of users keeps an eye on the present. For example, FGIC's earnings on a premium go up over time as the bond issuer pays its debt and reduces the amount FGIC would pay in the event of a default. FGIC must calculate its earnings over time for each policy it has in force. It then must report this data to regulatory and bond-rating agencies and calculate how much of the premium it should pass on to the reinsurers who cover FGIC against loss.

The mainframe-based system wasn't able to keep up with those changes and thus did not reflect the current status of the portfolio. It only reflected the status when the deal was first entered. It had no way to take into account changes in the tax code or for new types of insurance.

The LAN has helped FGIC streamline its business processes and reduce its staff from 200 to 180 employees, even while sales grew by 40%.

Downsizing from PCs

Another member of the New York financial community has found success in downsizing—not from a large system but from high-powered PCs.

Earlier, Royal Alliance had followed the usual path of giving users more and more powerful PCs. Along the way, it ran into many of the usual problems associated with stand-alone PC use:

- Users ran 17 different applications, with an equal variety of incompatible file formats.
- Users often failed to back up vital data.
- Maintenance costs were rising.
- Some users had both dumb terminals for mainframe access and PCs for word processing and spreadsheet work.

There was also a suspicion that many users were using machines that were too powerful for their needs. When a lease on the existing machines expired, the company took the opportunity to build a better system.

Going down

The firm removed the higher-powered systems from some users' desks and replaced them with networked 80286-based systems outfitted with only 3.5″ floppy drives. Other PCs were replaced by totally diskless workstations. Personal printers gave way to shared network resources.

The company had expected some objections from users who valued their stand-alone systems, but they did not materialize. Apparently, the users were happy to gain the advantages of being on the network. They had to access to standard versions of popular applications, huge amounts of server disk space, and direct connection to the mainframe.

Said one user, "You have access to the same software as everyone else, your files are compatible with everyone else's, and you have access to all these applications in one place on one terminal. Because you're hooked up to the LAN, you've got access to so much more data than you would get from just your hard drive.

OVERCOMING OBJECTIONS

From users:

• Give them access to more data

From IS professionals:

• Give them broader responsibility

The best way to succeed in office politics is to promise something to everyone.

Tailored to uses

The planning stage included interviews with users to see what jobs they were doing. The interviewers determined what hosts they were reaching and what information they were using. Officials consulted department managers, who made a seat-by-seat analysis of the users's actual needs. Assigned machines were then matched to those needs. If a user primarily did terminal emulation with a little word processing, for example, the PC was replaced with a diskless workstation.

In the process, the number of PCs was greatly reduced and the number of printers was cut by half. While users may have less CPU power on the desktop, they have easier access to data and applications through the network.

Remaining PCs are now linked to an AT&T 386-based NetWare server for DOS applications and for file storage. A Sun Sparcserver 390 connected to AT&T 6500 cluster controllers gives the terminal users access to a variety of mini and mainframe hosts, and to Unix versions of WordPerfect and Lotus 1-2-3.

The switch has cut the previous 17 applications to a basic four, and all data on the LAN is now backed up nightly.

Success has its price

The road to success is lined with speed bumps; those who blindly rush ahead are likely to break something. In fact, some who have carefully planned and considered downsizing projects have looked and backed away. They've found that the obstacles to downsizing can outweigh the potential benefits. Among their problems:

- The implementation process can be costly and complex.
- Many users lack the necessary expertise and technical tools—particularly true when they try to manage internetworked systems from a remote location.
- They encounter resistance, from traditional MIS personnel, from users, or both.

IT'S GOING TO BE BUMPY

Major problem areas:

- Complex installations
- Lack of tools (Particularly for network management)
- Human problems

Downsizing projects are likely to encounter three major problems.

The last issue can be particularly troublesome. Virtually every manager who has spearheaded a downsizing effort has had to overcome at least some initial opposition from someone. Employees fear the loss of their jobs—or if not their jobs, their current levels of power and control. IS professionals fear the decentralized aspect of downsizing, which hands more control to the users. In an equal and opposite reaction, users often fear the centralizing effect of linking stand-alone PCs into networks.

These opposing interests have become familiar enough to have acquired standard solutions. Users can be persuaded to accept downsizing if you demonstrate that the network will bring more power to their desktops, not less. MIS can learn that distributed platforms can enhance the department's role, making it more central to the organization and increasing the respect in which it is held.

In spite of problems like these, most managers who have been through the downsizing experience say it has been well worth the effort. Still, it's important to remember that others have encountered problems—and that you will, too.

Not up to the job

At least one company has run into trouble because it downsized too far. At Western General Services, a Chicago-based insurance company, officials decided to move one of their main applications, a benefits administration package, from several ADS-6000 minicomputers and an IBM System/36 midrange system to a LAN-based system. The basic idea was sound, and the project ultimately succeeded. Even so, Western General started by heeding what turned out to be bad advice.

Demanding application

On the advice of a consultant, the benefits application was moved to a 33-MHz 386 file server. By the time 10 users had logged on to the system, the 386 was running at 110% of its rated capacity.

This particular application puts heavy demands on a file server, the company's analysts determined. Each user simultaneously opens more than 30 files at a time. The server simply wasn't up to that kind of workload.

The company considered adding 386 more servers to boost performance, but there were two objections to that course. The cost could quickly escalate, and each new server would add unnecessary complexity, as well as maintenance headaches.

Instead, the company decided to install a 486 system, the Tricord Powerframe. Each 386 would cost nearly as much as the Powerframe, and would require two or three times the maintenance. The 486 system also solved the capacity problem. When it was tested with 47 users, it still was running at only 29% of its capacity. Average use in day-to-day service is only 6% or 7%.

Cautious approach

Having been burned by their first experience, company officials were wary. Even with those performance figures in hand, they hesitated to commit themselves. They persuaded the vendor to let them use the system on a 30-day trial basis.

The installation was a success, though; Western General has since bought a second Powerframe to use as a backup system.

Not without a fight

Downsizing at Pennsylvania Blue Shield has saved several hundred thousand dollars, just in the avoided costs of upgrades to the insurer's mainframes. It has also had the significant advantage of improving users' access to information. Networked PCs at the firm's Camp Hill, Pennsylvania, headquarters now are linked to statewide and national networks.

War zone

Achieving these results was not unlike a war, though, and Blue Shield had to win three major battles before it could succeed. Officials had to overcome:

- The resistance of IS personnel to distributed computing.
- A long debate among IS groups from four separate divisions on the selection of a network operating system.
- Problems with vendors, who wanted the network to be exclusively composed of their hardware and software products. They had to be persuaded to participate in a mixed system.

MAJOR HUMAN PROBLEMS

IS personnel:

- Fear loss of control

Users:

- Fear loss of independence

Vendors:

- Fear loss of business

Most human problems are rooted in security and resistance to change.

The lesson

As Blue Shield's experiences illustrate, you can't expect to create a trouble-free new downsized system overnight. Instead, it is usually a process of slow evolution that continues even after the first system is up and running.

This is particularly true in areas where the technology is not yet fully developed. Among these areas are:

- Internetworking, the connection of local area networks with other LANs and with wide-area networks. A uniform, integrated architecture for this process has been slow to develop.
- Network applications. Few packaged applications are available strictly for networks. Downsizing has done much, though, to speed up in-house application development.
- Network management tools. Managers need more and better ways to keep their systems running well.

A short breather

The Metropolitan Life Insurance Co. struck out on a downsizing project, then found it had to step back and take a more careful look at where it was heading.

MAJOR TECHNICAL PROBLEMS

- Internetworking
- Network applications
- Network management tools

Most technical needs can be filled, but there are some shortcomings.

The plan was—and still is—to replace a system of 1,000 minicomputers with PC-based LANs. One objective was to replace the minicomputers, which were becoming obsolete. That meant transferring their applications, including customer information, sales records, and management information to networked systems. Though the existing units were still performing well, they were being eclipsed by newer technology, and necessary upgrades were hard to justify.

At the same time, the company wanted to take advantage of new developments like laptop computers. It wanted to let sales representatives use laptops in the field, but without having to switch software environments when they came in to their home offices.

Networks and servers

A typical network configuration consists of several PCs connected to an NCR server carrying a Bull label under an OEM agreement.

All of the systems currently run using DOS. The LAN-based systems are to be used for all sales office applications, including those developed in-house and commercial PC software.

After about 50 of these conversions had been completed, the company decided to call a temporary halt to the process. The new systems were working well enough, but officials were beginning to see problems in managing such an extensive network.

Managing from a distance

The particular problem is how to manage remote computing. Many vendors could provide products to help the firm meet that need, but no one offered a complete management system.

Human as well as technical problems had to be dealt with. The downsizing project brought with it changes in the organizational structure. The company wanted to make sure the organization and its employees were prepared to manage the technology.

Remote management and training

The company's objective was to manage the networks remotely, from workstations. Because the linked networks would cover such a large organization, it was necessary to manage the system remotely from a central location. This included training the users, particularly in their personal responsibilities for security and data integrity.

Formerly, the minicomputer systems took care of most of these problems. With a PC network, individual users are responsible. Furthermore, PC users had to be trained to recognize that on a network, they had greater responsibilities to the organization; their personal computers were no longer purely personal. Among the responsibilities users must learn are those of backing up files and taking responsibility for security.

When PCs are being used for individual processes, such as spreadsheet applications, they are the responsibility of the individual user, officials pointed out. When that same PC is being used on a LAN as a business workstation, the user must take responsibility for more than the data on that one system.

Looking for trouble

Another reason for the pause was to give the company time to examine the system and its performance and to achieve what one official called a "zero-defect level." The objective was to buy some time, to see what improvements might be needed, and to determine what parts of the system were working well. At the same time, vendors would have a chance to catch up with the need for better network management tools.

A management crystal ball

Yet another purpose of the delay was to look into the future and anticipate possible changes. Since the technology is changing so rapidly, the company wanted to make sure that the investment it makes now will have value in the future.

In particular, the company wanted to avoid rushing into a quick-fix system that was available now, only to find that it would limit the opportunities later. Another question concerned the future development of PC operating systems.

The delay was only to be temporary, and even as it ordered the pause, Met Life had plans to convert another group of 50 installations within a few months.

"It doesn't exist"

Met Life is not the only company to have concerns about managing far-flung internetworked systems. The *Christian Science Monitor* has installed a complex internetwork of Ethernet, DECnet, and AppleTalk LANs networks. Linked by bridges, there are a total of 13 segments, with well over 500 nodes. What the publisher needs is an integrated network management system to oversee it all.

At a minimum, such a system would be a central repository for all network data, including statistics, status reports, alarms, and historical data. Ideally, the network manager could retrieve this information at a single console, while network operators at consoles in different areas would have simultaneous access.

It's a system that did not exist. The *Monitor* shares the frustrations of many users who have found that no single system can manage the entire span of interconnected, multi-vendor, multi-technology LANs many companies would like to use.

Anything but simple

Like many users in this position, the *Monitor* is using a simple network management protocol (SNMP), which is constantly being refined but has had trouble living up to its name.

SNMP, as defined by the Internet Engineering Task Force for managing transmission control protocol/internet protocol (TCP/IP) networks, provides a common format for network devices such as bridges, routers, concentrators, and modems. Using this format, these can communicate management data via an *agent* to the management station, or *host*. This host can be either a Unix-based workstation or a DOS-based personal computer.

Unfinished product

The problem: Though users and vendors have both widely adopted it, SNMP is just as widely viewed as an unfinished product that even in its final form might not have much of a future.

A major obstacle to its successful use is the proprietary nature of many SNMP products. Many vendors place proprietary data in their management information databases. These databases serve as the storage centers for management data about particular network devices. Consequently, host software from another vendor may not be able to read or display the network device's data. Few vendors make this proprietary data public.

As a result, a user who installs SNMP devices from a large number of vendors must choose a management station that either supports proprietary management information bases or offers tool kits to write applications that can.

The *Monitor* uses Lance, an SNMP management station from Micro Technology, Inc., to gather information from the firm's 3Com and Cabletron bridges and routers. Lance puts a "tap" on each network segment to be monitored. The bridges automatically send messages to the Lance system, so they provide an immediate alert when a line is down. What this system cannot do is monitor DECnet traffic.

Hope for the future

Some new types of management systems are being developed to handle these shortcomings. Still, the *Monitor's* experience may remain typical for some time. In fact, some authorities have predicted that a single integrated management system will never emerge.

There is, of course, another solution for those who are just beginning to plan and install their systems. Avoid the problems of diverse systems that have simply come together by accident. Integration and remote management should be major considerations in selecting system components.

Special networking applications

Most downsized projects are strictly business. They are designed to get information into the hands of managers, sales representatives, and customer service employees. While saving money, these systems improve a business organization's competitive stature by improving its employee's access to information.

That's not the only reason for downsizing, though. Medical, government, and scientific users have also found that downsized systems improve their own access to information and their ability to serve patients, citizens, and colleagues.

A hospital networks its networks

In an exercise better described as rightsizing than downsizing, Pittsburgh's Children's Hospital has embarked on a program to consolidate an impromptu assortment of LANs and individual PCs. In its place, says the plan, will be an organization-wide network.

The program is a response to the growing inefficiencies of running isolated networks in individual departments. These varying networks, with equipment from equally varied suppliers, placed heavy demands on support technicians. Many also maintained patient records and other information duplicated in other systems.

System goals

One of the hospital's objectives is to eliminate the duplication. Others are to:

- Provide wider access to available patient records.
- Let departments share their resources.
- Centralize administration and software distribution.

For example, many patient records traditionally take the form of dictated documents. These are printed and stored as part of the patient files. Only one physician at a time has access to a printed file. Under a networked system, any doctor who needs the information can retrieve it instantly by computer.

The hospital also has been standardizing its installations. For example, NetWare 3.11 has been established as the standard for new LAN installations. It lets a user communicate with a server on his or her own network, or gain access to other networks via TCP/IP.

Downsizing the database

As another part of the project, the hospital has shifted its patient database from a DEC VAX to SQL server running on a network database server.

The management functions of a relational database are important to maintaining the security of these confidential records, officials say. It allows the system administrator to manage access to particular tables, and even to specify certain rows and columns.

Collaborating on research

Academic researchers and government agencies have long had the services of the Internet communication network. However, the intricate address required to identify an Internet colleague can make even a DOS command with multiple switches look simple by comparison. To compound things further, access has traditionally been via campus mainframes that impose their own intricate command structures.

At Oregon State University, the College of Oceanography has downsized the process of preparing and editing research papers. Instead of the mainframe, the college now has a network of about 160 PCs, Macintoshes, and Sun workstations, running a TOPS network operating system. This network also provides easier access to Internet and thus to colleagues to research institutions throughout the world.

Changed methodology

Business organizations often have found that networking has changed and improved the way they work. OSU has had the same experience. In the past, an academic research paper was usually a one-professor, one-paper enterprise. Though Internet was available, only some professors were willing to go through the difficulties of using it.

The networked system makes access easier. It thus opens up new opportunities for collaborative research with scholars working on similar projects at other universities. Scholarly consultation that used to take days by mail now can be completed in as little as ten minutes. That also opens new opportunities in the continuing competition for research grants.

Group documents

The network has also simplified the process of writing and editing collaborative documents. Manuscript drafts can be sent out over the system so other participants can edit and add to them. The result is a cooperative effort in which everyone involved in the process has had an electronic chance to add his or her contributions.

Because researchers use a mixture of Macs, Sun workstations, and PCs, each person working on a manuscript saves his or her work in its native file format. Translation utilities included with the TOPS network handle any necessary conversions, and an InBox E-mail package shuttles the files back and forth between researchers. Although they'd like to move to a group editing application, professors say they have yet to find such a product that can run on all three platforms.

Decentralizing space research

The government is also taking a hand in making research and research data more widely available to the scientific community. A downsizing project at the Jet Propulsion Laboratories (Pasadena, California) is allowing researchers throughout the country to analyze data from the nation's space explorations on their own personal computers.

JPL receives and analyzes large volumes of transmitted data from satellites and space probes. Traditionally, it took a pair of mainframe systems to do this job: one to receive the transmissions, another to process the information.

Now, a decentralized data network, anchored at JPL, will maintain a directory of available data files. Scientists can use this directory to select and download the stored data to their desktop machines. At the same time, JPL is phasing out some mainframes that have outlived their usefulness.

Large systems still have roles

JPL's vision of its future mission is to evolve into a computational facility, doing calculations that can't be done on PCs. The JPL data center, which serves about 8,000 users, will still maintain its large data banks on high-end mainframes, which are available for off-line analysis. The center will also continue to serve as the heart of the downsized network.

However, as the LAN system expands, it will become the focal point of more activity and will serve as the main point of access to the central repository.

4

CHAPTER

Understanding
PC networks

The boom years of the personal computer are over. The ten years since IBM took PCs out of the hobbyist class and into the office were a decade of rapid growth and surging technical advancement. Now, diminishing returns have taken effect. The rapid growth of the PC's first decade has tapered off, with only a few exceptions.

One of those exceptions is particularly important, though, because it has made downsizing possible. That is the technological development behind the local area network. Developments in hardware and peripherals, operating systems software applications, communications, and connectivity continue to open doors for new kinds of PC uses and users, including local area networking.

Network fundamentals

Local area networks (LANs) carry data in much the same way the telephone system carries voice signals; in fact, many LANs use telephone wire. The biggest difference is in the way the two systems transmit their signals.

A voice signal coming over a telephone line is continuous. When you speak into a phone, the other party hears you almost simultaneously. Before a LAN transmits information, it assembles the data into *packets*. A packet serves much the same function as an envelope. The information is slipped inside; on the outside, the network operating system adds the origin and destination addresses and other data that will help the network get the packet to its destination.

Each type of LAN has its own type of *network operating system* (NOS) software to translate the electronic addressing and route the packet properly. Each NOS uses its particular kind of *protocol*. Like the rules of diplomacy, a network protocol establishes the rules for translating and dispatching the messages. The protocol establishes such things as how each computer is identified, how they verify the information they transmit, what they do in case of an error, and how the system can tell when the transmission is finished.

Usually, a single LAN will use a single protocol, but that isn't always the case. A downsized system, for example, may have a PC running Novell NetWare and a mainframe running its proprietary operating system. In that case, there must be a *gateway* between the two. The gateway serves the diplomatic function of an interpreter, translating the protocol of one machine into a form the other can understand.

Bigger bits and pieces

The last few years, and even months, have brought new power and functions to PC systems. This has made it possible for PC-based network servers to do the work of larger systems, sometimes including the largest mainframes. Only a few years ago, a large corporate database could not possibly have found room on the hard disk of any kind of PC. Now, superservers offer as much as 20 gigabytes (20Gb) of disk storage and eight microprocessors. Even lesser PCs let users develop and run major mainframe-scale applications for use on a LAN.

New designs and improved manufacturing processes have dropped the prices of PC peripherals. Laser printer prices have dropped about 22% in two years.

Operating systems

PC operating systems, even with the advent of DOS 5.0 and competing products, remain primarily single-user products. The same is true of Microsoft Windows Version 3 and its graphical interface. Windows simplifies computers for a new class of users, and its uniform interface simplifies training. However, it does neither job as well as was suggested by the great publicity blitz that accompanied its introduction, and it can be a bear to network as chapter 7 will explain.

Network operating systems have also matured. Many now provide security features and expanded capacity that let networks accommodate larger numbers of users. These users can run increasingly sophisticated applications.

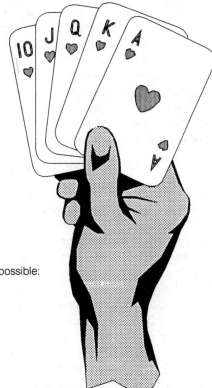

Upsized systems make downsizing possible:

- PC processors and storage
- Operating systems
- Applications
- Communication
- Client/server architecture

The increased power and capacity of PC networks has closed the gap with larger systems.

Work-saving applications

Groupware is one category of applications that directly depends on networking. Packages like Lotus Notes and AT&T's Rhapsody automate many of the manual steps involved in standard office procedure. Take the process of logging customer complaints and assigning responsibility for their solutions. Office workers once had to pick their way manually through multiple steps of such a task. Now, they can simply follow cues provided by the software.

Features such as hyperlinks, active documents, and object linking and embedding (OLE) now appear in some PC applications. These also free users from manual processes. They let users build intelligence into their documents so they can, for example, automatically refer to other documents or forms.

Better communication

Few forms of technology have changed business computing as much as electronic mail. Initially, a user could send E-mail messages to coworkers on the same network, which usually meant people working in the same department. Now, packages such as Network Courier and SoftSwitch Central connect LAN users to corporate-wide E-mail systems without the need for major in-house bridge building.

Speedier transmission also makes it possible to send more types of data across E-mail channels. Some can transmit images and handle voice-mail. There also are E-mail filters that minimizes users' workloads by automatic screening and routing incoming messages.

Client and servers

Client/server connectivity has also become a practical reality. Few network-related developments have been as great a boon to downsizing. Software has been designed to transparently link PCs with mainframe and minicomputer servers. That means these larger systems can remain valuable; not everyone needs a superserver to manage a large database.

PC users can now retrieve data from host systems without moving to dumb terminals or bothering with mainframe access and query languages. This has enabled more computer novices to use available online data. It has also increased the speed with which users can retrieve data from multiple hosts for processing on their PCs.

Another major new PC network application is electronic data interchange (EDI). This is the electronic transmission of orders, invoices, and inventory records between manufacturers and their suppliers; it is a boon to such efficiency-building techniques as just-in-time inventory management. PC-based EDI packages cost only a fraction of those designed for mainframes.

Many kinds of networks

Networks come in a confusing variety of sizes, types, hardware, and software, ranging from the simple to the complex. To begin to simplify the discussion, available LAN types can be placed in four major categories. Two of these are for light-duty use and normally would not be useful for downsized mainframe applications:

- Print and file sharing. These are simple switching mechanisms that let small groups of users share resources. They range from manual switches to zero-slot LANs, which permit file transfers via a cable between two computers. The network might have a single laser printer, for example, letting several users share this expensive, speedy resource. Or, representatives coming in from the field may plug in their portables to move information to the office system.

- Peer-to-peer network. This is a fast-growing form of local area networking designed for small businesses and departments. In this network, all workstations and other nodes are created equal. All users, for example, would have direct access to a word processing file stored on one system's hard disk. They could work with this file directly; they need not transfer it to their own systems. Network members can also share printers and other resources. Computers in this type of system are usually PCs running under DOS.

The main characteristic of a peer-to-peer LAN is that it does not need a designated file server—though it can have one. The low cost and efficiency of these smaller networks has made them popular, but most users downsizing large-system applications would find them too limited. More likely, the choice would be one of these two types:

- Client/server LANs. Here, one or more higher-powered units provide major resources for a network that typically would serve a single office or department. A file server is usually the minimum requirement. A client/server LAN can also have any number of specialized servers, such as those that manage communication or carry database files. In fact, client/server is usually associated with and most often used as a database management technique.
- Enterprise-wide internetworks. These are groups of LANs linked together, perhaps with wide-area networks (WANs) in the picture as well. They give users in one office or department access to corporate-wide data, perhaps from a database server in another location entirely.

This chapter will deal primarily with single client/server LANs, while the next will cover networks of networks.

NETWORKS VARY IN SIZE, COMPLEXITY

- Print and file sharing
- Peer-to-peer networks
- Client/server networks
- Enterprise-wide networks

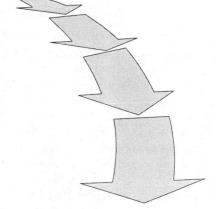

The smaller the network, the easier to buy and use—but downsized applications usually require top-line networks.

The client/server model

Those who like precise definitions will cringe at client/server computing. It's a concept with many applications and a definition to fit each use. It also includes peer-to-peer computing. While peer-to-peer LAN systems have been marketed as low-end products, in a large-system environment the equality of peer-to-peer is often seen as an ultimate objective.

Client/server architecture follows this basic pattern: Each application uses a pair of programs. One is a client; the other, naturally enough, is a server. This matched pair of programs is linked by an interprocess communication scheme. Through this scheme, the client makes requests for services, and the server fulfills those requests.

Software peers

The client program and the server program work as partners. The client makes requests. The server answers them. It's an simple as that. Though many database servers require high-capacity dedicated hardware, the client/server process can work on any pair of computers in the network.

Compare the client/server tandem with a single-purpose PC database program. The same program takes care of keyboard input, retrieves selected data from the disk, and displays it on the screen. This program must be designed to:

- Read the data file and understand its format.
- Make changes to the data file.
- Find and retrieve data from within the file, and do it in the most efficient manner.
- Execute its internal processing logic.
- Communicate with the user.

Serving the client

Though the two programs in a client/server relationship work together, normally an application developer need worry only about one of them. The server program already has its data management logic built in. The developer need only write a client program that taps that logic. In a database server, the usual vehicle these days is Structured Query Language (SQL). SQL is neither highly structured nor a complete programming language, but it has become the established way to communicate with the relational databases most often used in client/server systems. SQL is a means of contact with the database management program's application program interface (API). All the programmer must do is send the proper SQL instructions to the server. There is no need to worry about how the server processes those instructions. Other types of server programs have APIs of their own. For example, the X Window system has an API called the X Protocol, which works with a set of libraries called the xtib. Often, programmers will write mini-programs that combine several different xtib calls. Then the overall program can make calls to the mini-programs, which are called widgets (really). Widgets are reused and shared, and some are even bundled and sold. The Open Software Foundation's Motif and Sun's Open Look window managers, both of which use the X Window system, have their own widgets. Some developers also place widgets in the public domain, where they are shared freely.

Network traffic

One characteristic of all client/server programs is that they must run over networks. The client and server programs will usually reside in different computers. Since they need to communicate in order to work together, the interprocess communication must travel over the network. The X Window system's X Protocol was specifically designed to travel on a network. SQL was not originally designed for that purpose, but it can do the job if special networking software is written to carry the SQL commands.

File servers are similar to X Window servers. File servers were also designed specifically to use networks for communication. File servers take the normal disk access routines of an operating system such as DOS, and redirect those disk access requests over a network to a server process. The server process can run on a different operating system, such as NetWare, OS/2, or Unix. The client need not even be aware of the difference.

Many types of servers

A server is usually thought of as housing a large *back-end* database, to which the networked users have access through *front-end* systems on their workstations. This is the typical function of a database server. Servers perform other specialized functions as well:

- *File servers* are the central point of access to the network. Most network operating systems are designed to support these servers for DOS workstations. All access passes through this point, and this is where any security screening is applied. Originally, these were also the central points for network access, though this function is gradually going to workstations, particularly in Macintosh and Unix systems.
- *Database servers* are a special kind of file server. They store and manage database files. That's often a large enough job in itself for a dedicated server, and it spares the file server the workload of database management.
- *Communication servers* let users share modems and expensive outside access lines such as connections to wide-area networks.

- *Electronic mail gateways* are communication servers that provide access to E-mail and similar services. They run communication programs like CC:Mail, DaVinci and PROFS. They also can provide fax services, but fax produces large graphic-image files whose transmission can clog up a network.
- *Print servers* give larger networks the same printer-sharing facilities to which some smaller networks are dedicated.

Some newer kinds of servers are also being developed. They include:

- *Fax servers* use internal fax cards to transmit network users' outgoing faxes and manage the incoming messages. There still is one remaining problem: how to distribute the incoming faxes.
- *Voice servers* are an extension of the voice-mail systems now in use; they also can incorporate existing E-mail systems. The day may come when an employee can call in to pick up his or her electronic mail, though there is a human limit to this potential: It's hard to comprehend a message that plays for more than a few minutes. These systems may take advantage of a developing technology, the Integrated Services Digital Network (ISDN), which is designed to carry both voice and data messages over the same lines.
- *Video servers* could become important as document imaging spreads. Imaging systems store graphic representations of documents. Their storage and processing will demand a high-powered server.
- *Library servers*, which manage volume of archival data stored on CD ROM disks.

A VARIETY OF SERVERS

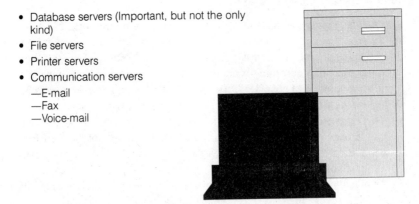

- Database servers (Important, but not the only kind)
- File servers
- Printer servers
- Communication servers
  —E-mail
  —Fax
  —Voice-mail

Servers can provide many kinds of services, some familiar, some not.

Principles of server planning

In years past, mainframe computers did all the work. They performed every function demanded of them. Should those demands come from more than one task, the mainframe lets each task use a share of its time and effort.

Adding a network and specialized servers has the effect of *exploding the box*. Functions that all were performed within the mainframe now are distributed among the servers. Each server is optimized to perform its particular function, and each directly devotes its processing time to performing that task. Where the mainframe is self-contained, the network is a modular system.

Most networks now are based at least on file servers. Other specialized servers provide such services as communication and printing. Though a server is often visualized as a high-powered PC, this isn't always necessary. Smaller units often can do some of the lighter, specialized work.

Normally, each server is a separate computer. It is possible, though, for more than one server to share the same enclosure. Each, however, should have its own dedicated bus structure.

Planning principles

There are three key concepts of planning a client/server LAN:

- The network should be *modular*. You should be able to add the special services you need simply by installing servers that provide those services.
- The system should have an *open architecture*. Proprietary formats limit the ability to add modular units for the specialized purposes you might need.
- The network should have a *sound, well-planned architecture*. Think of the network as a unit. Don't make unplanned, piece-by-piece additions.

CLIENT/SERVER DESIGN PRINCIPLES

Modular design:

- To add services as needed

Open system:

- To obtain these services from multiple sources

Planned architecture:

- So everything will work as a unit

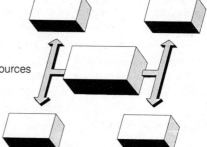

Multiple pieces from multiple sources should all work together.

Plans, not products

Planning for a client/server LAN should start with the file server. Then build out from there. Avoid the problems that plague many older networks. They are like the orphan Topsy of *Uncle Tom's Cabin*: "I 'spect I growed. Don't think nobody ever made me."

One reason that happens: System managers buy products instead of planning a system. Technology is a tool, not an end in itself. One example: System managers have chased the technology of E-mail; meanwhile, fax has established itself as the standard medium of communication.

What networks are made of

Clients and servers are the most visible and hardest-working parts of a local area network. These are, after all, the computers the network is intended to link. Connecting them, however, requires a confusing conglomeration of bits and pieces. Some are hardware, some are software, and some combine elements of both.

Nearly any kind of computer can function as a server, particularly when its task is specialized and light-duty. At the other extreme, heavy-duty database service can require one of the high-powered superservers with its fast processors, multiple disk drives, and other features that equip it for this demanding type of duty.

Short of that, the most effective PC-based servers will have these two main characteristics:

- An 80386 processor, or higher. Many network operating systems, and some network applications, take advantage of the capabilities of the 386, versus the earlier 80286.
- A large, fast hard disk. Nothing has a greater effect on the server's performance.

Network adapters

Every networked computer needs one of these interface cards. They translate the signals that travel along the network cables into messages the computer can understand and use; they also amplify outgoing signals and convert them between parallel and serial formats.

Generally, a card will incorporate one of three prevailing networking standards: Ethernet, Arcnet, or token ring. These are explained in more detail later in this chapter.

An adapter card has one other major function: media access control (MAC). This is a control system that keeps signals from different computers, or *nodes*, from interfering with each other. The process usually takes one of three forms:

- Carrier sense multiple access (CSMA). This is something like carrying on a conversation over the telephone: You wait for the other party to finish talking, then it's your turn. A CSMA board listens for traffic on the network; if it finds none, it is free to transmit its own signals. A CSMA board also, of necessity, includes a tie-breaker system for those times when two stations detect an opportunity and begin transmitting at the same time. Ethernet systems use a method called carrier sense multiple access with collision detection (CSMA/CD).

- Sequential station numbers. This method, used in Arcnet, assigns a number to each node. Access is like waiting in line at a deli. Each number is called in turn, and each station waits for its number to come up.
- Token passing. An electrical signal called a *token* is passed from station to station. When the token arrives at each station, that station is free to transmit. As its name suggests, a token ring network uses this system.

Network cabling

To have a network, there usually must be wires. That's no longer a universal requirement. No-cable networks use infrared flashes to transmit messages between nodes. For the most part, though, the circulatory system of a network is its cabling.

Like nearly everything else in networking, cable comes in an assortment of varieties:

- Twisted pair. This might sound like a rock group or something in an X-rated movie. Actually, it is the ordinary lightweight wiring commonly used in telephone systems. You may be able to run your network over telephone wiring that is already in place, though in practice you'll probably find that your needs exceed the available wiring. The best twisted pair wiring for data transmission meets the specifications for a version of the Ethernet protocol called *10BaseT*.
- Shielded twisted pair. Also called *data-grade twisted pair*, this type of wiring has an external shield to insulate it from electrical interference. It is common in token ring installations, where it adds insurance against damage and interference. The drawbacks: It is expensive and hard to handle.
- Coaxial cable. This is the cable in cable television. It consists of a single central wire surrounded by a shield. It has many of the advantages and disadvantages of shielded twisted pair. Some varieties are stiff and hard to install.
- Fiberoptic cable. If money is no object, this is the type to use. Since it uses light instead of electrical signals, this type is immune to electrical interference. It can also travel long distances without the need for amplification. It is particularly useful in areas where machinery is in use, or where there is a great distance between nodes.

The topic of topology

Topology refers to the physical layout of the network cables. There are three basic varieties:

- In a *bus* network, the network begins with a single strand of cable. At each station, a T-connector holds a wire that branches off to the station's adapter card. This format uses less cable than the others and is the least expensive, but it is also the least reliable. A cable break can shut down the entire network, and each of the many connectors is a possible failure point.

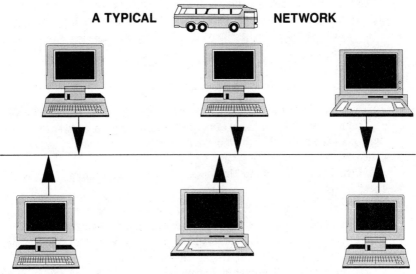

A TYPICAL   **NETWORK**

A bus network is simple and straightforward, but its simplicity does not mean easy maintenance.

- A *star* network consists of a single cable from each node, leading to a central wiring hub. It reduces the number of connections, is easier and neater to install, and a break in one cable doesn't affect the rest of the network. This system uses more cable, however, and the hub itself can be a costly, complex installation.
- In its simplest form, the *ring* topology is simply a bus whose ends are connected to form a loop. It rarely exists in this form, but it often is emulated. Here's how:

    A token ring network suggests that a token used for media access control is passed from station around a ring topology. That's a logical conclusion, and it's almost correct. Most token ring networks actually connect their cables in a star topology. As the token is passed, however, it emulates a ring, passing from node to node as though they were wired in a circle.

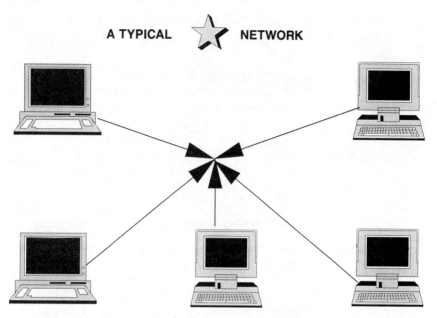

A TYPICAL ☆ NETWORK

A token ring also uses a star wiring configuration but circulates to each link in turn.

Networking protocols

As mentioned earlier, network adapter cards usually support one of three networking protocols: Ethernet, Arcnet, or token ring. The choice of standards tends to dictate other elements of the system such as topology, media access control, and the type of cabling.

These protocols are also sometimes known as standards, which is natural enough. Their official designation is *standard protocols*. They are the creation of committees established by the Institute of Electrical and Electronics Engineers (IEEE) and representatives of the electronics and communications industries.

Ethernet and 10BaseT

Ethernet, named after a poetic term for electromagnetic waves, has been on the market about as long as there have been personal computers. It has the appeal of low cost and simplicity. It will provide high-speed transmission at a reasonable price, and a host of vendors and products support it. Among its more important specifications:

- Data transmission rate of 10 megabits per second.
- Use of a bus topology.
- Maximum distance between stations of 2.8 kilometers, or about 1.75 miles.

- The use of shielded coaxial cable, or twisted-pair wiring, in the 10BaseT version.
- Media access control by CSMA/CD.

In its long life, Ethernet has spun off several variations. The original cabling scheme was used primarily to connect large computers with smaller terminals and workstations. The coaxial cable used as the backbone of these installations is thick, stiff, and hard to handle. Lighter cables run from connectors on this backbone to the individual stations.

A variation called *thin Ethernet* uses lighter-weight cable, which makes installation easier at the expense of transmission distance. More recent variations make use of fiberoptics or twisted-pair wiring.

The 10BaseT variation

Earlier, 10BaseT was mentioned as a specification for twisted-pair wiring. That's part of the story. The IEEE published this specification in 1990, as a standard for bringing this inexpensive form of wiring to Ethernet networks.

The purpose of this standard was to promote easier installation; technicians need not contend with the frozen-rope characteristics of coaxial cable. Network managers have found other advantages that probably are more important.

The greatest of these advantages is the ability to use a star topology instead of the traditional Ethernet bus. The star topology helps make a more reliable system; a fault in one line affects only the node to which it is attached. In addition, 10BaseT has become so widely supported it is almost generic. You can select adapters and wiring hubs from a variety of sources and mix them as you wish. For all this convenience, there is no significant performance penalty.

AN OVERNIGHT SUCCESS

What makes 10BaseT so popular?

- Easy installation
- Reliability
- Broad support
- No performance penalty

Reliability, ease, and widespread support make 10BaseT a leading network candidate.

The token ring

Token ring is the protocol that has IBM behind it. It is at the center of IBM's system of both local and wide area network architecture. With the right connections, all supplied by IBM, you can make a mainframe and a PC look like peers on the same network.

This standard is not strictly an IBM standard, though. Other manufacturers make token ring products, and the protocol is compatible with all major network operating systems.

A token ring system operates something like a parking lot shuttle at Walt Disney World. It uses a signal packet called, naturally enough, a token. This token makes the rounds, checking at each stop for messages ready to be transmitted. If the token finds something, it packages the data into a *frame* and takes it to the receiving station. This station acknowledges receipt, and the token drags the message back to the point of origin. The receiving station notes that the message was received and frees the token to pick up a new message from some other point on the system.

Though a token ring network uses a physical star topology, an error that blocks the token's circulation can effectively keep the entire network from operating. For that reason, most token ring networks use shielded twisted-pair cable to block out any possible contamination by outside electrical impulses.

Other key specifications include:

- Data transfer rates of 4 or 16 megabits per second.
- Maximum cable lengths of about 45 meters, or 150 feet.

Note: A system's maximum data transfer rates are like the top speed of an automobile—rarely achieved and even more rarely done safely. Only in the largest networks will differences in these specifications be reflected in actual performance.

Arcnet

Arcnet, originated by Datapoint, is a low-cost form of networking. It usually operates in a multiple star configuration: small hubs of two to four cables each, linked to other hubs of similar size. Arcnet hubs can use either coaxial cable or unshielded twisted-pair.

Arcnet networks can cover a lot of ground. Maximum cable lengths can be up to 2,000 feet; under the right conditions, the network can extend as far as 20,000 feet. Access control is by a polling system which contacts numbered stations in turn. The normal operating speed is 2.5 megabits per second.

That speed is slower than some superservers deliver data. There are ways to divide the network and use multiple channels to overcome that limitation. Users have found that performance is best when you keep consecutively numbered stations close to each other and assign the lowest numbers to the most powerful units.

Network operating systems

Just as a computer needs an operating system, so does a network. PC operating systems used in networking applications include DOS, OS/2, and Unix. The leading network operating systems (NOSs) include:

- The Novell NetWare family.
- Banyan Vines
- LAN Manager
- Unix, which is both a computer and a network operating system.

Top of the NetWare line

Novell has by far the largest share of the NOS market. NetWare comes in several versions for installations of different sizes, from large enterprise-wide networks to a handful of small-business PCs. The two most powerful, and the two most likely to be considered for downsizing are Versions 3.x and 2.x.

The senior version at this writing, NetWare 3.11, is a sophisticated NOS that can integrate diverse computing resources, including PCs, Unix workstations, Apple Macintoshes, and mainframes into a single enterprise-wide system.

This version of NetWare is designed with enterprise networking in mind. Version 3.11 is designed to take full advantage of the 32-bit environment of the 80386 and 80486 microprocessors, providing performance and capacity needed to build networks that span entire organizations. Available in 20-, 100-, and 250-user versions, NetWare 3.11 lets a user standardize on a single network operating system for both a central office and remote sites.

This is a powerful system. Before you reach its capacity limits, you'll probably exceed the limits of other elements of the system first.

Security is also an important element of this system. A network administrator can control who logs into the network, who has access to specific files and directories, and how much disk space a user can claim. There are built-in reliability features such as read-after-write verification, disk mirroring, disk duplexing, resource tracking, a transaction tracking system (TTS), and power supply monitoring. These increase dependability by safeguarding data against failure in critical parts of the network.

Other security enhancements include security auditing and encrypted backups. The auditing function maintains an audit trail of all security changes that take place on the server. As NetWare backs up files over the network, the data is transmitted in encrypted form. It is decoded only when it is used in a restoring operation.

Remote management facilities let the administrator manage remote servers from any workstation on the network. NetWare interfaces directly with IBM's Netview management application, allowing network alerts to be passed to a central administration console.

This version of NetWare also accommodates NetWare Loadable Modules (NLMs). These are software modules, some provided by Novell, others by outside suppliers. They link dynamically to the operating system and allow server-based applications to be added to the server while it is running. These applications include drivers for network cards, electronic mail gateways, and products that provide additional security, work group activity, and network management functions.

NetWare 3.11 also lets you add needed services such as communication, database access, and network management. Novell provides some of these add-on services, including NetWare for SAA, NetWare for Macintosh, NetWare NFS, and NetWare SQL 386.

NetWare Version 2

This is basic NetWare—the NOS that's been mainly responsible for Novell's leading position in the network marketplace. This version lacks some advanced features such as the add-on modules and features that take advantage of the 386 and 486 chips. It is designed for medium-sized networks with up to 100 users.

Security has generally been rated a strong point with this NetWare version. It assigns users to groups; each group has certain access rights. If someone changes job assignments, the network administrator can simply transfer that person to a new group. There's no need to go through all the specific access authorizations for that person. The system also lets the administrator restrict access to certain days and times and to require periodic password changes.

An add-on module adds disk mirroring and duplexing for added reliability.

The main rap against Version 2: It is a consultant's make-work tool. Installation is not as easy as Version 3, which is a later-generation system.

On the Vines

NetWare clearly shows its PC roots; Banyan Systems' Vines takes its cues from standard minicomputer software. Vines is a high-end system, most directly competitive with NetWare 3.11, in both price and features. Vines is a Unix-based system which handles all the common server functions including communication.

A Vines server can use just about any hardware platform you desire. Banyan sells its own line of server PCs, but nearly any PC from the 286 class up can be a Vines server. Like NetWare, Vines is available in separate versions for 80286 and for higher systems; there are also versions for Micro Channel computers and systems with multiple processors, like the Compaq Systempro.

One advantage over competing systems in a Vines feature that lets users find network resources faster by replicating directory information on servers throughout the network. This is particularly useful when the system has several servers. Another unique feature is the access to gateways, mail systems, print queues, fax gateways, and host gateways.

LAN Manager

This generic NOS should come with a plain, black-and-white label. Actually, it is sold under the labels of several vendors, including IBM, Microsoft, and 3Com. Though the systems are identical, each vendor implements it in a somewhat different way.

There is this requirement: All LAN Manager servers must run OS/2. Client workstations can use either DOS or OS/2. Since OS/2 is inherently a multitasking system, a Vines server conceivably can run OS/2 applications while also functioning as a file server. That would make it a leading candidate to become involved in the coming technology of *distributed processing*, a system that lets application programs take advantage of CPU processors wherever they may be on the network.

One major drawback: Except for database server products, there have been few OS/2 applications to capitalize on this opportunity.

Networking with Unix

The Unix operating system, originally developed by and for AT&T programmers, is often associated with high-powered graphic workstations. These stations usually feature reduced instruction set computing (RISC) designs, and graphic displays that use the X Window system and produce a visual effect similar to that of Microsoft Windows. Another increasingly popular use is to run Unix on a 386-class PC as a low-cost application or database server.

Unlike DOS, Unix was designed from scratch to serve multiple users, applications, and systems. One thing Unix does well is to mix with DOS operating systems on PCs. Unix can run on a variety of hosts, including minicomputers as well as PCs. In that role, it can act as the host to a network of DOS-based PCs. For example, you can create a database on a minicomputer running Unix; operators stationed at PCs can gain access to that database through a system that makes the same files look like Unix files to the minicomputer and DOS files to the PCs.

One popular way of linking PC and Unix systems is the Network File System (NFS) developed by Sun Microsystems. A DOS version of NFS running on each PC gives the PC users simultaneous access to the server's Unix files.

An alternative offered by both Digital and AT&T is a version of LAN Manager designed to run under Unix. Client PCs use the same software to connect with a Unix/LAN Manager server they would use if the server were running OS/2. You can map drives on client PCs to both types of servers at the same time.

Since LAN Manager is available in both Unix and OS/2 versions, it provides the ability to mix and match computer systems. This can be valuable if a large database demands a minicomputer server, or if writers and editors are using PCs, sending their output to a Unix-based publishing system.

There is this possible drawback: Any translation of files between two operating systems is going to take some time. Testers have found that the response is not quite as quick as you would get using DOS workstations and a NetWare file server, but in most applications the lag should not be critical.

Making network choices

Someone once devised a fictional organization called LEAN. It stands for Let's Eliminate Acronyms Now. A first encounter with networking is enough to make people ask, "Where do we sign up?"

The variety of available choices can be equally confusing. Then there's one more confounding factor: many networks are installed to suit a particular technological vision. Then the organization finds that the system is ill-suited to the organization and its mission. In planning a network, then, the first principle should be:

Let the network fit the organization.

In the first stage of planning, you can comfortably ignore the most difficult technical questions. Concentrate instead on:

- The nature of the organization.
- Its goals and vision.
- How the downsized system can help achieve these.

There's a tendency among technical people and traditional-minded managers to sneer at these "soft" and "wimpy" considerations; real managers don't need to get involved with it.

That attitude can be a serious mistake. Today's most successful organizations focus on people, not systems. In fact, one of the major objectives of downsizing is to scale corporate data processing functions down to a more human level where people take action instead of just waiting to be served.

Needs assessment

Human needs and the corporate mission, then, are major elements of the first phase of network planning: a needs assessment. In addition to these overall considerations, look closely at the users and what they really need to play their parts in fulfilling that mission.

FIRST PRINCIPLE OF NETWORK PLANNING

Let the network . . .   . . . fit the organization

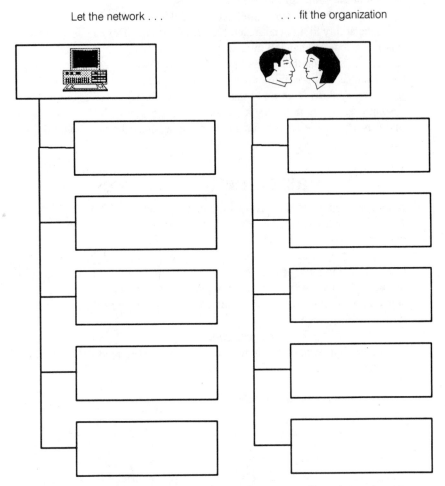

Network plans should be led by the organization's needs. Then choose the technology that meets those needs.

Though formal job descriptions are becoming less important (and certainly less descriptive) in today's team-oriented working environment, they still are a good place to start. A statement of what a particular user must do on the job every day is a key to deciding what kind of system will serve this user best.

Such an assessment will also be valuable when you are assaulted with the usual barrage of user requests. Understanding the specific jobs to be done can be essential when you try to distinguish between what users want and what they really need.

Choosing a network operating system (NOS)

A simple file-sharing or peer-to-peer network can be inexpensive and easy to install and maintain. For most downsized applications, though, a more robust client/server architecture will probably justify its cost in better operating efficiency.

A choice of operating system also entails some choices in cabling and network adapters. Here are the designs of two basic systems. Start your considerations by evaluating these alternatives against the needs you have identified:

- A client/server system using DOS workstations and OS/2 servers, using the 10BaseT version of Ethernet and the version of NetWare that best fits the size of your network.
- A mixed system of PCs and larger systems, using a token ring network that supports a mainframe protocol such as IBM's Systems Network Architecture (SNA).

That will serve a great many basic needs. Consider these variations when they will meet specific needs better than one of the basic systems:

- An alternative operating system when it must serve a larger number of users or variety of workstations and servers.
- A Unix-based file server system for database service, heavy-duty applications or such specialized operations as engineering or publishing.

There are no easy answers to network planning questions. However, making choices between the most widely used systems is easier if you make them within the context of the needs you must fill.

System envy

Relating system to need is important when selecting hardware, too. There's an additional reason here: Users sometimes measure their prestige by the power of the system assigned to them. The user of a basic system can develop feelings of inferiority when someone else is given what the computer press likes to call a "screamer."

There could be a very good reason, of course. The basic unit may be perfectly adequate for its user's job, while the more powerful system meets the heavier demands of a graphic artist or an engineer. Ironically, these specialists who can make good use of powerful equipment are often likely to understate their needs, saying they could get by with less.

Selecting systems to match the jobs to be done will not solve either problem by itself. It will, however, allow you to make the best allocation of computing resources and provide a rational basis with which to explain your choices.

5
CHAPTER

Networking networks

If you connect two or more personal computers, you have a local area network. The typical LAN serves a single office or department. If you connect two or more LANs, they form an internetwork, covering a larger department, an operating site, or even an entire multi-site enterprise.

At first, this might not seem to correspond very well with the idea of downsizing to smaller systems. The computers may be smaller, but the networks are getting larger. It does make sense, though, if you view it in terms of the basic objectives of downsizing.

Smaller systems cost less and, sometimes at least, demand fewer human and technical resources. The initial attraction of downsizing is to save money by switching to smaller systems. As many downsizers have learned, though, this is not always the best or most important reason. The cost savings often are not as great as expected. The real benefit of downsizing lies elsewhere: in giving more people more access to more information. The organization can use this information to gain a competitive edge, to more closely monitor the organization's performance, to improve quality and service, and to find and exploit new markets.

In that light, the expansion toward enterprise-wide networking is literally a natural outgrowth of the downsizing trend. Companies are discovering that they can multiply the benefits of downsizing by extending local data access to the entire organization. They connect LANs and tie these to networks at other sites. The result is an enterprise-wide network that can tap into the computing resources of the entire organization. It shouldn't matter whether these are in Portland, Oregon, or Portland, Maine, or anywhere else in the world.

Linking the links

An individual LAN is limited in size. Considerations like size, location, reliability, and performance effectively limit the number of computers you can connect to a LAN, usually long before you reach the network's rated capacity. In most installations, 20 to 50 nodes is tops. That's a bit small for an organization that has several thousand users. Such an organization will need more than one LAN, and it must connect these networks to each other. This process is called *internetworking*.

Traffic control

In its simplest form, an internetwork connects two LANs with an intelligent device, as shown on the diagram. This device might be a *bridge*, a *router*, or some combination of the two. The internetworking device performs much the same functions as an air traffic controller. It monitors all the packets of information that circulate on each LAN. When it detects a packet on the first LAN that is addressed to a station on the second, it forwards it to the other network.

Of course, if air-traffic control were really that simple, it would not have its reputation as a high-stress occupation. The same is true of networking. Even in a simple internetwork, things can get complicated. For

THE FIRST STEP

Two LANs make an internetwork. The internetwork device, usually a bridge or router, controls traffic between the LANs.

example, the two networks might be using different operating systems or protocols. In that case, the internetwork device will need the help of a *gateway* to translate the signals between the incompatible protocols.

Multiple networks

In a typical installation, several work group networks can be linked into departmental networks, as shown in the diagram. These, in turn, can be tied to an enterprise-wide backbone. This is the basic approach, but it can have many variations. For example, if you have a large building or a corporate campus, you will probably want to install a network to connect all the departmental LANs into a site network that is then tied to the corporate backbone.

This backbone can itself be a LAN in the form of a token ring network that has several internetwork devices connected to it. Each internetwork device, in turn, links one or more office- or department-level LANs. In this installation, they function as subnetworks. More recently, fiberoptics have become a popular choice for backbone service.

LINKING ONE BUILDING'S LANs

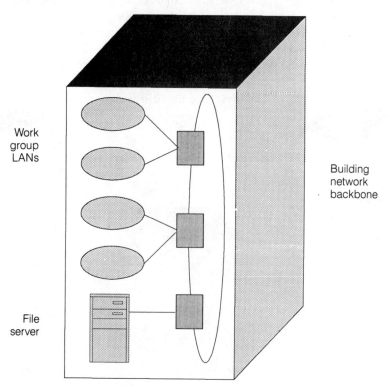

Work
group
LANs

Building
network
backbone

File
server

LANs in individual departments and work groups are linked to each other via a backbone system.

Data packets destined for computers on other subnetworks are redirected to the backbone by an internetworking device. Just as an airplane bound from Atlanta to Dallas is directed to a designated air traffic corridor, the backone serves as a direct route to the destination. There, another internetworking device—like another air traffic control center—takes over to serve as the approach control.

Some internetworking devices can direct messages among their connected subnetworks as well as with the backbone network. The direct routing minimizes traffic on the backbone, and the system usually performs better. On the other hand, you also can maximize performance by connecting widely used resources like file servers and gateways to the backbone network. Users from all over the system will want access to these devices. Placing them on the central network minimizes the amount of traffic and switching that is necessary to reach them.

Wider areas

When an organization wants to connect widely separated resources, another level of networking comes into play: the wide area network or WAN, as shown in the diagram. The WAN uses much the same internetworking principles as other networks. Internetworking devices detect and forward messages destined for other parts of the network. Like other networks, the WAN usually carries its messages in packets. Because of the distances they must cover, however, WANs generally use different types of protocols.

LINKING THE ENTERPRISE

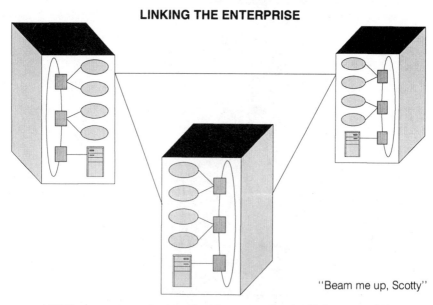

"Beam me up, Scotty"

A WAN connects separate elements of the same enterprise. To the users, all elements of the system would appear to be parts of a single network.

Managing the connections

The interconnecting devices are, naturally enough, key elements in any internetworking system. Whether they are bridges, routers or something else, they serve one vital function: moving information packets from one network to another.

This chapter later explores the variety of available internetworking devices. What type you have is, however, less important than how well the chosen device does its assigned job. Questions to consider in making a selection include:

- Reliability.
- Efficiency.
- Ability to select the best communication path between networks.
- Ability to control who may communicate with whom.
- Ability to identify network problems and faulty components.
- Sensitivity to LAN protocols, and the ability to mix protocols.
- Ease of use.
- Ability to monitor network use.
- Expansion capacity.

The larger the network, the more important these functions are. It's important that you choose components that fulfill these functions; the technology they use to do so is secondary.

Network organization schemes

Managing diversity has become a key concept in human resources management; it is just as important in managing interlinked networks. Corporate managers are increasingly recognizing the strategic importance of being able to interconnect diverse networks and computer platforms.

There are plenty of "solutions" you can buy. Any number of interconnection products are available, including varied types of bridges, routers, and gateways. With these, you can build a flexible, cost-effective backbone for enterprise-wide computing. Such an internetwork will connect LANs not only with each other but with diverse networking environments throughout the organization.

Internetworked systems usually have elements on all or most of these levels:

- Work group subnetworks. Typically, these are interconnected groups of PC LANs.
- Departmental subnetworks. Several work group networks may be grouped into an interlinked departmental system. This system uses one or more routers to provide the contact points between the work group nets.

- Site networks, connecting the departmental subnetworks at a particular location.
- The enterprise-wide backbone. This is an interconnection of the departmental subnetworks throughout the organization.

The working group

At the work group level, you can interconnect several LANs that let group members share data, information, and applications. Most network operating systems provide server-based routing plus *requester* services to let a workstation that uses one NOS contact a server that uses a different system. At this level, the servers can use a routing information protocol (RIP) to exchange routing information. In a larger network, RIP is inefficient enough to bring another meaning to mind; however, at this level, it is usually a cost-effective solution.

The departmental level

Internetworking at the departmental level can begin to involve subnetworks at remotely located sites like those in neighboring buildings. More intelligent bridges and routers might be needed, particularly if you must connect diverse types of networks.

One efficiency-boosting protocol that can be valuable on this level is called open shortest path first (OSPF). This protocol uses a logical grouping system that reassigns network resources according to ease of communication rather than physical location.

Showing some backbone

The backbone must be the sturdiest element of a corporate internetwork. It requires high-performance routers, including those that connect LANs to WANs. Your need here is for both high performance and the ability to link dissimilar networks.

The normal course in building an enterprise-wide system is to start at the department level. Link a few small LANs, then move up to increasingly larger networked systems. A downsized network is usually planned to accommodate a particular application. The nature of the application often determines the size of the network.

Still, the conventional advice for downsizing is a variation of that used for start-up networks. Start with a small application. Typically, this would be one used at the work-group level; logically, then, it would run on a work-group level. Once you have that application going, consider something at the departmental level. Only after you have installed several of these smaller networks should you consider downsizing a major application requiring enterprise-wide access. Once you do get to that large, mission-critical application, you will not only have the experience and confidence to handle it, but most of the systems to handle it will already be in place.

Downsizers face another complication, too. Many of the network elements already in place might reflect unplanned, haphazard installation. An odd mixture of PCs, workstations, LANs, WANs, minicomputers, and mainframes might already be in place, representing many different vendors, along with operating software of equally diverse backgrounds.

An evolutionary approach can gradually bring uniformity to what the orderly mind can easily see as chaos. The system plan must be able to adapt as technology changes. It must cover such issues as cable planning and maintenance, growth and capacity planning, and choices of standards.

Managing network diversity

The increase in networking scope has also meant an increase in complexity. Not long ago, the biggest LANs to be found were at the work group or departmental level. The only form of extended reach was usually for electronic mail or printer sharing. Now, these types of networking are coming into common use as well:

- *Distributed computing*, in which dedicated servers handle different computing, file management, or data storage tasks.
- *Work group computing*, in which users, often on different LAN segments, work in collaboration, such as in writing and editing a publication.
- *Enterprise computing*, where the work flow passes departmental and location boundaries.

To meet users' expectations, today's networks must support all of these types of computing, singly or in combination. The user wants to get the job done. It's up to the network administrator to provide the means. This means a network server that once was assigned to a single LAN must now maintain contact with both users and resources on other networks. The result is that where LANs used to be simple and uniform, today's enterprise-wide networks are complex and diverse.

In such a diverse environment, you have no guarantees that all the applications and communication links will work together. In fact, you should anticipate that they won't. You must make careful choices of network hardware, software, media, protocols and operating systems, so users can gain maximum benefit from widespread communication ability.

The layered look

To make these choices, take a step-by-step approach. Make use of the Open Systems Interconnection (OSI) model that separates network communication activities into seven layers:

1. **Physical.** This layer transmits the bit streams of data across the physical transmission medium.
2. **Data link.** Packages the data for transmission and defines the addressing scheme.
3. **Network.** Addresses and delivers the packets from one node to another, including routing between multiple networks.
4. **Transport.** Sends and receives data, and notifies the user of any errors.
5. **Session.** Establishes, maintains, and terminates the communication session.
6. **Presentation.** Converts and formats data for the user application.
7. **Application.** Provides an application program interface (API) for the user application.

OSI AND THE SEVEN LAYERS

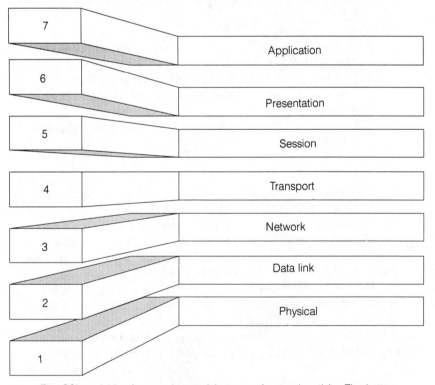

The OSI model is often used to explain types of network activity. The bottom three layers generally deal with network functions, the top four with applications.

The first step in making interconnection choices is to divide these seven layers into two groups: the application level and the network level. Application-level communication takes place at layers 5 through 7 of the OSI model. It refers to activities inside a server when a file server receives a NetWare request, a database server receives an SQL query, or when a print file reaches a print server.

Network-level activity takes place below the application level, at layers 1 through 3 of the OSI model—the physical, media access, and network layers. The physical layer administers the rules of sending signals over a given medium, such as twisted-pair, coax, or fiberoptic. Media access includes the protocols for using each medium, such as Ethernet or token ring.

The transport and network layers of the OSI model are where data streams from application layers are organized in packets and "enveloped" with address information to be used by bridges and routers to make high-speed delivery decisions.

Maintaining protocol

One of the most important internetworking questions is whether your applications and network devices support the right protocols to maintain communication across the system.

Protocols are the languages of networking. They establish the rules by which information is packaged for transmission. Major internetworking protocols include:

- **TCP/IP.** Transmission Control Protocol/Internet Protocol. This was originally developed for the Department of Defense, but since DOD is such a major computer equipment customer, this protocol has become almost universal. Actually, TCP and IP are two different protocols that perform different functions but work together.
- **NetBIOS.** Network Basic Input/Output System. This is an IBM-developed protocol developed for networks that use Microsoft products. It has become virtually a generic protocol for PC LANs, and most network operating systems offer NetBIOS compatibility.
- **IPX/SPX.** Internet Packet Exchange/Sequenced Packet Exchange. This is a protocol developed by Novell. Since Novell is dominant in PC networking, this system—again a combination of two protocols—has come into widespread use.
- **SDLC.** Synchronous Data Link Control. This protocol was developed by IBM to communicate among different devices within IBM's Systems Network Architecture (SNA).
- **DECnet.** Digital Equipment Corporation Network. A protocol developed by the Digital Equipment Corporation (DEC) for use within that firm's operating environment.

In the case of applications and network operating systems, there are usually few problems. For example, Novell, Digital, and IBM all support their systems' traditional protocols. They also support such generic protocols as TCP/IP.

The greater challenge concerning network devices is that an interlined network must be ready to support whatever protocols the applications and network operating systems in use might require. The network faces other demands, too:

- **Wide area LAN computing.** LAN servers and users can be located on different network segments and sites. Even so, users expect service unimpeded by physical or logical distances.
- **Distributed processing.** Client/server and other processing often takes place on multiple computing devices, which might be on different, and often distant, networks.
- **Multiple network operating systems.** As application interoperability increases, users buy a wider variety of products. The system must accommodate them all.
- **Increased demand for capacity.** Users are making more use of network applications. Graphic, image, and video applications demand more bandwidth. Wide area LAN connectivity, client/server, and distributed computing all add to the workload.

Meeting varied demands

Internetworking technology comes in the basic forms of repeaters, bridges, routers, and gateways.

Repeaters work strictly at the first layer, the physical layer, of the OSI model. Their main purpose is not to link networks but to increase the geographical coverage of a single LAN.

You'd typically choose a repeater to link LAN segments when there isn't much traffic on either segment, when the link between the segments is very fast, and when equipment cost is a more important consideration than connection cost. This means repeaters are usually local devices. You normally use one repeater to connect two high-speed LAN segments directly instead of using two repeaters to connect two LAN segments over a slower long-distance line.

Repeaters, with costs ranging from just under $1,000 for simple Ethernet equipment to well over $2,000 for token ring devices, are generally less expensive, as well as easier to install, than other linking devices. They're useful because they can connect different types of physical media, such as coaxial, fiberoptic, and twisted-pair cables. On the downside, all the traffic generated on each LAN segment connected by repeaters appears on all LAN segments, so the network segments can become very busy. Also, some kinds of problems on one segment, such as malfunctioning adapters that send out improperly formed packets, can affect all segments.

Bridges connect separate networks that have compatible addressing schemes. In effect, a bridge makes multiple networks look like a single entity, so that the connected networks generally must be of the same type, such as Ethernet or token ring. They also can connect different types of networks if the two use compatible addressing schemes.

Routers connect networks that may use different technologies but share a common protocol. For example, a router can connect an Ethernet LAN using DECnet with a token ring LAN using NetBIOS, if both use TCP/IP as an internetworking protocol. When a packet of information reaches the router, it accepts only the TCP/IP packets. The DECnet and NetBIOS packets remain on their own networks.

Gateways are primarily used to connect PC LANs to larger systems. For example, a gateway could allow employees on a PC LAN to gain access to an IBM mainframe on an SNA network. Gateways can also connect two LANs that run different communication protocols. For example, a TCP/IP gateway could give users of a NetWare LAN access to a separate TCP/IP LAN.

Building bridges

A bridge is a good choice when you need to link LANs, either locally or remotely, and you want to avoid loading each LAN segment with unnecessary traffic. Bridges discriminate between the packets or frames they pass, and they move only those packets and frames across the link that are

LOW BRIDGE

Bridge

Bridges work only at the lowest levels of the OSI model. They can't distinguish between different protocols.

addressed to nodes on the other LAN segment. They cannot, however, distinguish between packets created under different protocols at the network layer, as indicated in the diagram.

Like repeaters, bridges can move packets or frames between different kinds of media. The client PCs do not need any special software or hardware to benefit from the actions of repeaters and bridges.

A special type of bridge called a *learning bridge* has software that broadcasts a message that generates a reply from all network nodes. The bridge software reads the source address of each packet or frame and associates source addresses with LAN segments in an internal table. The bridge software uses this table to limit the traffic crossing between LAN segments and to prevent problem packets or adapters on one LAN segment from affecting connected segments.

Modern bridges monitor the traffic so closely, special software in the bridges can furnish information on both traffic volume and network errors. However, bridges are busy devices; they must evaluate packets on the fly.

Two OSI levels

A repeater operates only at the physical layer of the OSI model; the bridge operates at the data link layer as well. The bridge links two compatible addressing schemes, and these are identified at the data link layer. The bridge operates by forwarding packets between the data link layers of the connected networks.

Because a bridge works no higher than the data link layer, it is not able to recognize the difference between the packets sent under different protocols. This happens at the network layer. The bridge will simply forward a packet regardless of its protocol, and leave it to devices on the LANs to make the identifications.

Civil engineering

To function as a bridge, a PC must have two network cards, one for each of the two networks the bridge is to link. It also needs software that will enable it to bridge the two networks.

Choosing the right route

Like bridges, routers connect separate LANs, but they do so in a more sophisticated way. Routers work at three layers of the OSI model, including the network layer where packets can be addressed and directed to designated destinations, as indicated in the diagram.

Routers connect LANs that use the same protocol. These networks can operate on the same or different standard. Some common routers include:

- An *IP router* that handles TCP/IP packets.

- An *IPX router* that handles IPX/SPX packets.
- A *DECnet router* that handles, naturally enough, DECnet packets.

A router can be either a PC with network boards and appropriate software installed, or it can be a single-purpose device made strictly for this duty.

ROUTERS WORK AT A HIGHER LEVEL

Router

Routers work at the network level and can identify packets that use different protocols.

Smarter than smart

Routers are more discriminating than even smart bridges. Router software reads address information and decides how to route the data across multiple internetwork links. Routers don't examine every packet or frame, only those specifically addressed to them.

The programs in some routers always pick the shortest path between the two points. These are known as *static* routers. The routing information must be entered manually, however, so every change in the network system will require a corresponding change in the router information. More sophisticated products, known as *dynamic* routers, make packet-by-packet decisions based on the information they glean from other routers and network devices about the efficiency and reliability of different routes between the source and destination nodes.

Because routers don't read every network packet or frame, they don't work as hard as bridges; hence they put less of a load on the host CPU.

Because they allow only specially addressed packets and frames to pass between LAN segments, they put the lowest stress on the internetwork links.

Routing strategy

When a router determines the best path to a destination, it relies on a routing strategy. The best strategy is determined by a combination of two factors:

- The route with the fewest connections.
- The route with the fastest line speed.

Just as airlines direct most of their routes through hub airports, routers sometimes do much the same. For example, there might be a direct route from point A to the familiar point B, but it is an efficient, low-speed connection. The router might decide to send the message by way of point C, a central location served by high-speed connections with the other locations.

When a bridge is a router

The NetWare operating system has built-in bridges, but with a twist. What Novell calls bridges, most others would call routers. Actually, Novell named its bridge first. It was later developers who applied the name router to this form of internetwork communication.

Novell bridges route the company's IPX-standard packets from one network to another, operating at the network layer. This lets them work with many different networking standards, including Ethernet, token ring, and Arcnet.

Managing the gateway

LAN gateways translate data formats. They also open and close sessions between application programs. That means they operate at every layer of the OSI model. Sometimes a modem and PC form the hardware element of the gateway. The classic IRMA card is another type of LAN gateway hardware. A common type of gateway links the PC-based LAN to a device that uses a completely different data alphabet and signaling system, such as IBM's SNA communications system for mainframe computers.

In general, gateways provide two similar functions:

- They give LAN users access to other host computers.
- They connect network operating systems of different types.

Two major purposes

The traditional and most common use for a gateway is to give LAN users access to the data on a minicomputer or mainframe. They system usually lets the user establish terminal and printer sessions with the host computer. Other services can include file transfers and remote job entry (RJE).

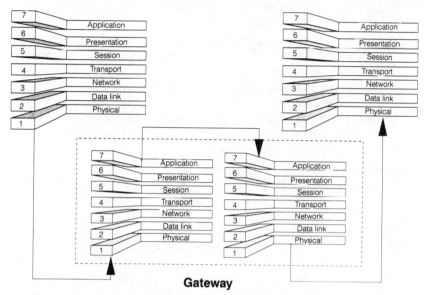

Gateway

Gateways work with all seven layers of the OSI model and can maintain contact with systems of all types.

Gateways also make several networks with dissimilar operating systems appear to users on the other side of the gateway as a single, uniform network. For example, a TCP/IP gateway gives users on a PC network access to a minicomputer on the other side of the gateway. At the same time, users of Unix workstations on the network with the minicomputer can gain access to a file server on the PC network.

The gateway PC

Personal computers often serve as gateways. A PC-based gateway uses both network and communication boards to connect two LANs, or to connect a LAN to a host computer. As with PC-based bridges and routers, the PC must also have communication software to link the two systems. In this case, users on the LAN will also need communication software to gain access to the host computer via the gateway.

Types of gateways

Gateways come in several basic types:

- *3270 gateways* connect LANs with IBM mainframe hosts on networks that use the firm's Systems Network Architecture (SNA).

They make network devices appear to the mainframe to be SNA devices.

- *5250 gateways* connect LANs to minicomputer hosts such as the IBM AS/400 series.
- *Asynchronous gateways* provide the services of serial ports and modems to LAN users. They are also sometimes known as asynchronous communication servers (ACS).

    These gateways can provide LAN users with such services as file transfer and terminal emulation. One of the most popular uses is to let LAN users share high-speed modems by way of a *modem pool*. The modems then provide access to bulletin boards, electronic mail, and database services.

- *TCP/IP gateways* let users on non-TCP/IP networks gain access to hosts that use this protocol. They then can gain access to such services as terminal emulation, file transfer, electronic mail, and process-to-process communication.
- *X.25 gateways* provide access to packet-switched networks, including public dial-up services and private networks.

Life on the WAN

Systems professionals who first encounter the speed and flexibility of the LAN for the first time are likely to be pleasantly surprised. LAN technology is, by and large, ahead of the development of older WANs. Those who are used to WAN transmission rates of, perhaps, 56 kilobits per second, will find a whole new world in a LAN that can transmit 10 megabits in that same second.

But the reverse is also true. As a networked system gets larger, it gets sluggish and less flexible. Once you've worked with a LAN, a WAN can seem frustrating and sluggish. Not only does it run more slowly, but every gateway, bridge, and other connector in the network will take its toll. That's particularly true in the case of standard bridges that pass along everything that comes their way. It can still be a problem with more selective connectors like routers and intelligent bridges.

Beyond issues of performance are those of compatibility. Not only do LANs and operating systems offer potential sources of incompatibility, but so do different E-mail systems, message formats, and other elements of a diverse internetwork.

Yet another factor: WAN specialists are used to the control and structure of the large-system world. PC people are used to working more independently.

As journalist Ed Foster puts it, "WANs and LANs are like the star-crossed lovers of romantic tradition—they come from such different worlds that it's hard to conceive of them having anything to do with each other.

There's a considerable amount of effort required to join them together even in a fairly tenuous way."

Networks need network managers

This is a place where systems professionals can apply their management talents to good effect. Network management has been identified as the greatest single hurdle in making enterprise networking work the way it should. Good network management is critical, but network managers, particularly those who have migrated from the PC side, don't always have all the tools they need.

Another issue that becomes much knottier in the WAN environment is security. Once you go through a gateway outside a LAN, you've multiplied the number of people who might gain access to your data. Local area networks tend to be closed campuses. When you open up an external gateway you expand the opportunity of someone else getting in. On the other hand, if you overcompensate and make security too tight, you defeat the purpose of having the link in the first place.

Higher performance coming

Two new forms of technology promise to help improve the performance bottlenecks that grow as a network expands.

Frame relay is a packet-switching technology that promises an improvement on the widely used but older X.25. The newer technology offers greater bandwidth and quicker response times.

X.25 was designed many years ago for telephone transmission lines whose error rates are relatively high for data transmission. Accordingly, X.25 regularly retransmits garbled packets. Furthermore, its top speed of 56 kilobits per second can be as frustrating as a 55-mph limit on an interstate highway. Frame relay products have been operated as high as 45 megabits per second, although the normal maximum is considered to be 1.5 megabits per second.

Frame relay is designed for digital, fiberoptic transmission lines that produce very few errors. That means it can operate at substantially higher speeds. Furthermore, because it can transmit large amounts of data in a single line, it can simplify network configuration and eliminate the number of connections, delays, and trouble spots.

Perhaps more important than operating speed is a "bandwidth on demand" feature. It allows multiple devices to dynamically share all the available bandwidth. A transmitting device has full access to whatever bandwidth might be available.

Switched Megabit Data Service (SMDS) is a new class of "connectionless" switched data service being developed by the telephone industry, specifically several regional Bell operating companies (RBOCs).

As with frame relay, the main advantage of SMDS for users is bandwidth on demand. For the RBOCs pushing SMDS, the impetus is account control; SMDS is a specification being driven heavily by the RBOCs. Their migration strategy is to have data connectivity combined with voice and video. SMDS is seen as a way for the RBOCs to extend their current core business.

Over fiber networks, SMDS can deliver throughput between 1.5 and 45 megabits per second. SMDS is a so-called connectionless service; it relies on *datagrams*, a packet-switched implementation in which the source and destination handle addressing and error detection.

Management tools

A growing product assortment addresses the need to manage more far-flung networks. Network operating systems display performance statistics and accounting information. You can remotely control servers and bridges, and receive reports on traffic conditions and errors. Many vendors have produced add-on management systems for networks that have not needed them in the past.

NOS vendors have also begun to agree on how to implement standards and to test interoperability, though these efforts have not kept up with the pace of network expansion.

Typical of these management tools is Novell's *Remote Management Facility* (RMF). RMF provides remote management of NetWare 386-based internetworks by distributing console control to network workstations. RMF is designed primarily for large, multiserver networks. Supervisors can manage all NetWare 386 servers on the internetwork from one centralized location, reducing the need for on-site network administrators.

The supervisors can execute console commands from a workstation over LAN-to-LAN links or asynchronous connections. They can also install and upgrade servers from remote locations, distribute software to multiple servers, and remotely execute and monitor unattended backup.

RMF is also a security management tool. The RMF password is separate from the individual server supervisor's password, so only authorized RMF users can administer servers remotely. The network supervisor also can install, upgrade and maintain the network operating system from a remote location, eliminating the need for a network supervisor at each satellite server. Network administrators can make one connection to a remote site to maintain multiple servers and distribute software across those servers. They can copy files to and from the servers via LAN or asynchronous connections.

RMF also lets remote sites with multiple servers share one or more backup devices, reducing the cost and effort of remote backups. Supervisors can perform unattended backups.

6
CHAPTER

Choosing
hardware platforms

The choice between a mainframe, a minicomputer, or a PC network is naturally based in large part on the respective merits of these technologies. The merits of the technologies, though, aren't necessarily technical merits.

No decision on downsizing hardware platforms should be made strictly on technical factors. The hardware you choose should also suit your business. The right choice can fit both your present and future needs. Nearly any system can be set up to do that, but some do it better than others.

Picking the best system

The two basic guidelines for choosing a hardware platform are:

- You should select a system that will solve today's business problem.
- Then, select the system that offers the best solution at the best price, or the best combination of the two.

One thing you need not worry about is that the system might soon become obsolete. Although PC LANs offer a high and improving price/performance ratio, no single type of interconnected system is likely to achieve an exclusive hold in the market in the foreseeable future. Much has been said about the imminent decline of mainframes and minicomputers, but all three hardware platforms have something to offer if they suit your business needs. Thus, most experts expect that larger systems will continue to remain in service at least until the end of the century.

For example, the increasing power and flexibility of PC LANs has cut significantly into the market share held by minicomputers. Still, minis have

FIRST RULE OF HARDWARE SELECTION

- Don't just buy technology
- Buy the technology that best fits your organization

Technology alone doesn't solve problems or create opportunities. Set your objectives, then pick the hardware to match.

a definite place as network servers, and you should not worry that their manufacturers will suddenly leave you with orphaned systems.

Much the same is true of mainframes. They are expected to remain in place for databases and compute-intensive jobs like transaction processing.

A commonly-held view of the future is that of an integrated, distributed network of machines of a variety of types, with workstations on every desk and servers designed for specific tasks to serve those desktop systems. That means a mixture of mainframes, minis, and PCs—some or all of the above. The most important problem will not be to choose between these platforms but to find ways to share information while running all those architectures simultaneously.

Where LANs work best

In most downsized organizations, PCs will be the hardware of choice. PC vendors have encountered firsthand the organizational and technical issues that face companies that have decided to downsize. As they often point out, the issue is not the technology, it's the application.

Analysts have identified areas like these where downsizing to PC LANs is likely to be most fruitful:

- When there is a need to deliver sophisticated MIS support to offices, departments, or other distinct parts of the organization.
- When cost-effectiveness is an overriding consideration.
- When you want the system to be more responsive to users' needs.
- When you need faster, more efficient application development
- Where there is need for greater control over operations, particularly for small units that share a larger group's central computing resources.

- Serve many corporate units
- Reduce cost
- Respond to users' needs
- Develop applications quickly
- Manage shared resources

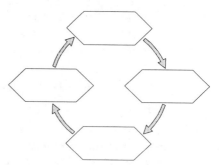

Networks are the heart of most downsized systems, but they can't do everything equally well.

Advantages of larger systems

Larger systems also have their places. Among them:

- When the reliability and integrity of important data are at stake.
- When a high-volume transaction processing application also requires safeguards to ensure that any recorded transaction is a complete one.
- When the company's "crown jewels" are at stake.

"BIG IRON" HAS ITS PLACE WHEN:

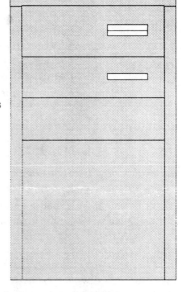

- Reliability and integrity are important
- High volumes require processing power
- Transaction systems require completeness
- Mission-critical data is at risk

Even in a downsized environment, large systems can have central roles.

While the raw performance of some PC networks may meet or exceed that of larger systems, the key difference is their functional differences. PCs must be versatile. Larger systems are designed for dedicated tasks. Their hardware is tuned with disk storage, cache memory, and advanced file systems to make database transactions operate faster.

Points to consider

Here's a checklist of points to consider in selecting hardware systems:

- Keep your objectives firmly in mind. Make sure your purchasing decisions reflect your corporate vision.
- Decide which types of systems will best meet the needs of your organization.
- Choose systems with future expansion in mind.
- Don't scrimp on servers, the heart of your system.
- Assign workstations to match the individuals' duties. Don't let the big system become a matter of pride rather than productivity. At the same time, watch out for the modest user who is willing to make do with less than the optimal system.
- Choose hardware that is flexible and easy to use.
- Make sure the chosen hardware architecture supports the application programs you expect to run.
- Select open systems that allow the greatest possible data interchange between diverse environments.

SELECTION CHECKLIST

- Identify and meet your objectives
- Allow for expansion
- Make sure servers are up to the job
- Match selections to tasks and applications
- Emphasize ease of use
- Allow for diversity

Keep these points in mind when selecting hardware.

PCs in a mixed environment

For many users, the right solution combines a strong server back-end database with a new-generation client front-end tool. These front-end systems will often run on PCs, but in a mixed environment that might include servers, and even workstations that run Unix or some other system.

Clients and servers

PCs used in a downsized environment will sometimes be the servers in a client/server relationship. If not, they will almost always be clients. It's a nice thought for users who think of it: Their client PCs can demand service from larger, more powerful systems.

An anticipated 20 million PCs will be connected to LANs by 1992. They will be expecting the computing equivalent of good customer service. Users will demand, with good reason, that their networked PCs not restrict their options but expand them.

In that vision, most PCs will function as personal workstations for their users. On one hand, that means you need the technical proficiency to build the kinds of applications that will meet these users' needs. But that won't be enough.

We run the great danger of developing a new generation of applications and enacting an entirely new set of rules for computer use that are just as inflexible as those that a downsizing project is intended to prevent.

To make people and their organizations more productive, and to implement the respective visions of employees and the organization, a downsized system must reflect the values of internal customer service. In a client/server relationship, it is always the client who should be served.

COMMON GROUND

In technology:

- The client/server relationship

In human dealings:

- Customer service

The relationship between client and server is a lot like the relationship between customer and employee—including internal customer service.

Variety of vendors

Unlike standard databases for PC LANs, these new combinations do not necessarily come from the same vendor, nor do they use the same operating system on the client and the server. In fact, because of differences in features and options, corporate information system staffs may choose assorted options.

For some applications, they may employ multiple front-end tools against a back-end database server, while other scenarios might dictate a single front end that accesses multiple back-end databases.

Technically, a client/server system operates differently on multi-user PC databases than on earlier-generation databases. Traditional systems, of which dBASE is the prime example, are primarily designed to operate on single PCs. They have some multi-user features, but these are added on, not inherent.

Client/server combinations split the tasks of database applications between a front end, which runs on the local PC workstation, and a back end, which runs on a database server.

That means for many users the hardware choice will not be a single system, but a diverse, heterogeneous networking strategy. This strategy should accommodate multiple architectures and converge on a single, standardized solution.

Which PC?

If you're buying PCs for network service, the conventional advice is to buy in at least the 386 class. The lower-speed members of this class make good clients. Mid-speed examples are usually the best choice to run Windows or other applications that make heavy demands on the system's resources. Heavyweight 386s are often all you need in a server. The 486 class is good for all but the heaviest server duty.

Meanwhile, thousands upon thousands of 286s sit in corporate offices. Next to them may be PC magazines which hammer away at a repeated message: The only good thing to do with a 286 is to replace it. Those magazines do a disservice. Though a 286 is hardly state of the art, it can continue to do many useful text-mode jobs, including client service on a LAN. For the record, this book was written on a six-year-old 286.

Higher-horsepower servers

Many PC LANs installed in the mid-to-late 1980s are now exceeding their capacities. The overhead caused by increasing the number of network users can push a file server beyond its performance limits and overload the network with traffic. Organizations that have encountered these crunch points are searching for cost-effective means to maximize the performance of the networks and equipment they already own. These users want increased LAN performance to maintain rapid user response time from the system, even as the user base increases. They want to allow users to get more work done more quickly. Basically, the two ways to this are:

- Replace file servers with database servers and servers for other specialized duties.
- Install higher-performance servers.

Servers aren't all alike

File servers let companies distribute data and applications across departmental or company-wide networks. Users can share expensive hardware resources such as laser printers, and communicate with electronic mail. File servers work well at managing small- to medium-size files for applications such as word processing and spreadsheets.

Database servers are much different. File servers do not usually offer the specialized data manipulation ability that is necessary to handle large database files.

Also, file servers send large amounts of redundant data across the network. For instance, if a user were to request a customer's telephone number from a customer record database on a file server, the server might transmit the entire customer list, and let the user retrieve the number from it.

This means file servers often pose exceptional data integrity and security risks. Needless data traveling across the network means a higher risk of data corruption should the hardware, software, or network fail during the transmission.

Database servers

The database server is a special-purpose system optimized for high-performance database operations. The clients send requests to the server via structured query language (SQL) queries. The server interprets the requests and returns only the data to the clients. This distributed architecture allows the client CPU to focus on running the application. The server performs the CPU- and disk-intensive database manipulation necessary to respond to the query.

Database servers improve LAN performance by handling data intelligently. When a client requests data from the server, only the specific information the user requested is returned; no redundant information travels across the network. That could mean the difference between sending several bytes or kilobytes across the LAN, instead of several megabytes.

The result is that database servers allow both the databases and the LANs to function more efficiently. With less data traveling across the network, database servers can improve the LAN's overall performance. Users get faster responses and simultaneous access to the same data. They also make better use of their organization's computer resources.

Enter the superserver

Another approach, and one that certainly has helped spur the downsizing movement, is the advent of the superserver. The Compaq Systempro has been the first and best-known example. This system, and others like it, add minicomputer features like multiprocessing and multiple disk arrays for higher performance and greater security.

A superserver is more than a hot-rodded PC. It is built from the outset to handle major file-sharing duty, to run large, transaction-oriented database operations or for similar heavy-duty work. The features that make a superserver a superserver include:

- Multiple processors in at least the 486 class. Some related systems have fewer or smaller processors, but these aren't likely to be the best choices for a large, downsized application.
- Up to 12 megabytes of system memory and a gigabyte of disk space.
- Extra hard disks and controllers to add fault tolerance.
- Enhanced buses to speed up performance.

The place you're most likely to find a superserver is as a replacement for a minicomputer in a downsized environment. Reasons for making the change often include the traditional considerations of cost and flexibility. Another factor that can be important: most superservers fit under desks; minis, despite their name, often require much more floor space.

At the other end of the spectrum, a superserver is not likely to be necessary, at least in file server status, for smaller LANs. A rule of thumb is that a network with more than 100 users could benefit from a superserver. Below that, you could probably do just as well with one of the more powerful members of the 386-class PC family.

Multiple processors

Superservers have more power than even top-of-the-line PCs. Though they are derived from PC technology, they are in no sense personal computers; for a single user, a superserver would be a waste. What's more, superserver owners can usually add more power as their needs dictate.

One fruitful way to boost that power is by installing additional central processing units (CPUs). Instead of the single CPU chip of a PC, a superserver can have two or more. This allows the machine to split up its work, performing different tasks for different users at the same time. Multiprocessing improves overall system performance by distributing the workload among processors instead of depending on only one.

Multiple multiprocessing

Now, throw in another wrinkle: There are two different kinds of multiprocessing, as shown in the diagram. In asymmetric multitasking, each processor is optimized for a single task. One might be dedicated permanently to computing operations, for example, while another handles all the I/O operations. If you're a NetWare user, you'll also be a user of asymmetric processing.

TWO KINDS OF MULTIPROCESSING

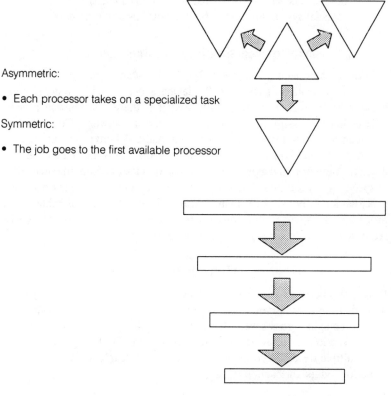

Asymmetric:

- Each processor takes on a specialized task

Symmetric:

- The job goes to the first available processor

Superservers—and network operating systems—determine how multiple processors are used.

A Vines network uses symmetric processing. Here, each processor's duties depend on the need at the time. When a task must be done, the system looks for a processor to handle it.

Multiprocessing in a file server

Processing on a file server is I/O intensive. The file server's main function is to move data quickly through the system. Sometimes it does. Sometimes it doesn't.

Consider a typical network read operation on a single-CPU file server. The CPU directs the transfer of data from a disk drive to data registers in the CPU. It then stores the data in system memory. Then when the network requests the data, the CPU loads the data back into its data registers, transfers the data through the bus to the network interface card, then finally sends the data out onto the network.

The problem is that the CPU does all the work as the data is moved multiple times within the machine. Some servers move data even more often than in this example. The same network read operation can be speeded up by dedicating a special system bus and 386 processor bus to the process.

Multiprocessing in a database server

An even greater need for multiple CPUs is in database management applications. Applications such as SQL database management systems make heavy demands on computing resources; it is these systems that process queries internally so it need not be done over the network. Compute routines can be two to three times faster in a dual CPU environment.

Another problem is that the results of the query must then be sent down the network, and a processor dedicated to faster computing does little to speed up I/O routines. Even so, tests show that in database service, dual processors can boost performance nearly 50% over a comparable single processor. In such applications environments as these, multiple CPUs really make a difference in the LAN environment.

Multiple disks

Disk arrays boost performance and provide a measure of safety. They do so by letting the superserver work with multiple disk drives. For example, a file can be split across several hard drives. While one drive is reading the current section, a second drive is already locating the next piece.

Multiple disks also provide a measure of fault tolerance by providing room for redundant backup storage.

All's not perfect

Just as a Ferrari is not the ideal car for heavy urban traffic, a superserver is not a universal or automatic solution to everyone's network needs.

One problem is that in spite of the superserver's advanced technology, not much software really capitalizes on it. Even those who want to develop their own applications will find few tools available for the purpose.

Another problem is that this is not shrink-wrap country. Putting together the hardware, the operating system, the network, and the applications can be a complicated endeavor. For example, a chain of video stores had a mainframe-based inventory management system that was run every night after hours. It took 3 hours, 25 minutes. When the application was transferred to a 33-MHz 386 system, it required more than 17 hours to run.

Switching to OS/2 brought the time down a little—to 14 hours. Moving it to a Systempro with dual processors, running under DOS, brought another inadequate improvement: The time now was 12 hours. Finally, the application was rewritten to run under Unix on the Systempro, and the running time was finally acceptably close to that of the mainframe: 3 hours, 43 minutes.

The RISC alternative

Reduced instruction set computing (RISC), based on Unix, has been developed into a strong competitor for superservers of PC origin. These are Unix machines that come in both server and workstation versions, though there is actually little difference between the two. The servers generally have higher memory, disk storage, and I/O capacities than their workstation counterparts.

Some major names are active in this market, including DEC, Hewlett-Packard, IBM, and Sun.

In speed tests, RISC workstations have compared in performance with high-end PCs. RISC servers were somewhat faster than comparable multiprocessing superservers.

Limited resources

If superservers have little dedicated software written for them, much the same is true of RISC machines. Fewer network operating systems are available, and those that are available aren't supported on all hardware platforms.

Adding Unix to the mix

Several operating systems and network environments, such as OS/2, VMS, NetWare 386, and Unix, have become popular for implementing database servers. Unix provides a solid foundation for running high-performance servers. It offers 32-bit addressing, multitasking, multi-user capabilities, and shared memory. It also can take full advantage of Intel 80X86 processor architecture.

New open systems such as Unix workstations are rapidly being added to the downsizing mix. They create another category of system with which managers must deal. These more powerful systems have many advantages, including better network-wide communication, increased interoperability, enhanced security, and much greater processing power.

They also present yet another challenge of how to make use of them along with PCs within today's diverse networks.

Rapid changes

A few years ago, things were simpler. Available hardware consisted mainly of mainframes, department-level minicomputers, terminals, and the ubiquitous PC. Most PCs were in single-user service, but some were clustered in LANs. A newer PC might have the processing power of an earlier mini, and some minis came to rival small mainframes. Even so, the distinctions among the various groups were reasonably clear.

This simple world has been replaced by one in which PCs are rapidly evolving, while RISC-based Unix workstations and servers have become available to take over many of the functions of the more traditional systems.

RISC-based servers provide the file and database services that were previously the domain of mainframes or minis. Meanwhile, RISC-based workstations lend themselves to a new generation of applications such as imaging and multimedia that require heavy-duty computing and graphics throughput.

Exploitation without excess

It's hard to ignore these trends. Systems that are more powerful and responsive, and that accommodate multitasking to boot, offer many new opportunities.

The challenge is to exploit them without going overboard. The opposite approach, to switch completely to RISC and Unix and replace all your existing systems is equally impractical. The cost would be prohibitive, making such a move a very poor investment, and the transition could actually reduce productivity.

Diversity in style

Diversity is thus becoming a way of life. Today, the mix includes Intel 80X86-based systems running MS-DOS, with or without Windows, or OS/2; RISC systems from Sun, HP, IBM, Digital, and others running varieties of Unix; and various proprietary computers with operating systems like MVS and VM.

The challenge for system managers is to determine the best way to organize these diverse and evolving systems into the most effective solution for the company. Managers must try to make maximum use of their existing base of hardware, software, and expertise without unnecessary disruption. At the same time, new technology is needed to meet the demands of users, and to do it in the most cost-effective way.

Criteria for a decision

The right mix of PCs, Unix machines, and other resources depends on these considerations:

- An *open* system. Can the diverse systems operate smoothly with each other?
- Availability of *standard services*. These usually include file sharing, printing, and remote log-in.
- *Application development* features that let programmers rapidly produce applications for the diverse environment.

Make best use of all resources:

* Existing systems
  —Proven technology
  —Trained personnel
* New technology
  —Improved service
  —Reduced cost

Something old, something new . . . many downsized systems are mixtures of new, existing resources.

Using larger systems

The increasing interest in downsizing doesn't mean mainframes or minicomputers are all going to be shelved. For one thing, they represent too large an investment; owners are not likely to scrap these units just for the sake of downsizing. There must be some other reason, such as an impending end to the large system's useful life. And in any event, a minicomputer or a mainframe still can be useful, even in a downsized environment.

Two major roles

Large systems still have two major interrelated roles in a downsized system:

* The client-server role. Client/server computing has become practical as software has been designed to link PCs with mainframe and minicomputer servers in transparent fashion. PC users can now grab data from host systems without moving to dumb terminals or bothering with mainframe access and query languages. This has enabled more computer novices to interact with online data and has increased the speed with which data on multiple hosts can be downloaded to PCs.
* The communication role. The second major role is that large systems can serve as important elements of internetworking. Not only can larger systems perform as database servers, but they can perform other key roles as well.

Improved communication and internetworking techniques will expand those roles. Groupware and electronic mail can take advantage of improving communication techniques between LANs and large systems.

The main problem is the list of useful applications for large systems in a networked environment is still a short one. Remember, though, that people buy results, not technology. As downsizing becomes more popular, more network-conscious applications should appear. These will kick off a cycling effect as the new applications attract more users.

How about a new mini?

It makes obvious good sense to make use of existing resources whenever you can, particularly if those resources cost as much as a large computer system. For many managers, though, another question presents itself: should you buy a *new* minicomputer for use in a downsized system?

On the surface, that might sound like a contradiction. The base premise of downsizing is that smaller is better—and usually less expensive. Still, a survey of 100 IS managers found that nearly a third of them had near-future plans to buy minicomputers as LAN servers.

More user friendliness

The industry has been working hard to encourage user friendliness. All the major vendors are working to change the images of their products: from specialized department-level stand-alone computing systems to powerful network servers. To do this, they are offering such features as better I/O performance, better communication with PCs and LANs, and more favorable software licensing terms.

Vendors are also working actively to provide better interfaces to their products and to ease the traditionally difficult task of installing and maintaining a mini.

PCs still have an edge

PCs still hold the advantage in many downsized applications. They are less expensive than minis of comparable power and capacity, particularly when configured as superservers. They also have the capacity to expand.

How minis compare

Still, minis also have power and expansion capacity. They can also claim these strong points:

- Strong systems management.
- Support of existing multi-user applications.
- High levels of service and maintenance.
- Better fault tolerance.

The minis also have two big drawbacks:

- Most of their features are proprietary. Much work needs to be done before they will work transparently with PCs, or any other system with which they might be linked.
- They are still expensive. Minicomputer manufacturers have been reducing the cost of their products, particularly at the bottom of the product line. Even these downpriced minis, however, are still substantially more expensive than comparable PC superservers.

EVALUATING MINICOMPUTERS

Strong points:

- Systems management
- Multiple users
- Fault tolerance

Drawbacks:

- Proprietary systems
- High cost

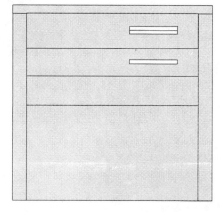

Minicomputers bring a mixture of advantages and drawbacks to a downsized system.

Integrating PCs and mainframes

Should a downsized system include a mainframe? The considerations are much the same as they would be for a mini—but on a larger scale. Again, the standard downsized architecture is usually a server based on some form of high-performance microcomputer connected by LAN to PC-based workstations. These dedicated servers offer an abundance of processor power, and their cost advantage over mainframes is even higher than it is for minis. You can get a capable PC server for about 1% of the cost of obtaining similar processor power on the leading mainframe platforms.

Thus, the economics of downsizing are even more favorable for PCs when you are jumping all the way down from a mainframe. Even minis have a price advantage, particularly in the types of database and communication service for which they typically are used in downsized systems.

Larger performance gap, too

Even the most powerful PC servers lack the sustained data throughput capabilities of even the smallest mainframes. As some data-heavy departmental programs are downsized, they can quickly overwhelm the data-handling capabilities of many LAN servers.

The real issue is not whether the mainframe will survive the downsizing trend, but in what capacity. A key role will be as a corporate data repository, consolidating all the information generated and used by thousands of PCs sitting on corporate desktops.

NEW ROLES FOR MAINFRAMES

- Increasing power
- Network communication
- Database service
- Security and integrity
- Global systems management

Mainframes are losing some of their traditional functions, but they can play important new roles in downsized systems.

Mainframe modifications

In their original form, mainframes were not particularly suitable for server duty. Still, manufacturers and vendors of add-on equipment are modifying the mainframe's structure, through hardware and software, to equip it better for that role. Among the areas where these developments are taking place:

- Computing power. IBM points out that in terms of power, large systems are still growing at a rate of more than 30% per year. This trend should continue. This means that today's mainframes might soon actually be too small to meet many demands.
- Communication. This will be a key element in the mainframe's evolution to a central role in a networked system. There must be a seamless linkage between the desktop PC and the organization's mainframe data repositories.
- Databases. If the mainframe is to serve as a data repository, it must gain the ability to store increasing amounts of data and to retrieve it more quickly. Some recently introduced systems include machine instructions that greatly speed up important database data manipulation activities.
- Security. New products automatically encrypt data and monitor the threat of computer viruses. As access to corporate data becomes

more transparent, data security will become an even more important issue than it now is.
- Global systems management. The ability to centrally manage a far-flung network of mainframes, departmental and desktop systems is vital to future success.

7
CHAPTER

Downsizing environments

In the beginning, there was DOS—or so it seems, anyway. Actually, several personal computer operating systems preceded it. Like its predecessors, though, DOS was designed for what now seems like a limited function: to let one person do one thing at one time on one computer.

The advancement—though certainly not the perfection—of Microsoft Windows has made DOS more useful and accessible. Windows can be somewhat easier to learn and use.

Somewhere along the line, Unix became a networking force. It offered multiple use and other advanced features, well suited to networks and larger systems. Unix systems commonly run under the X Window system that has most of the attributes associated with Windows.

OS/2 has many of the same multi-use features, and it was intended to replace DOS. That, of course, was before OS/2 became entangled in the PC industry's corporate politics.

Meanwhile, the Macintosh has its inimitable way of doing things.

Now, all four are available for use on downsized systems. Choosing between them isn't easy. You have many things to consider, the main ones being:

- Which features are important to you?
- Which of these features are built into each operating system, and which must be purchased separately?
- How easy is the system to install, configure, and use? Think of this from the standpoint of the least-skilled person who will use the system.

- Will the system run on your present equipment, or will an upgrade be necessary?
- Is this an open system, or will you deal with a single vendor? Which do you prefer? Does policy dictate the choice?
- How reliable is this system?
- Will the system run your application software?

ENVIRONMENTAL CHOICES

- DOS
  —Does one thing well
- Windows
  —Improves on DOS
- OS/2
  —The replacement that hasn't replaced
- Unix
  —Filling a vacuum

Which operating environment—or environments—to use is a multiple-choice question.

Most of all, there's the question of longevity. Will your networking environment last you for the long haul, or will you find yourself frequently trading it in because the ashtrays are full? Part of that question is whether the people who sell the system today will be around to support it tomorrow. The answer to that, unfortunately, involves you inescapably in the industry politics that have endlessly played themselves out in the computer trade press.

The evolution of DOS

In its original form, DOS had absolutely no networking features. The idea that one of the first PCs would be connected to another of those first PCs was never taken very seriously. IBM, if you remember, originally thought of its PC as a novelty item, not a serious business tool. Certainly, no one saw any reason to worry about what might happen if more than one person tried to use the same file.

Since then, the designers of DOS have at least recognized that networking is possible. Version 3.1, introduced in 1985, had built-in support for Microsoft's own networks. Version 5.0, the 1991 release, included network redirectors for the most popular network operation systems. Otherwise, such networking facilities as DOS offers come generally from third-party vendors.

MAKING THE CHOICE

Factors to consider:

- Features
  - —What does each have?
  - —What do you need?
- Ease of use
  - —Installation
  - —Configuration
- Is upgrading required?
  - —Is it worth it?
- Open or proprietary?
- Long-term service?

Consider all the costs. Upgrading and early replacement can be expensive.

Actually, these vendors may be contributing to DOS's longevity. DOS was written to be a completely open operating system that gives application developers free rein. Consequently, a lively third-party market in DOS networking sprang up, and a wide variety of DOS communication software continues to be available. In fact, DOS's long head start practically guarantees it a big lead in the number of available applications of all kinds.

Some strong points

DOS was designed for limited purposes, and it's never strayed far from them. Still, within its limits, it offers some worthwhile features:

- Compatibility that borders on the generic. DOS is deliberately designed to be compatible with almost every piece of PC software ever written. The Microsoft version is the clear standard. Only recently has it had any significant competition—from Digital Research's DR DOS.
- An undemanding nature. DOS claims few of a system's resources. You don't have to upgrade a computer to run DOS.
- It does the job. Users see this as a big advantage. DOS does what they need to do. It may not be the most technologically advanced product around, but it works.

EVALUATING DOS

- It runs almost anything
- It runs on almost anything
- It does almost anything

As long as it's only one thing at a time

Don't overlook DOS. It's simple, direct, and it often does the job.

Finding the limits

One way to quickly find the limits of DOS on a network is to implement an on-line transaction processing (OLTP) application. OLTP has not traditionally been considered a job for PC LANs. Nothing in the basic idea of a transaction exceeds the capacity of a DOS-based PC, but a lot of things in the actual day-to-day operation can easily go over the limit.

In an OLTP application, the user is accessing and changing a database. These operations require mechanisms to maintain concurrency and data integrity—including record locks, transaction logging, crash recovery, and deadlock control. DOS, with its single-user/single-task orientation, memory limits, and simple file-locking, is not usually up to all those jobs.

Even LANs with more sophisticated operating systems can find OLTP demands taxing. LANs have not been strong in concurrency, security, or making data readily available. Conventional LAN database applications have been hampered by the need to send whole files over the network. In an OLTP application, this makes concurrency impossible because the system must lock other users out of the data while it is being updated on one user's machine.

DOS will always be with us

DOS will, however, be around for the foreseeable future, even in a network-oriented environment. The leading network operating systems provide the multiple-use features DOS lacks. For many managers, the challenge today is to make use of existing DOS resources within the context of today's diverse networks.

In particular, DOS appears to have a future running on network workstations. At the same time, DOS's limitations are pretty much going to force it to cede the server marketplace to multitasking operating systems such as OS/2 and Unix.

Because some users continue to use traditional PC networks, managers will have to support these network protocols on LAN servers. One way is to add TCP/IP to each client PC. TCP/IP is standard in all Unix systems, and high-quality DOS versions are available. The major problem here is that TCP/IP demands its share of the always-scarce PC memory.

Maintaining network services

Another element to consider is made up of standard services, such as file sharing, printing, and remote log-in. These can be provided either by introducing a more network-conscious operating system as Unix into the PC LAN environment, or doing it the other way around: connecting the PCs into a Unix LAN.

In the first case, the file sharing and printing solutions are likely to be based on PC LAN practice, using NetWare or LAN Manager. You can run a companion service such as Portable NetWare or LAN Manager for Unix on the Unix system. In the second case, the Unix systems usually use Network File System (NFS) and related protocols. PCs can use DOS versions of the same networking services. Sun Microsystems' PC-NFS is one example.

Then, there's Windows

Microsoft Windows puts a pretty face over DOS' plain one. Consider these points:

- All Windows programs have uniform interfaces, more or less.
- Windows can make training and learning easier and more effective, though that is not guaranteed.
- It can take separate applications and make them work like one.
- Its sales success is largely the result of a publicity campaign that will go down in public relations history.
- It can be dreadfully slow.
- It often requires upgraded computers.
- It can be a bear to network.

ADVANTAGES OF WINDOWS

- Presents a uniform interface
- Makes training easier
- Integrates applications
- Manages memory

And it looks good doing it

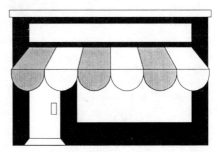

Windows fleshes out DOS very nicely and puts on a pretty [inter]face.

The early sales success of Windows 3.0 was not matched by success in networked applications. To some extent, that's only natural:

- Nothing about Version 3.0 specifically made Windows a networking tool. (That is being changed in later versions.)
- Windows is not an operating system. It is an add-on to DOS, suffering from many of the operating system's limitations and compensating for others.
- Many of the things that go wrong with Windows while on a network are just as likely to go wrong in single-user service. A particular case in point is the notorious Unrecoverable Application Error, whose dialogue box offers the user no option but to reply "OK" to a system crash.

PROBLEMS WITH WINDOWS

- Can harden network arteries
- Requires fine-tuning
- Often requires expensive upgrades
- Unrecoverable application errors

But it looks good doing it

Popular versions of Windows have not been ideal choices for networking.

Windows can be networked. In fact, Windows has several features that directly lend themselves to networking. A workstation running Windows can gain access to network disks and printers as though they were at the workstation. Network software can be multitasked and run in the background. Features like the file and print managers and the control pattern were written with networks in mind.

Nevertheless, Windows networking requires not just patience but endurance. You need not just pay attention to details; you must be obsessed with details. Those who have tried generally have not found it easy.

More potential than reality

For all its potential, Windows 3.0 proved to be immature as a networking product. It's a challenge to run Windows on a single network. It's even more of a challenge to make it work right in an enterprise-wide internetworked environment.

Among the problems: The official Windows manual says very little about networking. Users have reported problems getting help by telephone.

One person reported that when he ran into a problem, Microsoft's support staff offered little help beyond his existing knowledge. Novell's per-call charges were too high to justify. Online services were of some help, though.

Windows' vaunted ease of use can be a problem in itself, particularly from the point of view of network managers who want to maintain a high level of control. Any user can easily exit to DOS. Any knowledgeable user can add new macros and menu options to circumvent the institutional controls for security.

Locating Windows

One of the first and most important decisions in networking with Windows is where to install Windows itself. The three basic choices are:

- Install a separate copy on each workstation.
- Install common files on a server, with the workstation holding only those files that are unique to that station.
- Install the entire program on the server.

There's some argument over which of these is the best course, but a good case could be made for full workstation installation. Windows always exacts a penalty in operating speed, but in this configuration the penalty is the lightest. Another important consideration is that should the network go down, the station can continue to operate in Windows mode.

The second approach, splitting files between workstation and server, saves an acre or two of disk space, but the tradeoff is loss of speed. All those operations that make Windows performance sluggish on all but the most powerful PCs can reduce a network's data flow to oozing sludge.

The full-workstation option moves every signal Windows generates down the network. The overload causes performance to suffer accordingly. This is the only possible choice, though, if the network includes diskless workstations that have no hard disks on which to store their own Windows copies. The best solution here is to avoid diskless workstations with Windows.

Pitfalls to avoid

Here are some tips to help avoid Windows' many pitfalls:

- Install the network before you install Windows. When you run the Windows installation program, it will detect and recognize the type of network you are running. Then it can install the necessary configuration information such as drive designations.

  Windows obviously could not do that if the network was not installed first. The best approach is to make sure your network installation is sound and in order. Only then should you install Windows.

- Be careful on peer-to-peer networks. Servers on these small networks—if there are servers at all—can easily be victimized by Windows. It will drag down their performance, and sometimes might disable it all together. If you must run Windows on a server, make it a dedicated server.
- Load network drivers in high memory whenever you can. The latest DOS versions and several third-party products let you load drivers, TSR programs, and other memory consumers above the 640K limit of conventional memory. The more of that memory you can preserve, the more memory you will have for Windows and its applications.

Windows and the application developer

The same kinds of problems that create problems for network managers also make Windows more challenging to application developers. Some of the problems programmers have reported can be attributed to their unfamiliarity with Windows techniques. Along with their improving knowledge, programmers also have an ever-increasing number of application building tools at their disposal.

New methods

Windows has forced programmers to change many of their traditional ways of thinking. In traditional programming practice, the programmer controls, step by step, everything the application is to do. Typically, the program will cycle through a loop waiting for a key to be pressed. It will then execute the functions associated with that key, then return to the loop to wait for the next instruction from the keyboard.

Windows does things much differently. It uses an event-driven system, in which the operating environment controls the program's execution. The program is not a self-contained application but a collection of routines and resources that wait for instructions from the operating system.

In practice, Windows maintains an inventory of the various elements displayed on the screen. It also identifies the subroutines within the environment that have been designed to manage the user's interaction with those elements.

Now, when the user presses a key, Windows determines which window is active at the moment. It then calls the subroutine that has been registered for that window, and informs the subroutine which key has been pressed. The subroutine then makes the appropriate response.

This event-driven concept is substantially different from the step-by-step procedures most programmers have learned. Though it is possible to write new types of routines from scratch, Windows programmers usually will want to take advantage of the many programming tools that are now available to help them.

Programming the interface

The interface that makes Windows easier for the user to negotiate is not nearly as easy for programmers to create. Among the problems:

- **Windows is often incompatible with older products.** A great many vintage motherboards, add-on boards, and peripherals were designed long before Windows became popular. Uncounted numbers of them are still in service, bringing equally unknown sources of conflict into the picture.
- **There are conflicts with existing software.** Windows applications probably will have to run under a variety of DOS versions, each with its own set of configuration files, system files, device drivers, and other forms of environmental pollution.
- **Windows has to manage memory well—it consumes so much of it.** Both commercial and in-house application developers have had to fight this problem. Any kind of large-scale application will consume large memory chunks. At the same time, response will deteriorate from merely slow to molasses-in-January.
- **Icons are a mixed blessing.** It's great for a programmer to be able to create an icon that will execute multiple commands at the click of a button. Windows works fine as long as the icon clearly illustrates its function. Often, though, a drawing can be just as obscure as those user bugaboos, command line switches. Instead of clearly communicating their purposes, a set of poorly conceived icons can become nothing more than hard-to-decipher hieroglyphics.

Solving problems

The best thing a Windows programmer can do is to keep in contact with other Windows programmers. Call friends and professional contacts; keep in touch with bulletin boards.

One suggestion for application developers: Arrange to swap your product for those of other Windows developers, for mutual testing. You'll get the benefit of your colleagues' thinking. The program will also be exposed to a variety of operating conditions.

Future plans

All of the above is subject to change. Microsoft's product strategy includes expanding Windows' networking features by moving these from their current home in LAN Manager. Some of these features may also find their way into DOS and OS/2. Eventually, Windows should fully support network file management, printing, communications, mail, configuration, and transport protocols such as TCP/IP, IPX/SPX, and NetBIOS. Ultimately Microsoft will provide a distributed operating system with data and resource-location independence.

Windows and the mainframe

Surprisingly, one of the easier ways to integrate Windows into a downsized system is one that on paper should be one of the toughest. This is integrating the new, visually oriented, PC-based technology of Windows with the traditional structure of the mainframe.

It has never been easy to integrate PC and large-system resources. Older mainframe applications were never seriously intended for direct contact by nonprofessionals. Where PC applications from the beginning emphasized user friendliness, mainframe applications are noted for their user hostility. That has had one big effect on organizations who look to downsizing to gain the competitive advantage of distributing more and better information to their employees. If that data is on a mainframe, and if it is hard to get and use, it might as well not be there at all.

This is one place where Windows can make a major contribution, well worth the effort of making it work properly and reliably in a downsized system. Front-end products running under Windows bring the benefits of that environment to PC-mainframe communication. Though some believe Windows' ease-of-use claims are overstated, there is certainly this advantage over the typical mainframe application. There are also such features as a consistent interface, memory management, and hot links between applications. At a minimum, these products make data entry and retrieval easier, as well as make more information available to people who can make productive use of it.

From mainframe to spreadsheet

A major group of Windows-mainframe front ends is derived from older DOS products that make PCs emulate IBM 3270 terminals. Like their predecessors, programs like Rhumba and Irma for Windows provide such terminal emulation features as appropriate display modes, support for various cables and other media, and the ability to retrieve mainframe files and screen displays. As Windows programs, they do more, supplying such features as the common interface, icons, online help, and the ability to conduct multiple mainframe sessions. They also offer Windows' extensive data-sharing features.

On another level, there are application development programs that allow greater, more customized access to the mainframe's databases and communication facilities. These are not primarily tools for users; this degree of access should normally remain in the hands of IS professionals who fully respect the need to protect the mainframe's data from corruption and unauthorized access. A skilled professional can use these tools to import mainframe data into a Windows environment.

Some glitches

Early users have had to overcome some problems. This has been particularly true of networked PCs that are linked to the larger system through gateways. The same problems that have limited Windows in other types of network environments also appear here.

Performance sometimes is also a problem. Mainframe connections tend to be sluggish by PC standards; Windows often makes them more so. That can be a problem, because connection time with a mainframe can be costly.

The delayed promise of OS/2

As PCs began to acquire multiple uses and users, it became clear that DOS isn't the ideal operating system for relatively advanced uses.

OS/2 was announced in 1987 as a replacement for DOS. It was supposed to overcome the shortcomings of DOS, with the expectation that within a few years, it would become the dominant PC operating system.

Of course, it didn't work out exactly that way. OS/2 never became the dominant system; its sales have been comparatively minuscule. It does have some specialized uses, including one that is important to downsizing: running database servers. Even that success has been limited, though. Microsoft's LAN Manager and its IBM twin LAN Server were supposed to work with OS/2 to overcome Novell's networking dominance. That, of course, didn't happen.

Meanwhile, Windows was to be an interim product. It was supposed to give DOS a graphical user interface to serve until the better GUI of OS/2's Presentation Manager (PM) was available. But Windows has turned out to be good enough for most people. Microsoft's promotional barrage at Version 3.0's introduction helped bring about this result. Still, the marketplace reasons, it hasn't evolved as Microsoft and IBM intended for many reasons. OS/2 is demanding of system resources, it has few applications of its own, and though it has always run DOS applications, it has not always run them well. Windows, on the other hand, does run DOS applications—perhaps not perfectly, but well enough.

Feuding and fussing

OS/2 has another well-known problem, too. Microsoft and IBM originally were partners in OS/2 development. Then, their strategic goals came into conflict, leading to open warfare, a subject far more discussed by the trade press than the merits of their respective approaches to serving as PC operating systems. Meanwhile, users were left to feel that they had been conscripted as foot soldiers in someone else's war.

EVALUATING OS/2

- Has multi-use features DOS lacks
- Limited selection of software
- A victim of corporate warfare

Reflects vendors' strategy more than users' needs

OS/2's advantages have been offset by its lack of applications and its role as a strategic pawn.

In truth, the partnership failed because the two companies were pursuing different objectives. IBM is a hardware company. It wants to continue to sell and service computers. Operating systems help meet this objective in two ways: They allow hardware to be used, and they help tie the various IBM hardware platforms together.

DOS was not designed with this unifying purpose in mind; OS/2 was. IBM's goal is that every PC, from workstation to server, will run OS/2 and PM.

Microsoft mainly sells software. It also has visionary leadership. Its idea of the computing future is a multi-media environment with Microsoft software at its core. IBM briefly was the sole supplier of PCs; now it is no longer even the dominant supplier. Not only must Microsoft encourage the use of IBM PCs, it must keep everyone's PCs attractive enough to keep users away from competitors like Apple and Sun. It has no reason to lend particular support to IBM's hardware.

Hardy refugee

All this has left OS/2 in the position of a refugee. It's a hardy refugee, though, and users are beginning to recognize its value in a downsized, networking environment.

OS/2 has incorporated networking features from the very beginning. Microsoft's LAN Manager was announced on the same day as OS/2. IBM's Communications Manager, which provided PC-mainframe communication, was also announced early. Though these programs must be purchased separately, their functions were at least designed into OS/2, rather than being added later.

In fact, OS/2's first intended role was as a network server, and that continues to be its strong point. It is believed that there are more SQL database servers running OS/2 than running any other environment.

With Presentation Manager, OS/2 has enjoyed an easy-to-use interface similar to Windows—many rate it superior. In addition, in response to complaints about DOS networking, OS/2 was given several features that make it easier to install, configure, and manage.

Like Windows, OS/2 requires a more expensive platform than DOS, but don't always take the word of computer publications that push the Texas Nexus—the belief that bigger and more powerful—is always better. (That term originated with social critic John Keats, in a late-1950s critique of the American automobile industry.) On the other hand, OS/2's preemptive multitasking ability means it nearly always will perform better than DOS on comparable hardware. Furthermore, its addressing protection means that the crash of a single process won't take down the entire machine at the same time.

Filling the applications gap

The shortage of applications is also being corrected. In most cases, OS/2 can run applications written for DOS or Windows as well as for OS/2. In addition, more mission-critical back-end programs are available for OS/2 than for either DOS or Unix.

OS/2 2.0 includes functions designed to enhance its performance as both a client workstation and a server. On the client side, this version includes a graphical shell to shield the complexities of the network from the user. A user on one server can retrieve a file icon from a second server and drag it to the symbol of a printer attached to a third server.

Features to improve OS/2 in server use primarily enhance the operating system's original functions. These include improved speed through quicker initiation of multitasking threads and improved system and error management.

Unix: Getting wiser with age

Unix has been around for more than 20 years; it predates DOS by about a decade. It has followed a similar evolutionary pattern in which features and functions have been added as users have developed needs for them. In its present form, Unix is recognized as a source of many of the features that have been lacking in DOS—particularly true in large installations.

Unix is a protected operating system that offers better performance and larger capacities than DOS. It is available on a range of systems, from PCs to multi-processor RISC platforms. It has become best known for its use in RISC-based client/server systems. Like OS/2, Unix is also finding a role in servers connected to DOS networks. It runs many database applications much faster than DOS.

Designed for networks

In recent years, Unix has evolved into a system that emphasizes distributed processing. Networking functionality such as TCP/IP has been built into Unix for years. More recently, similar support has been available at extra cost for open systems interconnection (OSI) protocols.

Another major addition to Unix's networking ability has been Streams, an architecture that lets users and developers incorporate multiple protocol stacks. This has helped make the underlying character of the operating system very compatible with networking.

Many of the interoperability features that have been added to PC networks, including TCP/IP and Network File System (NFS), were first implemented in Unix and have been ported to PCs. Banyan Vines's network operating system is based on Unix. Likewise, some products that started out on the PC side, including NetWare and LAN Manager, have been ported to Unix.

Difficult reputation

One problem that has inhibited the widespread use of Unix is its reputation for being hard to learn and use. That reputation is not completely undeserved. Widespread use of the X Window interface has made things much easier for many users. Even then, learning the system can be a challenging exercise.

Unix partisans maintain, though, that the level of difficulty is primarily a learning problem; as users become familiar with the system, the unfamiliarity naturally disappears.

Operating features

Unix is similar to OS/2 in both its operating features and its system demands. Unix is also available from a wide variety of vendors on many types of hardware.

Unix has traditionally been known for having only a limited number of available applications—particularly business applications. One problem is that not all Unix applications are compatible with all Unix systems. Unix developers have had problems because different versions of the system have had different binary interfaces. That means programs written for one version of Unix won't necessarily run on another.

That may be changing. AT&T, Unix's developer and prime sponsor, has published a binary interface standard that can run applications written for earlier Unix versions.

- Networking is built in (Not added on)
- X Windows improve interface
- Limited number of applications
- Hard-to-use reputation

Unix, a much-criticized veteran, is gaining attention while filling a vacuum.

Running Unix with DOS

As with OS/2, one of Unix's main roles will be in servers on DOS networks. Unix is also in widespread service on workstations. Many users, however, want to retain use of the large and varied inventory of DOS applications. Converting humans to Unix can be just as daunting as converting systems to Unix.

Connecting DOS to Unix lets PC users gain access to Unix files, and to use either DOS or Unix applications. There are many options available to connect Unix systems to DOS networks. Depending on what package you choose, you can have two-direction resource sharing, full applications integrity, security features, and transparent operation. Naturally, the more costly systems offer more of these features.

Among the points to consider:

- Ability to meet *industry standards* for Unix-PC connections. On the Unix side, this includes standards such as X/Open and OSF/DCE. PC systems should meet NFS/TCP/IP or SMB and NetBIOS standards.
- Accommodation for your system's *existing protocols*. These can include NetBIOS, IPX, and Sockets. The connection system should also be compatible with the version of Unix you are using.
- The impact on *existing operations*. Watch out for additions that will slow down your network.
- The system's *functions*. Does it do the jobs you expect it to do?
- Overall *value*. Consider both initial cost, the costs of upgrading other parts of the system, and continued operating costs.

Integrating the Macintosh

PC networking has virtually meant the end of the one-vendor shop. One of the many kinds of freedom users have gained is the flexibility to use the systems that best enable them to do their jobs. One of these, of course, is Apple's Macintosh.

It's no longer unusual to see Macs and PCs on the same network. In fact, there are several ways to network them. The machines can coexist on Ethernet or token ring networks. Each can have its own kind of network. The Macs can be connected to their own LocalTalk system, with a bridge connecting that network to PCs on Ethernet or token ring. These linked systems can easily share files and printers. Often, they can also share applications, particularly those that exist in both DOS and Mac versions.

Still, there are problems. Since Macs and PCs take different attitudes toward computing, there are significant differences in their operating systems. Even when an application has both PC and Mac versions, these often are not completely compatible. Also, few shared applications share some of the things managers consider most important, such as electronic mail and work group scheduling.

To solve these problems, some managers are trying to standardize on a single network operating system to include cabling types and application software, for all networks, Mac and PC alike. Others have taken the bridging approach.

I want to be a client

As Apple's marketing approach makes clear, the networked Mac is best suited for duty as a client. It has enough computing power to handle high-end data transfers, not just for databases and number-crunching, but for image-based applications. Everyone's found they need more horsepower to run a GUI than to deal with the character-based interface PC users have seen in the past.

Apple has an advantage here. The company now has probably more commercial experience with the GUI than anyone else. It has also built the support for its GUI directly into the Mac's operating system. Windows is just a shell that runs on top of the operating system.

Macs and interoperability

Modern Macs have the tools to connect to nearly any kind of enterprise-wide network, whether it be DECnet, SAA, TCP/IP, or some combination. Often, it is possible to use the standard Mac interface, even when working with non-Mac services. This promotes ease of use and makes users more willing to extract value from the equipment.

The Macintosh has always had built-in support for the AppleTalk networking protocols. The addition of file and print services implemented the idea of an easy-to-install plug-and-play network.

Ease of use often came at the expense of performance. Users and network managers found that AppleTalk networking didn't meet all the needs of enterprise-wide computing. In some cases, AppleTalk, running on LocalTalk media, was slow and limiting. In others, the behavior of AppleTalk routers interfered with non-Mac computers on Ethernet. Still others found themselves facing a built-in limit: they could install no more than 254 Macs on an Ethernet backbone.

Apple has come to realize that it can penetrate corporate markets on a large scale only if its Macs can be connected to other computers. Apple addressed some of its early problems with its AppleTalk Phase 2 protocols. Not all of the wrinkles have been ironed out, but systems that run AppleTalk fit into enterprise networks better than they did before. Still, the job of fully integrating the Mac into a diverse computing environment is widely viewed as an unfinished task.

WHERE THE MAC FITS IN

- A client, not a server
- Two networking approaches:
  —Standardized network specifications
  —Internetworking diverse networks
- The big tradeoff:
  —Ease of use v. performance

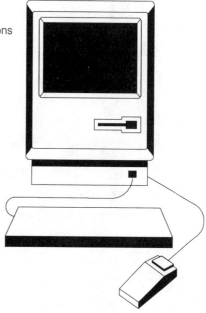

Macs, PCs and other systems live in different worlds, but they can be networked.

Dealing with remaining problems

The LocalTalk wiring system was a key factor in promoting Mac networking and internetworking, but its relatively slow performance has always been a limiting factor. Even more important may be LocalTalk's shortage of resources to ensure reliable file transfers.

More recently, Mac-Ethernet interfaces have been fast, more reliable, and more popular. There are many kinds of gateways to connect AppleTalk and Ethernet networks. Macs that are already on Ethernet can use widely available products to communicate via standard protocols such as TCP/IP.

A common practice now in designing large Mac networks is to connect each of several small networks to a larger-scale Ethernet backbone. This backbone then can play host to several LANs and TCP/IP services. In fact, Apple has a TCP software package that is more reliable than AppleTalk.

AppleTalk still is necessary, though, for WAN service. It includes the necessary routers and their accompanying software.

THE USER'S VIEW OF TECHNOLOGY

- What it is isn't vitally important (Though I might have some opinions)
- I just want to get my job done
- The system should help me do that

Never let technology get in the way of meeting user's needs.

8

CHAPTER

The client/server model

Networking once was a fairly simple idea. From a large-system perspective, a network was a hierarchy. A host system controlled things; it served dumb terminals that were clearly subordinate. Initially, the PC world stuck close to that example. Desktop systems were networked to communicate with file servers. In both cases, mainframe and PC LAN, there was a greater focus on how the network functioned than on what it did for its users.

Over time, that system changed. On the mainframe side, PCs supplemented, and in some cases replaced, dumb terminals. The PC took on the role of an intelligent terminal that could process the data it retrieved from the central host. Though that model is more flexible than the original, it still has shown its limitations.

Now, downsizers are making use of the newer and even more flexible client/server model. The client/server model goes further than its predecessors. It gives users direct access to the services provided by the information system, whatever that system may be. This has become the basic model for downsized systems. Typically, this model uses one or more servers, which may manage files or a database, provide communication, or act as a link to a host server, its information and its services.

The big difference is that now the users are in charge. They operate the client workstations. The server's function is to meet their needs. It's a coincidence, but an important one, that the abbreviation C/S could stand for either client/server or *customer service*. The two are much alike.

The advantages

The difference between this model and its predecessors is the use of LANs to gain access to a host system or server. The most familiar advantage of this model is reduced cost. The most important advantage often is flexibility.

Most users should find this model less expensive than its large-system counterpart. Some might find it a lot cheaper. It can be much less expensive to buy PCs and servers than large systems and dumb terminals. This is particularly true if you take advantage of the flexibility this system offers. You can tailor your purchases to meet the needs of particular individuals or work groups. Power users—or more precisely those whose work can benefit from power use—can get appropriately designed workstations. Users whose jobs are less demanding can be assigned less expensive units. This kind of modularity builds in flexibility. Systems installed under this theory have tended to evolve as the organizations and their needs have grown and changed.

It also can often be less expensive to provide technical support for PC LANs than it is to support larger systems. This is not always or automatically true, but it often does work that way. For example, when a mainframe needs service, you can't just take it down to the shop.

Advantages beyond cost

Cost, however, is only the first advantage, and it often is not the most important. The real advantage of downsizing and of the client/server model is that it lets you shift your focus. Instead of debating the merits of one technology over another, you can pick the technology that best suits your needs. The goal should be to give users easy access to information without regard to where it is located or in what kind of system.

Those who have successfully downsized have generally followed a common pattern. They have recognized that the PC makes a great deal of sense in the role of an intelligent workstation. It allows users to gain access to your data resources, and to make good use of the data they retrieve. Cost enters the picture as a secondary benefit, not a primary one. Once you have established the value of better data access, the relatively low cost makes such a system easy to justify.

Cost alone, however, is not a sufficient justification for a downsized system. Today's business environment demands additional advantages and benefits.

Assessing the technology

Typically, an organization's resources can be viewed in two ways:

- How these resources are managed. It can be done centrally, as in the typical large system, or the management can be decentralized.
- How these resources are used. From this perspective, you ask how these resources can be used to fulfill a business mission.

If you examine your resources from a use-oriented perspective, two other choices arise:

- The main value of the resource could be tactical. It must be put to use right now, or you will lose out on an opportunity.
- The main value could be strategic. In this case, your use of the resource would gain value over a longer time span.

THE COMPUTING RESOURCES MATRIX

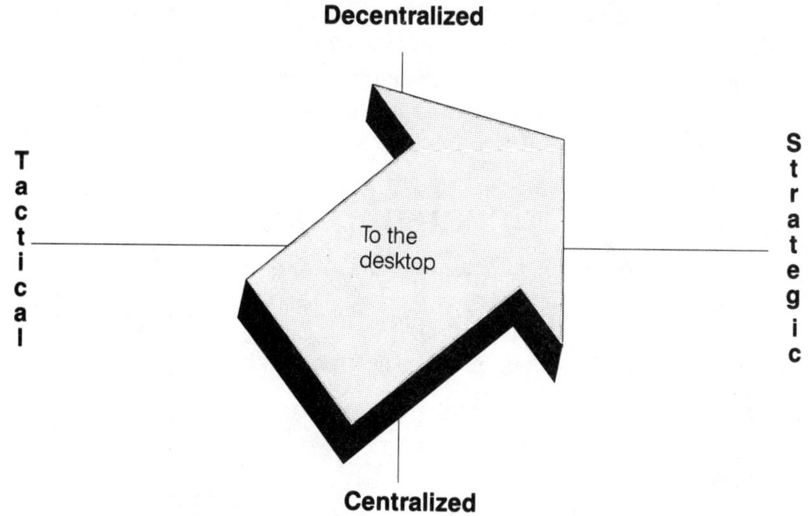

Decentralized

To the desktop

Tactical (left axis)

Strategic (right axis)

Centralized

Movement from tactical to strategic, and from centralized to decentralized processing, contributes to the downsizing trend.

Identifying these factors can be a big aid to selecting systems and software as here illustrated. You can assess the purpose and value of a particular information resource, then identify the type of system that would do the best job of achieving those goals. Consider these questions: How easy is it to maintain the system? What kind of variety does a particular system offer? Can you customize the installation? Can you easily adapt it to the specialized needs of individual users? How quickly can you implement this system?

The old highway safety adage, *speed kills*, is hardly appropriate to a downsized environment. Here, a shortage of speed could be a fatal error. A new system might offer a specialized, on-target response to the needs that are identified during initial planning. If that system can't be delivered until a year or more later, though, it will no longer be the best response to your situation. Circumstances easily can change in a year's time, and your new system will already be obsolete. Some say it can happen in as little as six months.

The real issues now are not centralized versus decentralized administration, or strategic versus tactical planning. These considerations provide a framework for analysis, but they are not ends in themselves. The real issue is how to provide access to users.

It has become an unfortunate habit to focus too strongly on technical issues. Selecting hardware and software has taken priority in systems professionals' thinking. This has been true on both the PC and large-system sides; in fact, it has been responsible for much of the tension between the two.

Employers and professionals alike have contributed to this process. In many cases, the professionals have just been dutifully responding to signals from their employers. Business at all levels lost sight of the idea that the purpose of an information system should be to provide information. That means that any downsizing plan should first consider exactly who shall have access to what information, and for what purposes.

The changing user

Changes in the conception of a network and its purposes have been accompanied by changes in the nature of the user. The modern user is a much different person than the person who used to simply type at a terminal. Compared with traditional users, the new user is likely to be:

- A professional or a manager.
- A more valuable person.
- More mobile.
- Assigned to a different type of job.

THE CHANGING USERS

- More professional
- More valuable
- More mobile
- More versatile

Users are changing. Information systems have to change with them.

The professional user

Over the last decade or so, there has been a very fundamental change in the nature of the user that professionals have been required to support. Consider the types of people you might have found sitting at terminals a few years ago. Some would have been programmers, of course. A great many would have been data entry clerks. Others would have been engineers, accountants, or others with specialized needs. It would have been rare to find executives (never mind secretaries) with terminals at their desks.

Today, these executives probably have networked PCs on their desks, and they use them to retrieve information for use in executive information systems, or to transfer the data directly to their spreadsheet programs. Generally, the older users daily performed the same tasks.

Today's users rely on their PCs to support a variety of tasks. Their jobs are fundamentally different. They require greater amounts of management analysis. They make use of different types of knowledge. Often, they work at higher skill levels.

USERS ARE MORE PROFESSIONAL

- Different types of knowledge
- Different tasks
- Different skills
- Different jobs

Users once were programmers, clerks, and a few specialists. Now, everyone uses data.

Meanwhile, organizations are changing, too. Along with downsized systems are downsized organizations. They are flatter and more flexible. In order to successfully give users the information they need, it's important to recognize that it's not just the users who have changed. It's their work and their organizational status as well.

The more valuable user

Anyone familiar with the *Workforce 2000* report or its widely scattered fallout is no doubt aware that we face a shortage of skilled employees. People can no longer be treated as interchangeable parts—if they ever could. People are an investment, and a very costly investment to boot. A primary goal of any information system should be to get maximum value from this investment.

It can cost an organization upwards of $6,000 simply to fill a position. Other estimates place the cost as high as the first two years' salary. That is only the cost of recruiting, interviewing, testing, and finally filling the position.

It costs even more to integrate the new employee into the organization. Training costs vary with the nature of the job, but there are always some costs—often substantial. There are continuing expenses such as the costs of supervision, keeping employees updated on new methods and technologies, and of course their salaries and benefits. Another potential cost is the value of information departing employees could take from the organization.

If there is a silver lining here, it is that personnel expenses are one class of costs that are well within the organization's control. But the process of cost control can itself be expensive.

USERS ARE MORE VALUABLE

- Good people are harder to find
- They're expensive, too
  - —Recruiting
  - —Training
  - —Supervision
  - —Value of knowledge

There's a shortage of skilled workers. Getting and keeping them requires a major investment.

The mobile user

One expense that is almost certain to decline is the expense of gold watches and other awards for long-term employees. Few stick around long enough to collect them. Few employers encourage them to do so. Statistically, any given person is likely to change jobs once every two to five years. Most individuals change careers at least two or three times in their working lives. That figure is rising; it is projected that those now entering the work force may change jobs as often as seven times before they retire.

Even those who stay with the same organizations do not often stay in the same jobs. In any group of employees, it's likely that at least half have experienced some kind of change within the last year in the responsibilities they perform for their organizations. They may be moved to different assignments or departments, or often they find the nature of any given job can change rapidly.

That means their requirements for information also change—often dramatically. Consider the well-documented trend toward an information economy, in which long-time mainstays like industry and agriculture become steadily less important to the national economy.

Other changes are in progress, too. One pattern U.S. business has begun to adapt from Japanese practice is that of developing generalists instead of specialists. The traditional American pattern is to rise vertically within your specialty—from sales representative to sales manager, for example. The prevailing Japanese pattern is to rotate rising managers among the organization's functions. By the time a manager reaches a senior position, this individual will probably have experience in sales, marketing, information systems, operations, and many other activities. U.S. employers are gradually adopting similar patterns.

USERS ARE MORE MOBILE

- Between tasks
- Between projects
- Between departments
- Between divisions
- Between companies

Users move around, and every change means a new kind of information need.

The second generation

Another characteristic of modern users is that increasing numbers of them are second-generation users. They have already encountered computers, often in school. Some developed healthy interests that spur them to look continually for better and more effective ways to use them. They can make good use of ready access to data.

Another group has had a much different reaction to the early experience. Typically, they come from the era when teaching "computer literacy" meant drilling students in BASIC programming and hexadecimal arithmetic. These people were often understandably turned off by the experience. Now, they will touch computers only with the greatest reluctance. If these users are to reach full productivity, they need easy, nonintimidating means of access.

Serving today's users

Today's users are being required to do more things with more data, and more types of data. The types of users who need access to information are different from the data entry clerks and specialized professionals of the past. This has also meant substantial changes in what data users need, and in what they do with it.

One way in which these trends are reflected is the increasing pressure on IS professionals to become more aware of their organizations' other functions. They are expected to learn more about the enterprise in order to apply their professional talents more precisely to meeting the organization's needs.

The demands of new kinds of users are also behind the downsizing phenomenon. The downsized system becomes a new and better way to give these users the kinds of information access they need. For the people in charge of providing this information, it means:

- Devising new means of access to existing information.
- Recognizing that these means must accommodate new demands from changed jobs.
- Providing for the use of multiple applications.
- Establishing a universal point of access to corporate information.

WHAT TODAY'S USERS NEED

- New means of access
- Ability to meet changing needs
- Ability to run multiple applications
- Universal point of access

New kinds of users have new kinds of needs. The client/server architecture helps meet them.

Providing access

The need for universal access is one explanation for the popularity of Microsoft Windows. Windows is not quite as easy to use as its sponsors would like it to be, and its interface is not quite as uniform as its users would like it to be. Still, as they say about money, it's way ahead of whatever's in second place.

Windows does eliminate the need to learn different access methods for different applications. In that, it is a model for front-end systems of all kinds. They can be either graphics- or character-based. For most purposes, that doesn't truly make a great deal of difference. What does count is that the access method makes the same response to the same actions, whatever the application.

The old way

Under a traditional type of architecture, the user had to go through a multi-step process to get access to the mainframe. Once the user logged onto the network, there was usually a shell program that allowed the PC to emulate a terminal. This, in turn, would allow access to the host. The retrieved information was transferred to a data file on the PC. Then, the user could retrieve it into a PC application, but would usually have to run some kind of file translation program first.

This is too involved for modern users. They aren't looking for fixed bodies of information, defined and controlled through application programs. As users change their needs, their jobs and even their roles in the organization, they need ad hoc, custom access. The old architecture restricts their ability to get what they need.

How to invent a better way

The client/server model uses *interoperability* as a means to encourage and control access. Interoperability is a large, important step beyond the older concept of connectivity.

Connectivity means, very simply, that two machines on different platforms are able to talk to each other. That's what the old architectural model provided.

A fully interoperable system lets users retrieve information painlessly from diverse sources. They not only need access to information, but they need it in a format they can manage and that helps improve their productivity, not restrict it. This means features like clipboard and file transfers, and the ability to cut and paste among various applications. Terminal emulation just doesn't do these things.

These features can be embedded into the clients' applications, as they are in Windows and the Macintosh operating system. Graphical front ends like these can have the ability to interface with multiple mainframe sessions at the same time. These applications also take advantage of architectural advances in remote procedure calls in which part of the program runs on the host while another portion resides on the client workstation. Through protocols such as LU 6.2, Novell's transport protocols, or transport tools supplied by database vendors, you can make interprocess communications across the network between the client workstation and the host, be it a mainframe, midrange system, or PC server.

Applications that fail to do this fall short of full interoperability, because they don't make the product transparent.

Other aspects of interoperability can be built into the system. These include such things as the way data repositories are managed. It can mean cooperative processing, in which the data is not located strictly on a host system but can be anywhere on the network—wherever it makes sense for the data to be. It also includes the ability to use common data dictionaries and directories, regardless of the platform, and interprocess communication across platforms. These are all server functions. That's the logical place for them to be.

BEYOND THE BASICS
Connectivity v. interoperability

Connectivity:	Interoperability:
• Provides ability to communicate (That's all)	• Easy retrieval from diverse sources
• Based on old model	• Custom formats
	• File transfers
	• Cut and paste

New concepts of interoperability go beyond the older, more limited, idea of connectivity.

Interoperability for clients

On the client side, where the users interact with the system, interoperability can start with terminal emulation. Even with advanced means of communication across platforms, this will always be needed some time.

Interoperability must not stop there; making file transfer as seamless as possible is even more important. The user should be able to retrieve information from one environment and use it in another, without regard to the varied platforms involved. In fact, the user should not even have to know from which platform the data comes. Ideally, the system should be able to remove a row of data from a server-based database system. It then will let the user manipulate that data by placing it in some application such as a spreadsheet. For example, the user should be able to insert retrieved information into, say, the Windows version of WordPerfect, knowing little more than how to operate WordPerfect.

Again, many managers are turning to Windows. They are trying to ease the process of obtaining mainframe data by using Windows as a front end to the host. Windows-to-host applications give users access to the data they need without their having to navigate through an unfamiliar host language. They need to accept the alternative of waiting until a trained operator can find the time to retrieve the data. Many IS managers have been striving to implement systems in which users can click on an icon and get logged into a host session, or click on an icon that represents the type of data they need, and go straight to that data.

Of course, it's not really that simple. You can't just install a Windows terminal emulator and suddenly get shelter from the host commands. Nevertheless, even basic Windows terminal emulators let users run host sessions in Windows, then use the clipboard to cut and paste the data into a spreadsheet or some other PC application. This application, in turn, might let them create graphic representations of the data.

Most terminal emulation packages further simplify the process by including scripting capabilities that let users automate tasks. Using a PC as a terminal emulator is one thing. You can also use Windows to mask the complexities of the mainframe from the user. Others find that Windows' user-friendly interface is less important than the operating environment's ability to multitask.

Managers make it possible

To achieve results like this, information managers must begin to look at themselves more as enablers and less as custodians of information. It's necessary to seek out those features and benefits that promote interoperability.

System features also can be enablers. They let a user make use of available information.

SQL is an important example. At its root, SQL is a limited-purpose programming language. It gives users the means to specify certain types of information they would like to retrieve from a relational database. In a client/server database environment, it then helps the user retrieve that information into a desktop application. For all SQL's reputation as a difficult, inhibiting language, it really serves only that clear, specialized purpose. It was never meant to do, or be, anything else.

The client/server model is another enabler. It provides a model and structure for giving users access to centralized sources of information.

A universal interface is another example. It makes the data easier to retrieve and use. Information is not really available unless the users can retrieve it in a form and by methods they can readily understand.

The local operating model

In a way, the newer, more flexible, model emphasizes the workstation. It's important not to overemphasize the workstation.

Consider what would happen, for example, if you were running a PC workstation as an intelligent node on a network. This workstation might run the operating system and a shell, plus the network files, all in RAM at that location. To perform an analytical operation, the user would have to open the database, sort or index it, retrieve it, and print out a copy. That doesn't even consider retrieving it into an application program.

That doesn't make much more sense than the older model in which the user must go through multiple steps to retrieve a small amount of database information from a central host.

Happy medium

The client/server architecture falls between these extremes. Some functions might be managed at a large-system host or by a PC file server. A database server might perform other functions. Some might be managed at the workstation. Still others might be managed at other workstations. None of this need meet any standard formula, only the needs of your own organization.

Issues to be addressed

That, of course, is an ideal situation. Before you can get there, you will have to address several other issues. They include:

- The operating environment. What kind of operating environment will provide the kind of interoperability that will meet your needs and objectives?
- Application program interfaces. These are the common interfaces that are necessary to make interoperability work.
- Communication protocols. These allow users to gain access to information across different platforms.
- Network operating systems. These, and how they interact with the operating environment, will no doubt become a key issue. Which one gives the best performance? Which provides true interoperability?
- Internetworking. How do you connect LANs and WANs, using PCs, or PCs attached to LANs, as gateways into host environments?

Look for benefits, not features

There is no right answer for everyone—not even a uniform way to find the right answer. One way to sharply increase your chances of success is to look for benefits, not features.

Much of the competition within the computer industry is based on features. Advertisements and trade-journal reports often compare products by comparing their features; some use elaborate tables for the purpose.

These comparisons can be valuable, but keep this in mind: Leading firms in the PC word processing market have competed for years on the number of features their products offer. As a result, the feature lists of competing products are very much alike. One long-time industry leader, Word-Perfect, has held its position not primarily because of its list of features, but on its reputation for customer service.

Customer service is not so much a feature as it is a benefit. Customers respond because they expect to take advantage of it. It's the benefit of having good service, not the service itself, that makes the difference.

Features are important, and the right features can provide significant benefits. Make sure, though, that when you make a choice, you look closely at the real benefits that are available.

FEATURES V. BENEFITS

Features: Benefits:

- NetBIOS   • Service
- TCP/IP   • Responsiveness
- Open systems   • Ease of access

Features are important, but pay closest attention to the benefits they provide.

9
CHAPTER

Downsizing databases

When downsizing is discussed, structured query language (SQL) cannot be far behind. SQL, however, is both more and less than a language.

As a language, SQL serves a limited purpose. It retrieves data from a database. Unlike more complete and conventional programming languages, SQL *describes* the data it seeks. Other languages, including database dialects, issue step-by-step procedural instructions for retrieving data that meets the user's specifications. SQL only transmits the specifications. It's up to the database manager to determine what it must do to meet those specifications and return the result to the user.

At the same time, SQL is more than a computer language; it is an entire system for recording, managing, and retrieving data. SQL is the key to the *relational* database system. All data is stored in tabular form. Data can be extracted from any of several related tables. For example, one table might indicate that an employee is assigned to the accounting department; the system can then look up the accounting department in another table and find the name of its manager. The process of extracting linked data from multiple tables is called a *join*.

If the user wants to do something with the retrieved data, the user must issue a separate set of instructions, perhaps by entering the names of the employee and department head in the spaces of a form. Traditionally, this has been done by embedding SQL queries in a procedural program that then acts on the data these instructions retrieve.

An increasingly popular method is to issue the query and retrieve the results into a Windows application. Those results can then be fed directly to an application program running at the PC workstation. Applications

WHAT IS SQL?

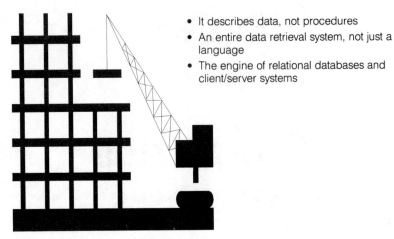

- It describes data, not procedures
- An entire data retrieval system, not just a language
- The engine of relational databases and client/server systems

SQL is both a language and a key to client/server database management.

such as the server edition of dBASE IV and Lotus' Data Lens are designed specifically to retrieve and use data from an SQL database.

Either approach can be particularly attractive for downsized applications using the client/server model. Among the reasons:

- It allows for the storage of large databases on dedicated servers or large-system hosts. The server, not the client PC, processes the SQL query.
- Only the response to the SQL query must travel over the network. This limits network traffic and improves responsiveness.
- Users can work with this data using familiar PC application programs.

A history of SQL

By today's standards, early databases were large and clumsy. They ran on central mainframes with access by way of dumb terminals, and later, through PCs emulating dumb terminals. This made good economic sense. Only an expensive, large system could accommodate the typical corporate database. The drawback was that user interaction with the large system was limited. The user could retrieve data and look at it, but there were few means to actually use it.

This began to change as PCs advanced in speed, power, and storage capacity. As these relatively inexpensive resources gained the capacity to manage ever-larger databases, there was less economic need to maintain only a single, large machine.

In addition, PC users had learned to use their own database programs. First came the dBASE line and its clones. Not far behind was the popular 1-2-3, which included data management as well as spreadsheet functions. dBASE, FoxBASE, and 1-2-3 initially operated as stand-alone applications on single PCs. Each PC program operated in isolation, using its own data format. This mode of operation will continue in many places for the foreseeable future. Many types of use, however, become more efficient when all users have easy access to the information on other systems and in other file formats.

Networking arrives

The next major development in PC technology was the LAN. Combined with increasingly powerful PCs, the LAN let users link their computers. One networked computer came to be designated the file server; it provided a hub for the system and stored shared data. When called upon by a workstation, it would ship entire files of data across the network.

When the workload grew—and on a network, it always does—the server could easily become a bottleneck. Ordinary file servers were not well equipped to maintain security or data integrity, nor were they strong when asked to deal with concurrent updates or other multiple uses of the same data.

Clients and servers

The tasks with which file servers had the most trouble were generally matters of database management. The response was to move the database operations to a separate dedicated database server.

This server is the back-end half of the client/server configuration. The objective is to make best use of both hardware and software resources by splitting the functions between two systems, the database server and front-end client workstations. Data on the server can be entered and stored once. Users can take advantage of many different types of front-end applications, including PC database managers, spreadsheets, graphics programs, and word processing/desktop publishing software.

The split duty lightens the workload on both ends. The database server processes requests from the clients and ships back only the responses to those requests; it need not send entire data files over the network as older server systems did. The specialized server can use the rest of its resources for protecting the security and integrity of its data, managing backup and recovery, and arbitrating multiple use.

Meanwhile, the PC application is receiving only the data its user requested. Instead of having to extract the desired data out of a transmitted mass, the application's resources can be put to use in ways that directly serve the user: transmitting queries, and reporting and analyzing the results.

SQL forever?

SQL has become the almost generic language of the database server. When a client application sends a query to the server, it almost always uses SQL. The client sends a single query to the server. The server interprets that query and returns the requested data. This query tells the server only what it wants; it leaves it to the back-end database manager to process the query and return the results.

As a means of access to database servers, SQL offers several benefits:

- Application programming is simplified. A programmer need only embed the appropriate SQL statements to retrieve the data the program needs.
- Network traffic is reduced. Only the query and the extracted data must travel over the network.
- Standardizing on SQL allows the use of different applications to retrieve and use data from a single source.
- SQL also permits the use of distributed databases, split between various locations. The same query can retrieve the appropriate data from each of several servers.

ADVANTAGES OF SQL

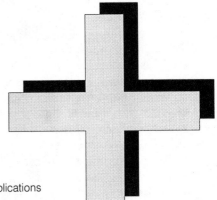

- Simplified application programming
  —Embedded statements
  —Front-end application builders
- Reduced network traffic
- Single data source serving multiple applications
- Distributed databases

SQL's specialized type of simplicity can aid users and program developers alike.

A varied "standard"

Though SQL is widely described as a standard way to retrieve data, in practice there is no such thing as standard SQL. Although the American National Standards Institute has published a standard, it is for only a barebones version of the query language. Virtually every vendor of an SQL product has added its own features, which mean nonstandard extensions and variations. This need not be a serious problem if you standardize on a single product at the server level. That product's version of SQL then can become your universal version of SQL.

Client/server computing

Both the downsizing movement and the advent of new front-end products are changing the way database applications look and work. These changes require that users adopt some new ways of thinking about how they design and use their networks.

The original purpose of PC LANs was to share costly resources like laser printers or large, fast hard disks. The newer, more strategic, purpose is to be able to share and use data. With the change in purpose has come a change in methods and practices.

THE CLIENT/SERVER MODEL

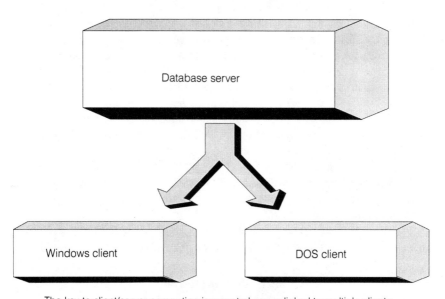

The key to client/server computing is a central server linked to multiple clients.

A new architecture

Downsizing activities have fallen into a generally consistent pattern. On one hand, application programs are being moved from large systems and servers to the individual workstation. The application itself is no longer centralized; it runs at the front end on desktop computers. In fact, different computers can use different applications, if they speak the same dialect of SQL.

In general, though, data files are not being moved to the desktop. There are few good reasons to do so. In general, large corporate databases are remaining on large systems. At most, they are being moved to high-powered PC servers. The usual objective is to install the applications, gateways, and other facilities that will give desktop users access to the central data storehouse.

That requires communication, not only between systems, but between people. Though most IS professionals have accepted the downsizing trend, there are some troublesome exceptions. Both parties can find it uncomfortable when a large-system database manager must deal with a PC LAN manager. Mainframe programmers must get used to the idea of writing applications that will run on PCs. They have to get along with the idea that a programmer's pay is not necessarily based on the size of the machine on which the output is run.

Old v. new

Under traditional large-system architecture, not only were the machines different, but so was the way they were used. A central host, be it a mainframe, a minicomputer, or a PC, was tied to a battery of terminals. The host managed all the screen handling, program logic, integrity checks, and security measures. A terminal did nothing; it only gave its user a view into the large machine's data.

The new model uses a common interface, often based on Windows. At the same time, database servers are in the middle of a migration from both directions. In addition to applications and databases that are migrating downward from larger systems, many PC LAN databases are moving upward to the client/server architecture.

Many organizations are now adopting strategies in which they integrate PCs into their core data processing functions. This lets users tie the data from a central database to their spreadsheet or word processor. Meanwhile, IS professionals can continue to manage the central data storehouse, maintaining the integrity and validity of the data while helping the users make use of that data to do their jobs more effectively.

Multiple benefits

Organizations that move to a client/server environment can benefit in two ways: cost and flexibility. LAN-based applications can be cheaper to build and maintain. But for many organizations, the issue is more than money. LAN applications can be much more flexible, providing hooks to tools like spreadsheets and graphics utilities. Users can not only get to their data more easily, but can make better use of it.

Many candidates for downsizing to client/server still reside on costly big-iron systems for one or more of these reasons:

- They were written years ago, when the big system represented the only possibility.

- Until recently, LANs were not safe havens for mission-critical applications, not yet able to fulfill security and data integrity requirements.
- Also until recently, LANs just didn't have the horsepower to pull off complex corporate applications.

Those days are over. Today, LANs can be built with enough horsepower to propel all but the biggest applications. And the necessary safeguards are available or can be built in.

And some drawbacks

Unfortunately, the dream of being able to connect any type of back-end database with any type of front-end client is only approaching reality. It took 19 months for the SQL Access Group, working in conjunction with the International Standards Organization, the American National Standards Institute (ANSI), and the X/Open Consortium, to develop a standard SQL server interface as a basis of interoperability and portability between back-end databases and front-end tools.

The SQL Access Group, founded in 1989, is a nonprofit corporation consisting of 42 of the largest systems and software vendors. The group overcame countless technical obstacles to achieve client/server interoperability. It did so with a prototype of recently completed technical specifications to enable front-end clients and database servers to work together seamlessly.

For starters, each brand of SQL is slightly different; the communications formats and protocols are different, as are the APIs. The SQL Access Group's technical specification addresses and resolves all of these technical issues.

Unfortunately, this technical breakthrough will not immediately let loose a flow of new products to take advantage of it. These must still be developed, a process expected to take at least a year.

Where SQL fits

In this picture, SQL is the underlying technology that enables everything else. If SQL didn't exist, we would have to invent it.

Basically, SQL is an architecture that lets you make the separation between the client and server functions; you are allowed a great deal of flexibility. For example, there are several database applications designed for back-end service on a database server. Among them are Oracle Server, the Microsoft/Sybase SQL Server, Gupta's SQL Base, the extended edition of OS/2, or Novell's NetWare SQL. Large systems can also use mainframe-oriented databases like IBM's DB2.

To use the contents of these back-end databases, you have your choice of tools. Among them are Windows applications that can issue SQL queries and receive the results, applications like dBASE IV that are designed to incorporate retrieved data into your own application programs, and products like Data Lens that retrieve information into conventional application programs like 1-2-3.

At Sara Lee, client/server systems have allowed the organization to take advantage of each platform's strengths. Using such products as Channel Computing's Forest and Trees, and executive information system, and conversion utilities like Lotus' Data Lens, client/server projects give users the ability to make good use of more of the organization's information resources.

Any organization can use this flexibility to customize its selection of front-end tools. Target the key users in each work group of the department. Ideally, there will be at least one sophisticated user who not only understands the system, but knows what the users in that group really need. Make use of such experience and insight; select the method that best meets their needs, and those of their less knowledgeable coworkers.

TWO KINDS OF PROGRAMS

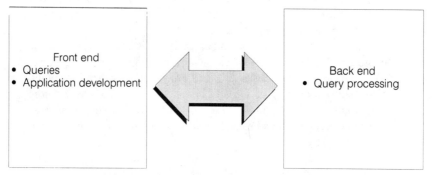

The client and server use separate programs that split the database duty.

Law enforcement

Another choice to be made is where to maintain the "business rules" that help enforce data safety and integrity. For example, a program should provide in some way that if a department is deleted from the database, its employees should not remain on file as members of the no-longer-existing department.

One school of thought, identified primarily with Sybase and SQL Server, is that these rules should be maintained and enforced at the server. That way, users and even application programmers need not worry about them. The server enforces them in the course of processing a database query. In addition, this approach places this rule-enforcement function in what is probably the network's most powerful unit.

An opposing school of thought points out that even powerful servers can be swamped by heavy workloads. In addition, the rules are not always universal. They can vary from application to application. Accordingly, people who hold this view enforce the rules at the workstation. This approach avoids imposing extra work on the server. It also gives programmers more options for enforcing rules—as well as more responsibility.

Front-end alignment

For users at the front end, the division of labor between client and server can have two advantages:

- Better operation of the application, particularly when large databases are in use. Depending on the hardware and operating environment, response time for queries can rival that of a minicomputer or mainframe.
- Updating mainframe applications in the shortest amount of time. Many users are turning to front-end tools that are powerful enough to avoid further programming in time-consuming third-generation languages such as COBOL or C.

This division represents one way in which the available front-end products vary. Some are designed primarily to support users in retrieving and using data. Others are primarily application builders that use graphical and object-oriented techniques to speed up the development process. While the distinction is often blurred, certain products are more appropriate for one audience or another.

FRONT ENDS FOR APPLICATION DEVELOPMENT

Consider these criteria:

- Full SQL implementation
  - —Integrated with client/server applications
- Variety of tools for major tasks:
  - —Creating application
  - —Database administration
  - —Client/server communication
- Portable client applications
  - —Operating systems
  - —Hardware platforms

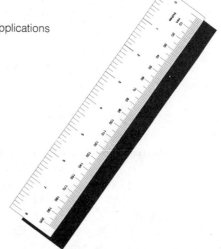

Front-end software used for serious application development requires extra features.

The developer category goes deeper than the end-user category because it incorporates many tools that help create sophisticated applications. Products in this category often provide a comprehensive language, report generation, forms generation, a debugger, and access to external programming languages.

Products for the end user generally contain fewer application development functions. This category does not provide as comprehensive an environment for building new applications, but it gives the user an ad hoc query capability that usually includes simple form and report generation. On the other hand, front-end software that's intended for serious application development should have extra features for that purpose, as shown.

Some front-end tools were built from the ground up for a client/server environment. Others were ported from a DOS environment. Although most products can perform ordinary queries and updates, some have features that make data administration easier. These are more often found in products built from the ground up as front-end tools.

Graphic v. character

Another difference in products is whether they use a graphical user interface or a character-based orientation. A GUI includes many features not normally associated with character-based systems.

For example, GUI products lend themselves more readily to the development of object-oriented databases rather than structured, line-by-line programming. Databases and other applications can communicate through internal communication protocols found inside the GUI environment, such as Windows' dynamic data exchange (DDE).

That shouldn't discourage the consideration of character-based front ends as well. The best of these—FoxPro, for example—are quicker, can run on smaller systems and have many of the features of their graphic counterparts.

How to support SQL

Another difference, and one that could affect performance, is the way various front-end products support SQL. You'll rarely see a user typing a query in SQL. Most often, SQL queries are made by programs written in other languages, such as COBOL or C. The SQL code, which is *embedded* within the program, is sent directly to the database engine to perform database operations. When SQL is embedded within the front-end application, the SQL statements are processed without intervention by the front end. The only thing it needs to do is send the query to the back end.

The link between SQL and the host language comes in two main varieties: precompilers and application program interfaces (APIs). In systems that use precompilers, the programmer writes SQL statements directly into the program, preceded by a command such as "Exec SQL". Then, a precompiler is run to translate the SQL statements into function and procedure calls that are intelligible to the host language's compiler. Finally, the host language compiler is run to produce the finished program.

When an API is used, the programmer explicitly calls a library of functions in the host language rather than using the precompiler to create those calls. An API tends to produce tighter code than a precompiler.

Neither approach produces a universal, portable application. Both have pitfalls that can make it difficult to port existing code for use with a different database. Precompilers tend to be picky about proprietary language features, and APIs differ so widely that most of the code for a new front-end application must be rewritten from scratch.

In addition, some products provide far more transparent access to the back-end server data than do others. Ideally, the front end should be able to let the end user or developer have access to the data on the back end without knowing where the data resides. It shouldn't matter where the data is located, whether locally on a PC server or remotely on a database server, a minicomputer, or a mainframe.

Also, because many companies have a mix of DOS, OS/2, Macintosh and Unix environments, some users will be more sensitive to the need to run applications on multiple operating systems.

Client/server planning principles

There are no free lunches, in client/server or anywhere else. Many companies have found many advantages in downsizing their databases to client/server systems. Still, the process is not risk-free, and there are pitfalls to be avoided. Richard Finkelstein, a Chicago-based consultant and writer, offers four rules to help minimize the risks of a client/server conversion:

- **Start small.** Don't risk your organization's critical applications in your first downsizing project. First, try downsizing a simple project with low risks, low costs, and low visibility.
- **Start early.** Don't wait until the last minute. Leave yourself time to evaluate alternative approaches and products.
- **Don't mix and match.** Stay as mainstream as possible and choose products that were designed to work together and have been tested together.
- **Don't rule out options.** Be comfortable with your hardware and software choices, but don't automatically exclude any potential solution without at least some investigation.

Picking the project

Departmental decision-support applications, or those that provide for ad hoc queries by users, are good candidates for the first downsizing projects.

There will be a minimum amount of new technology to learn. Developers can concentrate on installing the new database server and its supporting network and application tools. They won't be distracted by the added problems of installing more complex applications like online transaction processing (OLTP) systems.

The database server facilities aren't overly taxed and should require a minimal amount of tuning, Finkelstein points out. This approach allows your organization to become familiar with downsizing issues while deploying much-needed applications into the user community. You'll face lower risks and reap increased benefits—exactly the type of equation you're looking for.

Get an early start

As Finkelstein points out, an organization often will wait until the last minute to begin preparing for downsizing. By then, the new system is needed immediately, and a traditional mainframe system would be impractical. That leaves downsizing as the only practical option.

Last-minute downsizing, in turn, can lead to panic-stricken responses. These organizations will scramble for quick solutions—a sure prescription for failure.

Long before downsizing is necessary, you should begin evaluating your organization's strategic needs. Build a prototype of a potential application to validate the correctness of your choices and the stability of the software. Expect to spend some time learning about the new technology and introducing it to your users. Also expect bugs.

Don't mix and match

At least be careful, Finkelstein advises. Though a client/server system is designed to let diverse front-end systems interact with equally diverse server systems, the linkage does not come automatically. Here are some of the problems you can encounter:

- Even if it works today, you have no guarantee it'll work tomorrow. Software and hardware are constantly changing.
- It's impossible for vendors to test their software on all possible software and hardware combinations.
- In a client/server environment, user workstations can have a potpourri of tools, memory-resident software, networking drivers, and hardware. Anything can happen in these environments—and it almost always does.

Finkelstein's advice: Stay as mainstream as possible and choose products that were designed to work together and have been tested together. This includes the operating system, database manager, network operating system, and application development tools.

Look for the best answer

Many organizations limit themselves because they explore too few options. For example, organizations with PC expertise often lean toward DOS or OS/2 when downsizing. These can work well, but they don't always offer the flexibility or power of Unix platforms. Unix and PC users will often overlook the DEC VMS system.

Also, don't limit yourself to the commonly known database servers. All database servers are not the same. Each database server has vastly different transaction management capabilities, performance aids, administration tools, programming and development environments, and connectivity software. Take time to understand the database server.

The distributed database

In its basic form, a client/server database has one database server that works on behalf of a number of clients, possibly on a number of networks. There's no rule that requires, though, that the database tables all reside on the same server. A client/server system can reach databases on servers all over the organization, using internetworking to create a *distributed database*.

Users can retrieve information from these dispersed databases using a *distributed query*. A distributed query gets data from more than one database server, but does so transparently to the user. The distributed query may not look significantly different than a query of a single database.

THE DISTRIBUTED DATABASE

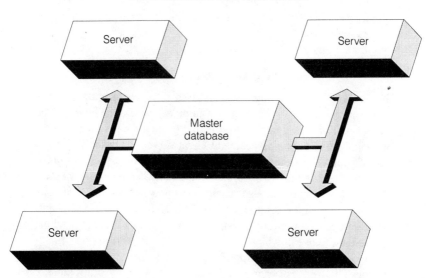

In a distributed database, a master server sends queries to databases at other locations, then assembles and reports the results.

For example, here's how it works in the Oracle system: For an Oracle database to support a distributed query, the database must have a valid network link to a second Oracle database. It must also have a special database object, called a database link, which refers both to the second database and to the network link.

A distributed query first goes to one of the linked databases. If that query includes a reference to the database link, the first database will generate a query to the second database, asking it for the relevant data. When the second database responds with that data, the first database then performs any necessary processing and sends the final result to the client. The client doesn't even have to know that there is a second database, or how to access it. The first server also acts as a client, submitting a request for data to the second server.

Some server products cannot use SQL to communicate between servers. These server products satisfy distributed queries using Remote Procedure Calls (RPCs), which means that they have to precode all possible queries ahead of time.

Mixed messages

Like any kind of technology, distributed database is a mixed bag of advantages and drawbacks. On the plus side, it extends the client/server principle of letting one server take on a specialized job and do it very well. Instead of a single database server handling data from all parts of the organization, a distributed system lets a single server specialize in a single subject.

More important for many users, splitting up database duties creates smaller bodies of data and makes it possible to make use of inexpensive server platforms. You can use these relatively inexpensive platforms to set up databases in offices all over the country.

Go with care

Nevertheless, going from a single server-based database to multiple databases, even on the same server, is a long jump across a deep chasm. The problem that will probably appear first is that of incompatible databases.

The techniques for gaining access to client/server databases vary from vendor to vendor. The vendors even disagree on exactly what distributed processing is. Nearly all provide ways to read and update remote databases. This facility can be limited, though; some allow you to work with only one database at a time in any given transaction. This is the basic form of client/server access. It provides for quick response from dedicated servers, and the results can be put to use in windowed environments on workstation PCs.

The process becomes more complicated when a second or third database becomes involved. For example, one database might include a table of customer data, with the customers identified by standard codes. Another, on a different server, might include a table of shipments, including the codes of the customers to whom they are sent. To retrieve a list of shipments to a particular customer, you must look up the customer code in one table, then query the second table for a list of shipments identified with that customer's code.

Though most of the widely used back-end database products would perform this operation, not all will do so. Those that do may use different, incompatible means. Remote database operation is much, much easier when every database uses the same system. When that is impractical, at least make sure the varied systems are compatible.

DISTRIBUTED DATABASE DRAWBACKS

- Incompatibility
  —Vendors' products vary
- Multiple databases
  —Multiply hazards
- Multiple updates
  —Can produce conflicts

Distributed databases are harder to administer. Use them only when you must.

Why distribute?

Consultants and columnists Martin Butler and Robin Bloor offer this "prime rule for distributing data": Do it only to improve performance. "Usually," they say, "it is far better to have a single database that services all the applications an organization runs."

There are times, however, when this advice is not practical. Sometimes even the most powerful platforms are not adequate to handle the quantity of data or the transaction volume of a large corporate database. This problem can arise even when the database remains on a large system.

When that occurs, most organizations first try a limited form of distribution. They split their databases in such a way that it is only rarely necessary to work with more than one database.

Nevertheless, some organizations need more sophisticated distribution systems. For example, a company may ship goods from several regional warehouses. Each has a local computer with databases to manage that warehouse's inventory and operations. If large numbers of transactions involve more than one warehouse, the company would do well to link the databases at the individual sites into a distributed system.

Ideally, this system should appear to the user as a single database. A query of the distributed system will retrieve the requested data wherever it might be located, and present it in standard SQL form as a single table that holds the results.

Distributed commands

As explained earlier, a distributed query typically goes first to one database, which itself then acts as a client. It passes queries to the other database and retrieves the results.

But how is this master database chosen? Some SQL systems include routines to optimize this choice. If the query retrieves a customer's name from one database and a list of 500 shipments from another, it makes sense to send the query first to the shipment-record database. It then can retrieve a single item, the customer's name, from the secondary database and forward the entire block of information to the client.

Should the query retrieve the customer's name first, it would then have to collect those 500 shipment records, link them with the customer, and forward the results to the client. In either case, one set of records will have to cross the network twice, from the secondary database to the primary, and then to the client. In the first instance, only the single customer name must make the trip twice; in the second, it would be all the shipment records.

Multiple updates

Updating can present even more serious problems. A distributed query that fails at least leaves the database intact. An update operation that fails can corrupt the data. Say, for example, an operator wants to update the distributed customer/shipment database to reflect a new shipment to a new customer. The system records the new shipment in that database, but before the customer's record can be added, a power failure interrupts the process. You are left with the record of a shipment to an unidentified customer.

To avoid that type of problem, a distributed system should use a *two-phase commit*. It should collect all the data to be added to both databases, then verify that each is ready to receive its changes. The system should lock these databases to ensure it has exclusive access to them until the transaction is complete. Only then does it add the data.

Then, it makes a second check of the database status to determine whether both databases properly recorded the information. If not, the system rolls back the transaction, and the databases are left in the original condition they were in prior to the operation.

The process is far from perfect. This type of transaction can slow down network performance, particularly when it spans a wide area or a large number of servers. There is also the increased danger of a global deadlock.

A deadlock occurs when two users fall into unwitting competition for the same resources. An operator in San Francisco tries to record a sale from the Atlanta warehouse to a California customer. When this system issues the update command, it locks the San Francisco customer database for its exclusive use. Then it tries to do the same with the shipment records in Atlanta.

Meanwhile, an operator in Atlanta is similarly trying to record a sale from that site's inventory to another California customer. The Atlanta system locks its inventory record, then tries to do the same with the California customer file. The result is that each user has placed an exclusive claim on data the other needs to complete the transactions. The result is a deadlock; early database programmers called it a *deadly embrace*.

This can be a serious enough problem when all the contested data is on the same server. When it reaches across the nation, it can paralyze the entire network. Most systems have the means to detect a deadlock and to get the competing parties to back off and try again. Even so, it can keep anything else from happening until the situation is cleared up.

Evaluating SQL

As client/server and distributed databases have risen in popularity, SQL has become an almost universal language of database access. Even products for which SQL is not a native tongue have learned it as a second language. Nearly all database vendors either offer an SQL interface for access to their products or are now developing one. Potential clients see lack of SQL support as a serious defect. A positive incentive is that SQL has the potential to open up their products to wider user bases.

In particular, SQL promotes interoperability between software products. However, SQL is not without its problems and controversies. Potential users should be aware of them. They include:

- SQL is often promoted as a portable language, a universal standard that can be run on any platform. It seldom works that way.
- SQL is often criticized as being excessively complex, for programmers as well as users.
- SQL is often perceived as too slow, compared with other database systems.
- SQL is often seen as too old, and unable to handle developing concepts like graphics and object orientation.

The myth of portable SQL

SQL has been described as the Esperanto of computer languages. It is supposed to be a universal language, but few people actually use it that way.

SQL ISN'T PERFECT

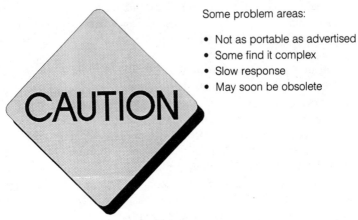

Some problem areas:

- Not as portable as advertised
- Some find it complex
- Slow response
- May soon be obsolete

Though SQL does many things well, there are some things it does not do quite so well.

The ideal for many users is *portable SQL*, a universal query language that can be used on PCs, mainframes, Unix machines and any other system where a database exists or is used. In practice, it simply doesn't work that way.

Strictly speaking, SQL abides by a standard published by the American National Standards Institute. The ANSI standard is universal, but it is also limited. You will hardly ever see an SQL system that adheres strictly to the ANSI specifications. Nearly every vendor extends or alters the language to add value or fit it onto a particular platform. Even commands that look identical might behave differently in different systems.

Often, this stems from a desire to make the vendor's package more versatile than standard SQL. Some vendors add unique functions or data types, most of which work well but tempt the programmer to write code that won't work on another vendor's platform. Other vendors add features that let programmers fine-tune the way a query is processed in order to get maximum performance. More differences crop up in application programming interfaces (APIs) between SQL and application programs written in languages such as C or COBOL.

Other differences stem from vagueness in the ANSI standard, which does a good job of specifying the language's syntax but is less exact in describing what the commands are actually supposed to do.

Limited standard

Many of the problems with the SQL standard stem from what is also one of its strengths: its solid grounding in mathematical theory. E.F. Codd, SQL's strong-minded inventor, insists that SQL should make relational databases completely independent and invisible. Ideally, the system should not even be aware of things like file names and network drive specifications.

While such independence would be theoretically ideal, working programmers do have to worry about such matters. They need to optimize their systems to make the best possible use of available resources. Most SQL implementations add statements to help programmers accomplish these tasks. Many SQL databases also differ in the way they handle null, or empty, fields. These are only some of the ways in which different implementations of SQL cause programs that work on one system to fail on another.

Another problem is that the ANSI SQL standards aren't the only ones in town. In 1987, a standardization group called X/Open came out with its own version of SQL for Unix. IBM's DB2 is a well-recognized de facto standard.

Other differences are designed to help SQL perform functions it would normally do awkwardly if at all. Consider the company that owns a fleet of automobiles, some of which are assigned to certain key employees. You cannot use a basic join to produce a list of all automobiles and their assigned drivers. It would omit those cars that do not have assigned users, and those employees who do not have assigned automobiles. There is a function called an *outer join* which would do that, but it is not part of standard SQL. It is an add-on, provided only by vendors choosing to make use of it.

The complexity factor

All these variations from the standard theme contribute to a widespread perception that SQL is overly complex.

Some people find SQL to be an easy, intuitive way to describe data. Others simply don't get it. Their numbers aren't limited to untrained users. Many programmers accustomed to issuing step-by-step instructions run into perceptual problems with SQL's descriptive approach.

A related problem is that SQL is designed to work with *sets* of data. One of the cardinal rules is that it return its data in the form of a table. The system treats it as a table even if it has only a single row and a single column. Most procedural languages, including the dBASE variations, return only one record at a time. Programmers who are used to this standard need to adjust their thinking if they are to use SQL effectively. This is particularly important in transaction processing, which normally does deal with only one record at a time.

A growing number of front-end products can help both users and programmers overcome much of the complexity. A graphical front end helps users specify the information they want to retrieve, and the program constructs the proper SQL query. More advanced forms of these same products help programmers build applications that can inherently manage the difference between record and set orientation.

The performance issue

Another SQL issue is how to define performance. IS professionals are at home with concepts like benchmarking and quick response. They tend to think that the faster the database responds, the better the system performs.

One large-system programmer was heard to complain that an SQL database runs too slowly. It would take two or three seconds for the response to a query to appear on the user's screen, while the older system displayed the results almost instantaneously.

The problem there is not with the system's response, but with the definition of good performance. It's important to look at response time from the user's perspective. The proper measurement is not how long it takes the system to retrieve the information but how long it takes the user to do the job.

To be sure, some SQL databases might take those two or three seconds longer to react. But they will regain those seconds many times over if an improved front-end application makes it easier and quicker for the user to complete the job. It's not system-to-screen time that counts. It's the time the user needs to complete a report, update an employee roster, or complete some other task.

The user who can complete a task more quickly does not think of the system as slow. Neither should its manager. The system's response time is only a tiny slice of the whole.

SQL and object orientation

A future SQL standard is expected to include some of the newer concepts of object-oriented programming (OOP). Meanwhile, some vendors have been including OOP extensions in their products, and more will probably follow suit.

Neither approach is ideal. The vendor add-ons simply add to the problems of complexity and incompatibility. The coming standard probably will provide only for limited OOP functions. And there's another problem even bigger than these: SQL and OOP are two entirely different kinds of systems. They simply do not work very well together.

SQL is tailored to a client/server environment. Here, the interface between client and server processes is predictable, well-defined, and static. The object-oriented environment probably will function much differently. It is more likely that objects and their data will be distributed over networks. They will send messages around the network to invoke each other. In these circumstances, the most important relationships will not be between client and server, but among various objects.

One possibility is this ironic result: Just as SQL hits its stride in client/server applications, it might have to give way to a newer, object-oriented system yet to come.

10
CHAPTER

Other downsizing applications

The client/server database with an SQL engine is the most dominant form of downsizing. Nevertheless, many other types of applications can find valuable use in a downsized system. They fall into several classes:

- Database applications identified primarily with the PC world, but that have increasingly gained SQL capabilities. Most now are fully equipped to serve as front ends to client/server systems.
- Executive information systems (EIS). These provide a form of database retrieval for the special purpose of presenting and interpreting management information.
- Electronic mail and other types of communication and work group programs that can take advantage of the networked architecture used in downsizing.
- The products of custom application development, making use of productive new tools that have been rapidly reaching the market.

Downsizing applications

Downsizing may or may not save money, and it may or may not reduce your personnel requirements. It has had one important consequence, however. As consultant Cheryl Currid puts it, "New technology is providing cost-effective alternatives to a mono-mainframe mentality. That means it's time to take a fresh, careful look at the technology, people, procedures, and policies that corporate America uses for computer applications."

The process will not be easy, she adds. "In the final analysis, no matter how good you are or how buttoned-down the organization is, downsizing computer applications is a challenge."

Still, there is a wealth of potentially useful applications available, and downsizing greatly expands their numbers and variety. You are not limited just to large-system database operations, or small-system personal applications, or even to custom applications written expressly for your organization. This is one instance when "some of the above" is usually the correct answer.

Identify goals

That doesn't necessarily mean "all of the above," although it might. It is still necessary to be selective and to look for applications that will meet your goals. Remember, research indicates that cost-cutting is not the major reason companies have chosen to downsize. The greater motivation is to give users the data they need, when they need it, in a form they can use.

Currid says she has seen evidence that it actually takes more people to run LANs than it does to run minicomputers. The reason is that large systems are often installed to run just a few applications. LANs usually run multiple applications and serve as the base for connecting everything to everything else. It stands to reason that the more you do, the more support you'll need to do it.

DOWNSIZING GOALS

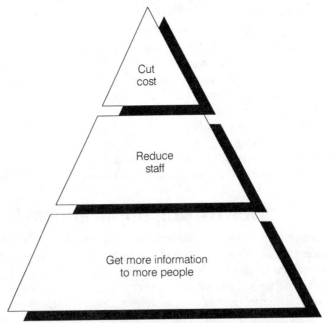

Firms that look to downsizing often think first of cutting costs and staff levels. Most find, though, that the greatest benefit is to make more information available.

It's easy to make mistakes and misjudgments. Just as some firms have installed over- or under-powered systems to handle their downsized applications, some have made similar mistakes in selecting software, installing programs that either are too weak or too powerful for the job.

A 1991 Downsizing/Rightsizing Corporate Computing Conference focused on determining which obstacles stand in the way of corporate downsizing projects. IS executives expressed doubt that downsizing leads to cost savings. They also worried about the limited number of tools available to expedite software migration to LANs. As important as the tools, they added, were trained professionals who knew how to use them. For instance, mainframe programmers can require up to one year of retraining before they can work competently in object-oriented computing environments.

Look for enablers

The best guideline for deciding on an application: does it *enable* the organization and its employees to do their jobs better? Does it give them resources they need to gain access to corporate information, and to put it to good use in ways that contribute to knowledge and communication?

Software connections are really what connect people. Initially, only a handful of meaningful applications could use the LAN as an enabling technology:

- E-mail has achieved this status.
- Database applications make up the other large group.
- Large internetworked groupware packages are now making a move into corporate America.

AVOID MISTAKES

Common mistakes:

- Too little power
- Too much power

The best solutions

- Focus on goals
- Consider software as an enabler

To avoid expensive misjudgments, focus on your goals, and select software that will enable the organization to reach them.

More kinds of enablers are being developed. At Sara Lee, distributed client/server platforms give departmental employees the flexibility to choose the method and tools by which they use the corporation's information resources.

Users are also being encouraged to create their own reports, data inquiries, and decision-support questions, using the tools with which they are most proficient. They can use the familiarity they already have gained with such common PC programs as spreadsheets, databases, word processors, accounting applications, executive information systems, and decision support software. These systems move the responsibility for gathering and manipulating information away from the MIS staff and into the hands of those who use the information to do their jobs. As a result, downsizing gives Sara Lee's users a substantial increase in flexibility.

WHAT ENABLERS CAN DO

- Improve access to information
- Create new kinds of inquiries
- Create more useful reports
- Let users work with familiar applications

Enabling software improves employees' efficiency and effectiveness.

Programmers have not been forgotten. Graphics-based programmer tools are becoming more and more powerful, but they're also becoming simpler. They enable professionals to do more work more quickly, and to build better programs. Meanwhile, users can create their own personal utility applications.

Good applications enable an organization to improve its competitive situation. For example, a networked system allows the fund-raising consultants for several environmental organizations to analyze client lists and determine which type of mailing and which potential donors will generate the best results for a particular campaign.

A warehousing firm is linked to most of its major steel company customers via an electronic data interchange (EDI) connection that enables vendors and their customers to gain remote, real-time access to each other's inventory and order databases using inter-LAN communications. Up-to-the-minute information about shipment and delivery of goods enables

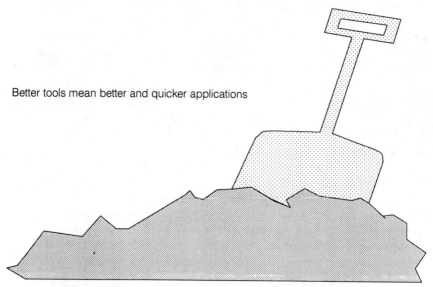

Better tools mean better and quicker applications

Modern programming tools let professional programmers create better applications, more quickly.

the firm to get the invoices out to its customers that much faster, which ultimately means that revenue comes in more quickly.

Enabling power can also be useful to peacemakers in the continuing warfare between advocates of large and small systems. Showing users that bringing more power to individual desktops will enable them to perform their jobs better is one way to quell these fights.

The shrink-wrapped world

One of the great potential economies of a downsized environment is the ability to use standard, shrink-wrapped software. It is lower in price than large-system equivalents. Applications of every type are available for the PC and Mac; increasing numbers are available for Unix platforms. The latter, however, tend to be more expensive and might be earlier versions than those available for PCs.

These off-the-shelf products are familiar to many users, and it's easy to find advice on how to use them, and on how to use them better. One of the greatest advantages, though, is that these shrink-wrapped applications are often application development platforms in their own right. The dBASE family is the most notable example, but some spreadsheet jockeys write elaborate collections of macros that nearly qualify as independent applications.

Linking databases

As described in the previous chapter, there is a strong trend toward using client/server technology, limited mainly by still-developing technology, to establish a point of contact. Often, client/server technology combines a PC-based front end with a database management system running on a larger system or a more powerful PC.

For example, Novell's server product, NetWare SQL, lets you select the applications best suited to your needs and preferences. You can choose a spreadsheet program, accounting package, fourth-generation programming language, database manager, and application program generator, all sharing a common database with other users, using other front ends.

In the 1980s, a number of very successful stand-alone database management products became available for PCs and LANs. The best-known, of course, was the dBASE line, plus other products like FoxBASE and Clipper, that adapted the dBASE language. In fact, many people used the Lotus spreadsheet as a database; 1-2-3 does include a flat-file database function.

Many of these former single-user products have now evolved into front-end database servers, incorporating the means to send SQL commands to a database server.

PC DATABASES EXPAND THEIR SCOPE

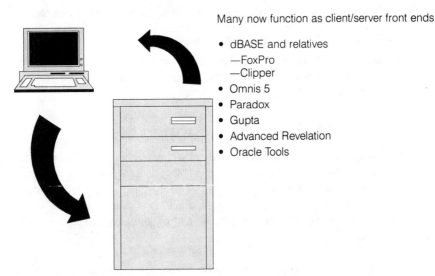

Many now function as client/server front ends

- dBASE and relatives
  - —FoxPro
  - —Clipper
- Omnis 5
- Paradox
- Gupta
- Advanced Revelation
- Oracle Tools

Many database managers that once were single-user PC products now have client/server ability as well.

The dBASE connection

After several clumsy attempts, Ashton-Tate (just prior to its fall 1991 takeover by Borland) had developed a version of its dBASE family that provides for access to database servers. The dBASE IV Server Edition lets developers embed SQL statements into their dBASE code. SQL Server was the only back end supported by the initial version, but Ashton-Tate said support of other popular database engines will be added to future releases.

This is the product that was supposed to have played a key role in launching SQL Server. It was to have been the first to let dBASE programmers build applications for SQL Server.

The server edition was delayed first by Ashton-Tate's inexperience with the SQL world, then by problems with the regular dBASE IV release that was to form a base of the server edition. Tired of waiting, dBASE programmers defected to compatible products such as FoxPro and Clipper, and Microsoft ended its exclusive SQL Server relationship with Ashton-Tate.

Meanwhile, several other vendors filled the dBASE vacuum and produced front-end products of their own. Among them have been Blyth Software's Omnis 5, Borland International's Paradox with SQL Link, Dataease SQL Professional, Gupta Technologies' SQL Windows, Oracle Tools for MS-DOS, and Advanced Revelation 2.0 with SQL Server Bond.

In spite of the growing competition, the server edition brings some new abilities to the field. Applications can be developed entirely on a stand-alone machine, using the dBASE SQL programming language. Then, they can be moved onto a network to run SQL Server without any alteration, a feature that makes it useful for prototyping client/server applications.

Tailored products

Front-end products vary widely with respect to how, and how completely, they support SQL. Those built from the ground up for client/server service generally have the strongest support. Those that were ported from older DOS products usually support basic SQL operations, but may not execute some of the most sophisticated commands.

They come in two distinct groups. dBASE, and FoxBASE, and Clipper are designed primarily as developer's tools, although the first two have some features designed to improve their ease of use in less knowledgeable hands. SQL Windows, Oracle Tools, and Omnis 5 are also more oriented toward developers.

Paradox and Dataease are primarily end-user tools. Advanced Revelation spans both the developer and end-user categories.

Any of these can serve one important role: If you follow the conventional advice and downsize a small application first, these front-end products all offer added ease of use that can make that project easier. Once you've gained experience, you can use them for more expansive projects.

Executive information systems

The basic purpose of an EIS is to give senior executives an overview of their operations. Like other front-end products, an EIS retrieves data from a corporate database. In an EIS, the object is to consolidate the wealth of information that answers the question,"How well are we doing?" and to present it in an on-screen version of the executive summary.

A basic EIS system pulls information from corporate databases, analyzes and compares it, and presents it as a summary or a graph. More advanced systems also retrieve and integrate information from outside sources. These systems use such techniques as hypertext, text and data integration, and presenting multiple views of related data.

The system consolidates the retrieved data and presents it in an easy-to-understand form. The key is to consolidate information from various sources into a meaningful pattern. The best systems let their users examine patterns and relationships not obvious from the mass of raw data itself. Increasingly, this takes the form of a graphic presentation that makes use of point-and-click techniques, touch screens, and other features that make the system easy to use and its information easy to understand.

Most systems also let managers *drill down* through their corporate databases to retrieve increasingly finer levels of detail and examine the figures on which the summaries are based. Users then can conduct what-if analyses, discover patterns, and look for exceptions to established models.

Ease of use is another important feature. Most executives are presumed to be experts at something other than operating computers. The best EIS systems have user-cordial interfaces and are designed to catch the errors made by inexperienced users.

EXECUTIVE INFORMATION

EIS helps managers analyze data:

- Retrieved from corporate databases
- Prime candidate for downsizing
- Uses client/server techniques

Executive information systems are a type of database retrieval operation that is a prime candidate for downsizing.

Downsizing the EIS

EIS has definitely been caught up in the downsizing trend. It's one of the many applications that are being moved from large systems to PC networks. For example, Pilot Executive Software (Boston) has been one of the leading vendors of mainframe-based EIS software. Pilot now offers a version called Lightship designed to run under Microsoft Windows on a networked PC.

There are differences between the two versions. David Friend, Pilot's chairman and founder, describes Command Center, his firm's mainframe product, as "a cooperative-processing product, which IS staffers can use as a fourth-generation language to build EIS applications." The PC product requires less expertise. "Anyone who can build a spreadsheet can build a Lightship EIS," says Friend.

Typical of downsized EIS products, Lightship operates in a client-server relationship. The program itself can reside entirely on a PC workstation. It then can gain access to LAN- or mainframe-based database servers using SQL server. The two EIS products work together as well; mainframe applications have been rewritten to run on Lightship, which in turn can act as a client to Command Center, which will function as an EIS file server.

Another downsizing EIS vendor is Comshare (Ann Arbor, MI), which has announced Macintosh and OS/2 versions of its Commander EIS.

Windows-based EIS

The SAS System (Cary, NC), known for its statistical-oriented product line, is one of several vendors to adopt Microsoft Windows for graphic displays of EIS data. SAS is marketing a package of data analysis, spreadsheet, and application development tools, collectively called the SAS Applications System, to run under Windows 3.0.

Pilot's Lightship is also a Windows application. So are Forest & Trees from Channel Computing (Newmarket, NH). Several other PC-based systems also are Windows applications. Corporate View from Sterling Resources (Paramus, NJ) is a client-server system whose workstation components run under Windows.

Electronic teamwork

Many applications can take advantage of networking to multiply their potential. One of the most popular and effective is electronic mail. Network users learned early that when they sent electronic messages to each other, they could relieve themselves of hours' worth of telephone tag.

Like nearly every LAN-based endeavor, though, E-mail has become much more complex. Until recently, most LANs were limited to group and departmental levels. E-mail was one of the few purposes for which these self-contained LANs were connected with others of their kind. Remote printing was the other.

Like networks themselves, E-mail was originally a relatively simple application. Now that networking is being extended enterprise-wide, it is becoming much more complex. The original departmental LAN with its simple E-mail system has mutated into several new versions:

- Distributed computing, where dedicated servers handle different parts of data storage and computation.
- Work Group and collaborative computing, where users on different LAN segments and sites work in common on documents, programs, and other projects.
- Enterprise computing, where the work flow transcends departmental and corporate boundaries.

GETTING PEOPLE TOGETHER

Network software supports group efforts:

- Electronic mail
- Scheduling software
- Group projects
  —Project management
  —Joint documents

Networked software in a downsized environment spurs group dynamics.

Software must grow, too

Previous chapters have dealt with the technology of this expansion. But physical LAN expansion through bridges, gateways, and other internetworking technology would have no real value unless the available software also grew into more expansive roles. The software expansion has led to a concept called *work group computing*—whatever that might mean.

As yet, no firm standardized definition of work group computing exists, and perhaps none is necessary. Users do have a useful sense of what it means to them. This fluid category of software is generally acknowledged to include these general types:

- Software used in joint projects, in which several people collaborate. Project management software falls into this category. So do programs that manage the production of group-written documents.
- Group scheduling programs that help coordinate meeting schedules and other joint activities. These usually include group phone directories, both conventional and E-mail, and electronic mail itself.
- Pure electronic mail software, expanded to cover ever-larger numbers of people.

A related development in software applications is work-flow management software. Packages such as Lotus Notes and AT&T's Rhapsody Business Orchestration Solution automate the many manual steps involved in an office procedure such as logging and delegating customer complaints. Office workers who once had to pick their way manually through the multiple steps of a particular task can now take cues from the software.

Keeping on schedule

Scheduling programs relieve their users of the nagging question, "When can everybody get together for a meeting?" Simply finding a time when every member of a group is free to meet can be a more daunting project than anything to be discussed at the meeting. The person responsible for this task faces long, frustrating, and unproductive hours, just getting in contact with everyone.

If only you could hold a meeting to pick a meeting time. In a way, scheduling software lets you do that. Every user keeps a personal calendar with appointments and other obligations noted. The meeting coordinator can feed in the names of those who are to meet. The program will look for blocks of free time and suggest them for the meeting. If there is no time when everyone is free, the system suggests the times that have the fewest conflicts. Some packages go further and ask the attendees to verify that they can be there.

How effective these programs are depends on how well they are used. You must encourage users to maintain their calendars complete and up-to-date. That means the calendar should be easy to use—ridiculously easy, if possible.

Modern electronic mail

Most scheduling programs include electronic mail features that let users communicate with each other. These generally work fine as long as they communicate between similar systems. Mixed systems and larger networks generally require a more robust E-mail system with added features. This is particularly true of long-distance E-mail systems, such as those linking branch offices or that keep you in touch with customers or suppliers. Most E-mail systems can keep coworkers at the same location in touch. It takes a good system to extend your reach.

What you gain, of course, is freedom from the tyranny of the telephone. While the phone nominally offers immediate, person-to-person contact, it really succeeds only when the parties make contact at the first call. Experience tells us how rarely that actually happens. Thus the participation sport called telephone tag, plus the proliferation of answering machines and voice-mail systems.

E-mail functions

The basic functions of an E-mail system were defined long ago. A standard system will:

- Create a message.
- Read the messages addressed to a user.
- Send replies to these messages.
- Forward messages.
- Acknowledge the receipt of a message.

Other useful features include:

- Automatic notice of waiting messages.
- A pop-up window for reading messages.
- The ability to transmit an existing file as part of a message.
- The ability to use familiar word processors to create messages.
- Verification that a message has been transmitted and received.
- The ability to classify messages by subject.
- Password protection and message encryption.
- The ability to set up special-interest bulletin boards.

The message handling service

The most advanced E-mail systems include the ability to cover long distances and maintain contact with diverse systems. The usual means of doing this is message handling service (MHS).

MHS is sometimes sold as a separate program, but it is also often bundled with popular E-mail software and network operating systems. MHS can connect homogeneous LANs over telephone lines, but its real value is its ability to connect an E-mail system over gateways to large-system E-mail.

The program resides on a dedicated MHS server, which communicates with the network E-mail application and operates gateway software to gain access to outside E-mail resources. MHS users automatically have the ability to exchange messages with each other, regardless of their platforms. For example, a user with a Windows-based E-mail system can communicate readily with someone on another network who is using a character-based program. In the same way, MIS can make the necessary links between this user and mainframe E-mail systems, or commercial services such as MCI Mail.

Truly downsized applications

Most downsizing programs make use of available PC software to perform the functions formerly handled by large-system equivalents. The major exception is the client/server database, in which a PC-based front end maintains access to a server that, in many cases, is still a mini or mainframe. This is not the only exception, though. In some cases, standard mainframe applications are being ported to PC LANs.

Among them are data retrieval and report-writing systems from Dylakor (Chatsworth, CA) and Pansophic Systems (Lisle, IL). Both were originally written for IBM database products running on S/370 mainframes and are now considered classics of independently-produced software for large IBM systems. Both firms have been working on PC equivalents for their mainframe products.

Initial versions have concentrated on linking PC front ends to the existing mainframe products, but both vendors have been working on full PC equivalents. The products let users bypass mainframe IS tasks such as job control language, mainframe operating systems, and connectivity technology. The new software will keep such matters behind the scenes, so the user is isolated from that technology.

For Dylakor, the goal is to keep the functions of its successful existing software while downsizing it to fit into a PC box, which maintains IBM compatibility complete with an IBM-approved graphical user interface. The PC front end will let users invoke any of four components of Dylakor's mainframe product, depending on the users' needs, not on their knowledge of the product's functions.

Pansophic's PC front end, called Easytrieve Plus Workstation, lets developers write Pansophic programs to be run on either a PC or the mainframe. Users choose PC or mainframe execution from a menu. The application itself looks the same, regardless of the platform on which it's running.

Developing applications

The one problem downsizing can't solve by itself is making business applications faster, better, and less expensive. The reasons for this continuous challenge include:

- A mounting backlog of mainframe applications even after years of trying to reduce it.
- Increased user demand for applications that are sophisticated yet easy to use.
- Rising costs of software development and maintenance. In addition, MIS is faced with data proliferation on disparate platforms and few applications with which to manipulate this data.

One of the big advantages of a downsized environment is that it lets programmers build applications easily and more quickly on their PCs. At the most basic level are PC COBOL compilers that let programmers write and test their applications on smaller systems. That, however, is only a very small beginning.

Application-building tools and strategies now available for PCs not only streamline the development process but can produce more functional, easy-to-use applications. To build applications more quickly, you need only to follow proven development methods. While doing so, you can also take advantage of advances in fourth-generation language (4GL) environments and automatic application generation. Among the features of this approach:

- Developers can build and maintain applications more efficiently with structured development techniques and tools.
- They can promote economic efficiency by using efficiently-sized development platforms.
- They can create better software by bringing the development process closer to users.
- Users can be so close, in fact, that they can develop many of their own applications.

A traditional application

A traditional monolithic application program is simple, in a way. A developer could write a single program that takes keyboard input, manipulates data, and produces screen and disk output.

Though the programming process is simple and straightforward, this method requires that the programmer insert a great deal of knowledge. Among the things this program must know are:

- How to read the file format of the data file.
- How to make changes to the data file.
- The best ways to find and retrieve data from within the file.
- What its own internal processing logic is.
- How to communicate with a user.

A client/server application

A conventional application is usually a single program, doing everything itself. A client/server program looks like two programs, one running on the client station and the other on the server.

The originator of this matched pair of applications has more work to do. The programmer must write two programs, and the portion that runs on the server must be full of extra functions. Once all this has been done, however, programming is much easier for the application developer who uses this two-phased tool. The developer actually has to write only one of the two programs; the originator writes the server portion.

All the application developer need care about is:

- How to send requests to and read answers from the server program.
- What internal processing logic it uses to talk to a user.

Meanwhile, there are many things the application developer does not have to worry about. The originator who wrote the server program should already have taken care of them:

- Data access methods, such as what index to use and where the data is on the disk.
- The internal format of the data file.
- How to maintain the data file, such as managing the adding of tables or columns, and dropping tables.

GUIs make it even easier

If client/server makes life easier for application programmers, the next step is to make things easier for users. The newest GUI application tools help both parties. Developers can use the same click-on-a-button techniques to build applications as their clients do to operate them. If a GUI application program can be easier for users, a GUI application development environment can be easier in the same way for developers.

Take the most-used GUI, Microsoft Windows. A typical Windows application typically has features like these:

- Each program is represented as an icon. These are the equivalents of menu choices.
- The program manager provides an umbrella or shell function, which contains groups of icons. There is a natural hierarchy of groups, group boxes, and individual icons.
- There is a more or less standardized system of pull-down menus. The menus will vary from application to application, but they do follow the same general pattern.

That means that when developing applications in the Windows environment, there are certain things a programmer can't do—Windows has already done them. The purpose is to standardize the environment for the users' benefit. It eliminates, or at least minimizes, the confusion that can set in when a user switches from program to program with different user interfaces.

Windows applications, and their creation, are standardized in other ways, too. The title bar and system button are top-of-the-screen staples. The bar is colored when the application is active—something referred to as the *focus*. A uniform system of controls also lets the user change the size of the display, move between programs, and open or close applications.

While the Windows environment limits some of the programmer's actions, there are also many new features to be learned. These also represent opportunities to provide new functions and flexibility. Among them:

- Message and dialogue boxes with pushbuttons and other visual cues.
- Free-form text areas that can be much easier to program than when using conventional methods.

- The ability to work with images.
- Active links with other programs.

Windows as a programming language

Most major Windows applications are written in C. Various products offer libraries and other facilities to write custom code that will produce all the visual effects for which Windows is known. C is certainly a language professional programmers should know if they want to work in Windows. For less serious work, a graphics-oriented language like Visual Basic may do the job.

In truth, however, it isn't necessary to know C or any other low-level language to program with Windows. There is an ever-increasing variety of application generators, from the simple to the complex, that put application development in the hands of everyone from ordinary users to senior professionals. These have come to be known as toolkits—an apt metaphor. Simple toolkits help the amateur achieve worthwhile use; the most advanced kits let professionals take full advantage of their knowledge and talents. Both use visual techniques as major elements in application building.

Most of the work of building the visual interface and other common functions of an application are built into these systems. The programmer need worry only about the unique features the application will bring to this environment. Also, as soon as one of these applications has been generated, it's ready to be run on a network.

The construction process

A typical product of this kind, Gupta's SQL Windows, presents the program construction process in a typical windowed environment. One displays the program code in an outline format. The product generates this code automatically, though the programmer can also write or edit it directly.

One piece of code, for example, might define a single window. Others could draw the data fields to be retrieved from a database server. Dialog and list boxes help the programmer select the appropriate items and operations.

To perform some activity on a data field, the developer can draw and name a pushbutton. By clicking on available selections, the developer can specify that when there is a click on this button, a certain action should be taken on the data field—perhaps to copy the data to a list in another window. The final application will present this button to the user.

Programmers can use the same techniques for their own purposes, such as to set a break point while they are testing the program.

All this is done with a series of C routines written to manage the graphical interface. Of course, you could also program these routines yourself. The advantage of a GUI development environment is that they are already written and optimized. There is a good chance they will perform better than anything similar you could have written yourself.

11
CHAPTER

Taking that fateful step

There have been many reports of successful downsizing programs. There have been fewer reports of unsuccessful downsizing projects. That's only natural. Corporate public relations departments aren't fond of putting out press releases that document failures.

Even successful project leaders say the obstacles to moving mainframe applications to LANs often outweigh the potential benefits. Few users have downsized key applications, because the implementation process is costly and complex. Many lack the expertise and technical tools necessary, and resistance from both internal management information system (MIS) personnel and end users is common.

Every manager who has spearheaded a downsizing effort had to overcome at least some initial opposition. Employees fear the loss of their jobs, or of power and control. Some fear added responsibilities. MIS personnel tend to fear the loss of centralized control.

In spite of all this, the managers said downsizing is worth the effort.

Pursuing the goal

It makes no sense to downsize without a reason, particularly when there are so many good reasons available. There is the cost advantage brought by smaller systems with higher capacity. Maintenance and personnel costs can be lower, too. What's more, there are the even larger long-term payoffs in terms of improving competitive position by giving more people access to more information. These are all worthwhile goals, but they do not make a downsizing plan.

To reach any goal, you must have a plan. When considering a downsizing project, it's easy to become too tightly focused on technical issues. Someone decides that the organization should buy certain types of hardware and software. That's an easy way to get off the track. Downsizing is largely a technical process, so it's only natural to focus on technical issues.

Another way to get sidetracked is through failure to understand why the organization is considering downsizing. When you ask an IS manager why the organization is planning to downsize, all too often the answer will be, "because management wants it done."

WRONG REASONS TO DOWNSIZE

- We have the technology
- The boss made me do it

Neither technical reasons nor knee-jerk reactions make a sufficient reason for downsizing.

The real question

The real issue, though, is not which technology to adopt but what business purposes you hope to achieve. Downsizing is really a type of business initiative. The basic question to ask is how you can adapt the business to today's rapidly changing conditions? Then the second question becomes: How can downsizing help you do that?

Working together—with difficulty

To achieve a focus on the business benefits of downsizing, IS and business management will have to learn to work together. Given their relationships in the past, this won't be easy. It will be necessary. The two conflicting forces at work are:

- Many IS professionals still believe standardization and control are essential if downsizing is to be an orderly, healthy process.
- Users, often represented by corporate management, want more access to data, on their own terms.

To resolve this basic conflict, some organizations have instituted mixed systems. Under this type of plan, both IS professionals and users are brought into the process of deciding which applications and resources should be distributed among networks. IS can maintain a measure of control, placing limits on ad hoc application development, but users have more opportunities to make sure the system responds to their needs, not to goals established elsewhere.

THE BASIC QUESTIONS

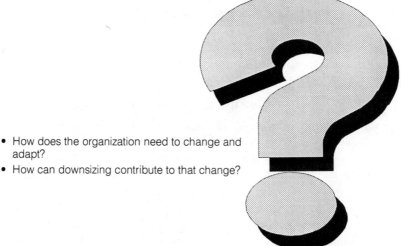

- How does the organization need to change and adapt?
- How can downsizing contribute to that change?

A plan should be based on business issues, not technical questions.

Tactical v. strategic

In today's prevailing practice, most systems have been implemented as tactical tools. They help collect the bills, which in turn helps make the payroll. They coordinate factory production and facilitate efficiency measures like just-in-time delivery. They provide the numbers for reporting and analysis—numbers then used as a basis of future projections.

All of these systems are tactical tools, and are of great value to an organization. They lead to more efficient ways to get products and services to the people who will pay for them.

Downsizing can play a role in all these activities. There is a larger role, too, however, and it represents a large opportunity. That is the ability—with the help of downsizing—to transform tactical activities into elements of an overall business strategy. This now makes them strategic tools, instead of just tactical tools.

TACTICAL TO STRATEGIC

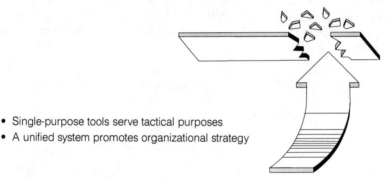

- Single-purpose tools serve tactical purposes
- A unified system promotes organizational strategy

Tactical tools help get the job done, but strategic tools promote a well-directed effort.

Downsizing's role

The way to do this is through enterprise-wide computing, a system of linked networks replacing central data administration on one side and local-service networks on the other. Ultimately, all users should have access to the information they need, when they need it, and in a format they can use.

WHAT USERS SHOULD HAVE

- The information they need
- When they need it
- In a form they can use

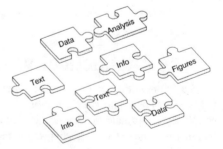

When users have access to more kinds of information, they expand their thinking and play greater roles in corporate strategy.

When users have this kind of universal access, they gain the ability to become more strategic in their thinking. They will no longer focus entirely on how to schedule processes or get products out the door. They will have the means as well to think about what those products should be, who will buy them, how they should be priced, and how they should be delivered to the marketplace. This kind of thinking can help set the course of business strategy. Not all users will expand their thinking this way, of course. Still, a downsized system can be an asset to those who do. It allows them to make greater contributions to the overall organization.

These contributions add another important benefit to downsizing. Cost will always be a consideration, and often a justification, for a downsizing project. After all, reduced cost is a tangible benefit everyone in business can appreciate. There will also be an important, if intangible, further benefit which comes from a more flexible enterprise. Downsizing can enhance the ability to respond to new and developing business conditions. They can speed that response, too, by offering more rapid turnaround on developing the applications to capitalize on opportunities. These applications can be up, running, and responding much faster than they could under traditional mainframe practice.

The long-range goal is not so much immediate cost savings but to accomplish things like these:

- Increase corporate communication.
- Improve access to data.
- Create a flexible atmosphere that can respond to change.

These are the goals successful downsizers have pursued and achieved.

Examples

There are many examples of how downsizing can improve an organization's strategic position. Applications like E-mail improve communication. Client/server techniques and distributed computing provide ways to split applications between various platforms, providing new ways to retrieve and manipulate data.

At the professional level, standardized application tools, available on PCs, provide the flexibility for rapid change. Many organizations have cut application development time and expense by as much as 66%.

The user as a customer

The main reason for downsizing is to deliver information to users. Though that should be explicit enough, implementation can have many problems.

Even more obvious to many people is a continuing conflict of values between users on one side and IS professionals on the other. Contrary to many rumors, most IS professionals do not fit the stereotype of terminally stubborn, and often fearful, defenders of the status quo. Surveys show most professionals want to keep up with the advances in their profession, and downsizing is a leading-edge movement. If they appear restrained in joining the trend, it is usually in the interest of maintaining professional standards and traditions.

It is no accident, though, that the stereotype remains. That's because it does fit a significant minority, an influential group that personifies resistance to change. Their presence creates human problems that are explored at length in the next chapter. For planning purposes, the conflicting groups can be classified according to how they perceive their roles in life.

Members of the traditional group believe, as they were taught to believe, that their function is to deliver resources to the users who need them. Downsizing reflects a different perspective of an IS professional's job to support the organization by helping users find and create their own computer resources.

These views are not necessarily in conflict. There are many times when the users' need for information can best be met by letting them develop their own applications. This is particularly apt with the large number of application development facilities now available, which let them construct useful applications without advanced programming knowledge. There has been a definite trend toward providing users with these tools. IS thus primarily plays a supporting role. However, sometimes a professional is the best person to serve those needs.

The important thing is that the needs be served. This is one of the major objectives of downsizing. User flexibility is an important foundation of enterprise-wide computing. PC applications, the LANs that support them, shared peripherals and information, and interconnections among departments all form the enterprise-wide infrastructure.

Internal customer service

The users are the remaining element in this structure. They are the information system's *internal customers*. American business has learned to emphasize customer service. It has also learned that you can't effectively serve external customers unless you also support the customer-contact employees. That has led to the idea that employees responsible for customer service are the internal customers whom others in the organization are expected to serve. The level of customer service should be just the same internally as it is externally.

IS has many internal customers. They are the users, line management, senior executives, and ultimately the board of directors. By serving these internal customers, you support the organization in serving its external customers. In particular, you provide the basis for an increasingly popular and necessary sales pitch.

It has been reliably estimated that information supplies more than 70%

of the value of a typical industrial product. Raw materials and other input account for only about 30%. Information is an even greater percentage of the value of the typical service, which of course uses few raw materials. This increasingly means that the most effective sales approach would be to say, in effect, "I'm smarter than the rest. I can get my products to the market faster, and I can deliver a better-quality product—and deliver it on time." You can back these claims, in large part, by the contributions of the IS department.

Thus, when a company puts its information in the hands of as many employees as possible, the company literally gets smarter.

Delivering the goods

For example, Nike has become a leader in athletic shoes, in part through effective advertising, and in part because it is geared to respond quickly to developments in the marketplace. Nike can get new designs into the stores earlier than anyone else. The firm initially installed a mainframe system to run graphics and design applications, but these have since been transferred to PCs. This means Nike is able to deliver new products with the speed of the athletes who perform in its commercials.

Though the systems support this effort, it is Nike's people who actually deliver. The system doesn't do the work. It has simply been geared most effectively to support the people and improve their ability to perform.

The system is the user

To put it another way, *the system is the user.* In today's systems architecture, serving today's business environment, the user is the primary component. Downsizing supports this human element by bringing information directly to their desktops.

This is a big departure from traditional practice, where a major part of the effort had been to restrict access to data in order to protect it. Now, it is more important to improve access to data in order to make use of it—and to protect the data at the same time. It is important to protect valuable information, of course, but not at the expense of denying access to people who could use it productively. This can be a difficult transition for IS professionals to make. Like eating oatmeal, it might be the right thing to do, but to some people it still doesn't seem very appealing.

This doesn't mean that everyone has to have access to everything. Focus first on getting people who work in tandem to share information with each other. Let managers talk to managers, engineers to engineers, and so on. Once the departmental and functional links have been set up, you can provide internetwork/interdepartmental pathways between groups. This, then, becomes the foundation of enterprise-wide computing and of a downsized environment.

Although you should start out a downsizing project with something small and simple, not a grand overhaul, the overhaul should be the ultimate goal. It is essential that you build internetworks—both human and technical—between all your departments. As one consultant said, "It just might happen that you'll get better market response for your next product if R&D actually talks to marketing during the design process. It might be worth a try."

A systems approach to planning

Developing a downsizing plan is largely a matter of answering a lot of questions. These are mostly questions about yourself and details of what you hope to achieve from the implementation. Among them:

- What system requirements and file structures do your applications require?
- Do you have or expect a high level of transaction processing?
- How much disk storage capacity will you need? How much more than you expect to need do you think you ought to provide?
- How many sessions will be in progress at one time?
- Now many users will be logged onto the system at the same time?

ELEMENTS OF A SYSTEMS APPROACH

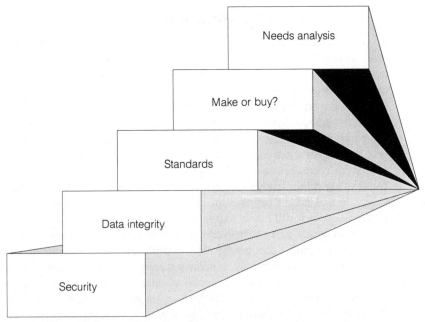

A systems approach is a systematic approach that addresses the major elements of your goals and plans.

These questions and their answers are preludes to the *systems approach* to a downsizing plan. True to its name, this approach systematically identifies, then addresses, all the issues and concerns the downsizing project will entail. These include:

- Conducting a needs analysis.
- Choosing between packaged software or developing custom code.
- Providing for security and disaster recovery.
- Maintaining data integrity.
- Setting and observing standards.

Analyzing the need

A needs analysis can be a detailed review of what types of systems and other technology the downsizing venture will require. That's an important consideration, and for many people it's the one that comes to mind first.

A needs analysis is not only, or even primarily, a technology assessment. The most effective type of needs analysis starts with a definition of the business need to be addressed. Only after you have identified the business need is it time to worry about the technology that's available to solve it. Start by deciding what the business problem is. Only then can you make responsive technological decisions.

Involve users in this process. Start by asking for a list of their information requirements. Almost inevitably, the first report will be a wish list. Give it some respectful attention, then go back to the users and separate their real needs from their wishful thinking.

Only after you've identified the most important needs can you match the technology to the needs. Then, be sure you leave room for the growth that is inevitably going to occur.

Make or buy?

The chances are that you will be creating at least some of your own code for your downsized applications. Many shrink-wrap applications are available, particularly for PCs. Even so, you may find yourself writing code to supplement or expand these applications. In particular, most database management programs are actually application development platforms requiring your provision of some code to implement them.

Another factor is the availability of better application development tools, and the ability to develop programs on PCs within the networked environment. The newest tools are easier to use, and they can sharply reduce implementation time.

When it becomes increasingly easier to address your particular business needs specifically, doing it yourself makes more and more sense. Even if you're not going to be writing applications from scratch, you might be writing internal macros and kinds of enhancements to various kinds of shrink-wrap applications.

Observing standards

Few things are more characteristic of the IS profession than its dedication to standards. Some call it an obsession. It has often been a source of conflict. Professionals call for standardization for the sake of data integrity and other worthwhile causes. Users chafe at the same standards, feeling—often correctly—that these inhibit their ability to do their jobs.

Some standards are necessary. The trick is to determine which ones. The GUI, particularly its Windows implementation, is a notable and widely used standard. It is supposed to present the same type of interface every time, no matter which application is being used.

Windows application developers have created a notable number of exceptions. For example, of the major Windows word processors, each takes a distinctive approach. While Microsoft Word has naturally stuck closely to Windows' uniform approach, WordPerfect transferred the distinctive characteristics of its character-based products to the Windows version.

Even where exceptions have become the rule, however, there is enough uniformity to make standardization worthwhile. Though WordPerfect has made notable departures from Windows standards, it is uniform within its own product line. In a training situation, for example, users who have learned the mechanics of one Windows application, or one WordPerfect application, need not learn a new set of commands and functions when they move to new applications that share the same environment. That means instructors can devote more time to teaching the new application as opposed to things like the use of function keys. The time saved can be used to teach how to get better results.

Networking technology is another area where standardization can be important. To a large extent, it is taking place in the twin fields of internetworking and interoperability. Here, the standards are expansive, not restrictive. They specify ways in which diverse networks, interconnections, and applications can interact with each other, regardless of the platforms on which they run. This is also a case where it can often be more important to maintain communication between departments than to require that every department use the same platform.

The approved software list is another form of standardization. Users cite advantages like these:

- **Volume discounts**. Standardized packages are usually purchased in quantity.
- **Reduced support workload**. Technicians need only work with a limited number of applications.

- **Backup resources**. With volume purchasing, it is easy and inexpensive to arrange to have spare software copies on hand to meet unexpected needs.

How one firm evaluates software

In selecting software for its approved list, Martin Marietta goes through these steps:

- Decide which products to evaluate, and set priorities for reviewing them.
- Select experts to work with individual products.
- Define the business-related needs that products are expected to meet.
- Acquire evaluation copies.
- Perform preliminary evaluations that identify the leading candidates for adoption.
- Conduct extensive field tests of the selected final candidates.
- Review the test results and make final recommendations.
- Make selections based on those recommendations.
- Keep records of the review and approval process for use in future evaluations.
- Update the list of approved products and active candidates every three months.

Maintaining integrity

Maintaining data integrity is a major concern of IS professionals. They traditionally have considered this one of their most important responsibilities. They are understandably uneasy with the likelihood that widespread user access threaten the accuracy and usability of the organization's data resources.

Some companies go so far as to prevent user uploads as a way to keep the core company data pure. It seems simple but effective: Don't allow users to upload data at all.

That approach helps keep the data uncorrupted. But it is just as effective in screening the core data from necessary updates. The database fails to reflect the research and development users have been doing. It is in direct conflict with the major downsizing objective of deriving the maximum possible value from the maximum available data.

A better approach lets concerned IS professionals act on their concerns. Establish a dedicated group of professionals who are skilled in both business and systems needs. Let them act as gatekeepers to ensure the accuracy of the data passed up to the server or mainframe. These can be teams of specialists who can monitor uploads and make sure they are not going to put everything else in your system awry. At the same time, they can let the system reflect legitimate changes being made on the desktop level.

Maintaining security

Security and disaster recovery are allied with maintaining data integrity. Often, though, they tend to be forgotten, particularly in downsized systems. One reason is that it is harder to protect a network than an isolated larger system. Another problem, more serious in a downsized environment, is a tendency to think of network resources as inexpensive and easy to replace. That's true of typical PCs and much of their related hardware.

The story is not the same when you consider the increasing power—and cost—of network-level superservers. These machines represent major investments in their own right, not to mention their contents. Even though they still do not approach the price levels of large systems, they are worth protecting. They not only need physical security, but environmental controls and maintenance programs to ensure their long life, and to make sure they will be up and running when you need them.

For this reason, security is not entirely a matter for security officials or IS professionals. Other people like building managers and electricians also have roles in keeping your resources secure. Include them in your planning. They probably can give you some good ideas about things to do or avoid, to make the system more secure.

Justifying the project

Not all downsizing efforts succeed. Those companies that have enjoyed some success have concentrated on the organization's needs and the benefits it could gain. They have balanced these against the technological demands and the project's likely costs. The key is to start by considering business factors, not technical ones.

Business considerations

No downsizing plan can pass any reasonable justification test unless it responds to a business need. Don't do something just because you have the means to do it. Act because you can respond to an identified need and improve your competitive position.

Even better, look for opportunities to gain a future competitive advantage as well as a current-quarter edge. We exist in a highly competitive global economy. A single remark about interest rates has sent the stock market into a tailspin the next day. Good news from the Middle East shot the market back up again just as quickly. The ideal project puts you in position to respond as quickly as conditions change.

The ability to promote internetworking might seem like a technical consideration, but this too, first and foremost, is a business issue. The technology of internetworking promotes communication. If a plan would promote communication, particularly between diverse elements of the organization, it will enable them to work more closely and to cooperate in a common effort. This, too, improves the organization's ability to compete.

On the other side

Weigh the potential advantages against the cost and difficulty of implementing them. Even a beneficial project may not be worthwhile if the systems necessary to implement it would be too complex and hard to manage.

FACTORS TO CONSIDER

Compare:

* Business need
* Possible competitive advantage
* Internetworking with existing systems

With:

* Complexity
* Cost

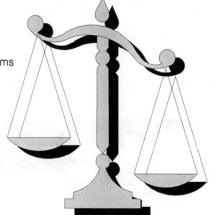

When selecting a potential downsizing project, compare the business advantages with the technical and financial needs.

Another factor can be labeled, "If it ain't broke, don't fix it." For many purposes, that folksy saying is too simplistic. Even good-running systems can often stand improvements. At the same time, don't underrate the value of a system that already works well. It might not be worth the risk of upsetting a delicate balance to try to build in a new project that will give you only a limited return. At least, look for a return that is worth the risk.

Don't try to downsize, either, when an application truly requires large-scale computing power. A large system may ultimately evolve into a server role, but it still will be there to run the applications that require its power.

Costs v. benefits

The traditional form of cost-benefit analysis in data processing compares the cost of computerization with the cost of doing the same job manually.

The analysis for downsizing must be somewhat different. Turn the traditional method around and consider *opportunity cost*. Examine the potential cost savings of downsizing the application. If there are none, that would end the analysis right there. But if there are significant savings, failing to take advantage of them would be a cost in itself—the cost of missing an opportunity.

Pick a winner

The universal advice of nearly anyone who has attempted a downsizing project is, *start small*. Look for an application that involves only a few users, and where the risk of failure is small. This is no time to take chances

THREE PLACES TO DOWNSIZE
Take it from the top

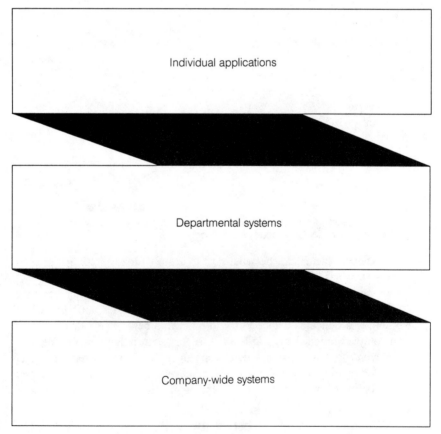

Start your downsizing program with small-group or departmental systems. Anything larger invites problems you may find hard to solve without more experience.

with vital applications and data. It's much more important that you come up with a winner the first time. You need to gain valuable experience at small risk. Your success will build morale, and make doubters less reluctant to participate.

Three basic places you can start are an individual or small-group application, a departmental system, or something that extends enterprise-wide. It makes a lot of sense to start with the smallest possibility that has passed the justification test. You can experiment, you can work at a reasonable scale, and should you fail, it will be a localized failure.

A single department or user group also can provide a good candidate for the first downsizing effort. Here, the users know their needs and are likely to be proficient in using their systems. In fact, many good ideas for downsizing come from small user groups who can make direct, specific suggestions about how to meet their needs. These groups also are often under pressure from above to produce more results or solve nagging problems. People in that situation will be anxious to work with you if it means a solution—or better yet an opportunity—will result.

Selection guidelines

Aside from the admonition to start small, here are some other guidelines for selecting a first downsizing project:

- **Be prepared to be flexible**. The first project will be a learning process, no matter which target you pick. Allow some room for creativity of your development team. Let them explore. Let them find better ways of doing things.
- **Don't restrict yourself**. Starting small doesn't mean limiting your options. For example, it's all right to work with more than one package at a time. Use the opportunity to learn the ins and outs of two or three packages, though probably no more than that. You can use the experience to pick one that best suits your needs.
- **Target the initial training process**. Start first with a few internal gurus who will run the application and help other users once it's implemented. Make sure those folks are trained and are ready to carry the ball whenever the new system comes on line.
- **Let developers and users work together**. Assign some developers to work with the prospective users. Get some user analysis to guide the implementation and development process. Give the professionals an opportunity to talk with the people who are going to have to live with their work. At the same time, help users better understand what the developers can and cannot provide.
- **Don't pick unnecessary fights**. Avoid projects that can become battlegrounds for alternative technologies. Pick one where there's going to be a single, clear-cut way of achieving the goal.

Beyond a good start

Once the first project or two are completed, the nature of the downsizing plan will begin to change. Now, you will have two main responsibilities:

- To extend the process to larger, more widespread applications that can have greater impact on the organization.
- To help the managers of departments where projects have been completed manage their systems and improve their effectiveness.

The management challenge

Some managers may be unintentionally troublesome. A downsized application should be one that requires less involvement and support from the IS department. That is one source of cost savings, and it will be an opportunity lost if the users aren't able essentially to take charge of their own system.

Some managers will be slow to do this. One of your challenges will be to persuade these managers that their departments must accept full responsibility for the downsized system.

One clear sign that this is not happening is the department's failure to train its users and maintain necessary records and procedures. The department that is most likely to turn its downsized system into a success is the one that is willing to take responsibility for achieving that success.

Still go slowly

Early success will build confidence, but be careful not to let it build over-confidence. Don't rush into a wholesale makeover. Make changes on a single system, then a single department, and then a single division. A careful approach lets you build on your success to date and helps you gain the support necessary for continued success.

Continue to look for appropriate business areas where it might be fruitful to install a downsized system. It doesn't even have to be a fully downsized system; sometimes a partial changeover will meet the need. Continue to work within the specific selection criteria you used with the early projects. These criteria can be expanded and amended as you gain experience. Don't be too quick to assume, though, that you can begin to wing it on the basis of your early success and experience. Continue to maintain a set of criteria against which to evaluate all new proposals and requests. Your adherence to such definite standards can save you from the familiar experience of learning from your mistakes.

Remember training

If users are going to accept responsibility for running and using their own systems, they must be trained to do so. Start by training a cadre that will support the department's other users.

In many cases, you'll find computer expertise spread among the users, sometimes in surprising places. A manager might have gained only minimal knowledge of how to operate a desktop computer, while a junior employee has become a self-taught expert on Unix or internetworking.

Certainly, the problem is not the manager's lack of capacity. Managers and professionals can, and should, learn how to use their own systems. They can then contribute to the development of the company's business. They need to learn only the basics; they need not become computer experts. The object is to empower them to use their business knowledge, backed by the flexibility and information access of the downsized system.

The new role for MIS

The managers and users of downsized systems will be taking on some functions that traditionally have been performed by MIS. That doesn't mean the skilled professionals of this department will have nothing to do. Like the system, their jobs will change.

MIS could continue to support the effort, but on a larger scale than the downsized environments provide. They should continue to be the setters of standards, the guardians of the database and the headmasters of the training program. Instead of acting in the direct role of developing mainframe systems, IS professionals should think of themselves more as consultants, advising and supporting users who want to pursue downsizing.

Meanwhile, advances in network technology allow downsizers to shift the development and operation of computer systems out of the data center and into the user organizations. Downsizing should reduce the need for traditional mainframe programmers. It will not eliminate them, and it should create new demands for more business-oriented systems professionals to work in partnership with the user community.

From talk to action

As they teach in every management school, planning is a "Good Thing." The more planning you do before you act, the more successful your action will probably be.

Nevertheless, excessive planning can be too much of a "Good Thing." It can easily happen in downsizing: You spend so much time planning the transition you never actually get around to doing the deed. Cheryl Currid calls this NATO: no action, talk only. To negate this tendency, Currid offers a step-by-step plan for making the move from talk to action:

- **Secure top management support**. Win over the CEO, CFO and anyone else in top management who will listen. Make sure they understand the flexibility and economic benefits of downsized computer applications.

- **Be sure you have a willing CIO**. Like it or not, the information kingdom is about to be transformed. An uncooperative CIO could launch too many missiles and destroy the project.
- **Build a winning team**. Handpick a talented team of volunteers. A downsizing project, particularly a company's first one, is likely to be full of unexpected glitches. A strongly committed and competent clan needs to be formed. Secure the latitude and resources they need to get the job done.
- **Don't buy cheap stuff**. Build a strong LAN platform that is WAN-able. Don't fool around. This is not Tinker Toy technology. You'll need an industrial-strength LAN and good standards and procedures.
- **Get procedures in order**. This means backups, security, audits, support, and professional management. If you can't do it yourself, contract with a systems integrator who can.
- **Start assessing the desktop environment**. If you have a bunch of monochrome-monitored 286s out there, you have a problem. You need powerful workstations that can share the processing load of the new applications. Remember, the whole-cost economics of a LAN are different from those of a mainframe. With LANs and client/server applications, it's what's up front (on the desktop) that counts.
- **Select a strong client/server back-end database**. The best bet is to pick a database that is robust, supportable and can be plugged into the network easily.
- **Find the right front-end development tools**. Chances are you can avoid programming in COBOL or C if you take a look at some of the graphics-oriented front-end tools now available. Survey the market and select what you need. Don't be surprised if you end up with a multi-vendor arrangement between front ends and back ends. Also, it's no crime to have different tools for users and developers. The beauty of the client/server environment is being able to have something for everyone—and it all fits together.
- **Choose a downsizable pilot application**. Survey the current applications development project list and check out the gas guzzlers on the mainframe. Select a project that can be accomplished in a few months; you don't want to wait years for results. And don't take the company's largest database down first. Instead, pull down something that's realistic from the standpoint of size and complexity.
- **Consider outsourcing the mainframe**. The sooner you go on meter charges for mainframe use, the better. That way, people will realize the benefits of downsizing right away.
- **Reorganize MIS**. Start blending the new technology into mainstream MIS, but be sure to play by the new rules, not the old. LANs and client/server computing create some jobs and displace others. Don't try to force-fit a 20-year-old MIS organizational structure onto the new platform.

How Sara Lee proceeded

On the basis of its downsizing experience with multiple business units, Sara Lee has developed a set of procedures that both corporate and MIS management feel can boost the success of any such project:

- Form a committee of MIS staff members, corporate management, departmental management, and users to define, review, and monitor the project. Many divisions have found this approach to be effective for both short- and long-range planning.
- Identify the applications best suited for downsizing.
- Start with a project that has a limited scope and is easy to define and control, and whose success is easy to determine.
- Don't try to implement too much too quickly.
- Identify the work and information flows that are currently in place for the existing system and determine the effect the project will have on those processes.
- Determine who will be the owners of the data and who will be responsible for maintaining that information.
- Clearly identity the project's objectives and quantify the benefits these objectives will provide.
- Get upper management involved in the project from the beginning and secure a commitment from them about its objectives and benefits.
- Make sure the rationale for downsizing is based on strategic business goals rather than political ambitions.
- Regularly review the progress of the project with the multi-departmental committee, making modifications to the plan as the committee deems appropriate.

Don't do this

Downsizing also offers plenty of mistakes to avoid. Consultant Patrick Corrigan of the Corrigan Group (San Francisco) offers these examples:

- **Do-it-yourself installation**. Too many companies install their own LANs, without sufficient experience or knowledge. Hire a professional well-versed in network design and installation to help you, or to take over the entire process.
- **A bargain basement approach**. Shopping for the cheapest hardware and operating system may ease the initial pain, but bargain shopping will cost you when you run into the inevitable incompatibilities.
- **Using an untested reseller or system integrator**. Too many people are orphaned by a dealer, VAR, or consultant when things don't go right. Get references, and look for someone who has implemented a LAN in a similar environment.
- **Poor planning and design**. Most networks just happen, says Corrigan. But as the network gets bigger and takes on a more critical role,

the lack of planning becomes evident. Issues such as user account information, directory structures, and deciding who has access to different types of data should be hammered out when the network is installed. Do it with an eye toward future growth.

- **Unrealistic expectations**. Most organizations that install networks expect the process to be quick and easy. Neither is ever true.
- **Assuming everything will work on the first try**. This hardly ever happens, even when you have a professional network installer handling the project.
- **Assuming that anyone can manage the LAN**. Every network, regardless of its size, requires the ongoing attention of a trained network administrator. This administrator will have to deal every day with problems like backups, application installation and maintenance, management of user accounts, and hardware and software compatibility.
- **Lack of user training**. Users need to be schooled in issues such as dealing with shared peripherals and shared applications. Instead, users often are simply given passwords and shown how to log onto the network.
- **Improper backup**. A major source of trouble for networks of any size is a failure to follow proper backup procedures.
- **Ignoring disaster recovery**. Every company needs a comprehensive disaster recovery plan. This is particularly critical when the business depends on the smooth operation of the network.

12
CHAPTER

The human challenge of downsizing

Anyone who even remotely contemplates downsizing will soon learn one important reality: No matter how hard it might be to integrate large systems with PC networks, it can be infinitely harder to integrate the people who run them.

A downsizing project walks right into a running feud between advocates of the two types of systems—often strong advocates who don't just disagree with the other side. They operate out of fear and mistrust. One big source of conflict: Standards are the mainstays of most MIS departments. Yet if PC users feel confined to particular programs, they can feel very frustrated when more attractive options present themselves.

Thus, mainframe people are known for their belief that "micro" people have too little respect for proper controls and standards. Meanwhile, those on the PC side (who rarely use "micro" any more) perceive the large-system people as stubbornly standing in the way of change and flexibility, and interfering with their ability to make maximum use of computing power to better do their jobs. Neither stereotype is entirely correct. Most large-system people accept the need for change, and most PC people recognize that it has to take place with some order and control.

Still, there are just enough people who do fit the stereotypes to cause some serious trouble when you try to get them together. It is sometimes a matter of prejudice or of trying to protect an investment in one's skills and experience. For most IS professionals, though, this attitude is the result of a lifetime of professional conditioning. They have been taught that computing activity should revolve around the large central computer. Modern knowledge and practice have strongly challenged that belief. The network and the individual user is becoming the central focus, and this change of focus requires that many people reject a lifetime of teaching and conditioning. No, it's not easy, either for the subject or for the organization that's trying to bring about the change.

People problems in downsizing

Perhaps more importantly, this is only the most familiar source of human conflict in the downsizing environment. Floyd Stanley, in a seminar sponsored by Wave Technologies Training, has identified a full half-dozen "problems with people" with which a downsizing manager must contend. Turf wars and office politics are part of the problem, but far from the only part. Stanley's people problems include:

- There aren't enough of them.
- They don't have the right skills.
- They're afraid of change.
- They have to work with other people.
- They play political games.

Downsizing, says Stanley, can be described as systems democracy in action. Thomas Jefferson, in turn, once described democracy as organized anarchy. The two quotes together appear to describe the downsizing process. At the same time, though, there is a potential opportunity. Downsizing gives you the means to tailor the resulting system to support—and work with—the revamped organization.

ONE VIEW OF DOWNSIZING

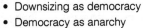

- Downsizing as democracy
- Democracy as anarchy

Moral: learn how to live in a less orderly environment

New systems give users more freedom and flexibility, but some might miss the loss of structure and control.

Too few good people

It seems incongruous that even in an economic recession, there is a shortage of skilled people to fill critical positions in downsized systems.

Yet the labor force as a whole has simultaneously experienced large-scale layoffs while at the same time employers anticipate a shortage of employees with the right kinds of skills for an evolving business climate. IS is no exception. It's not so much that the profession lacks people; it lacks the *right kinds* of people. There is still a shortage of the kinds of employees who must make things happen in a new environment.

TOO FEW PEOPLE

- Qualified employees in demand
- LANs often increase their workloads
- Solutions:
  - —Divide tasks
  - —Assign specialists

It's not that there are too few people in the workforce. There are too few qualified, well-trained people.

Being unprepared

A complicating problem is that companies haven't built up the necessary human infrastructure to support their new LANs correctly. All too often, PCs have been viewed as toys, not serious business machines.

Few companies have developed adequate PC support departments. At many places, the entire LAN support responsibility rests on a couple of self-selected in-house gurus. They become jacks-of-all-trades and end up doing nothing well. They also find themselves spending most of their time troubleshooting and responding to emergencies. Long-range planning stops the instant the beeper goes off. In other words, they are so busy fighting fires they never have the opportunity to practice fire prevention. There are no adequate procedures for capacity controls, backups, off-site storage, disaster recovery, or security administration.

Fearing layoffs

Many people fear downsizing, believing it to be a way for management to eliminate a lot of systems jobs. This is not usually the way it happens.

According to a 1990 *PC Week* survey of more than 200 companies, central MIS staffs were cut at 16% of the sites that had downsized. Another

69% said their central MIS staffs remained the same, while 14% said IS staff had increased at their firms.

Those results might be skewed toward the rosy side. Follow-up interviews reached several MIS directors who anonymously suggested that staff cuts were still possible. Perhaps more important, many employees were worried about their jobs—enough to cut morale sharply. When layoffs do happen, PC technicians and support people are just as vulnerable as large-system staff members.

Heavier workload?

Downsizing can also mean that the workload for the IS organization will actually increase. The department will have a broader diversity of systems to support. They will need to maintain multiple links, and the system has more places for something to fail.

A suggested approach is to list the tasks that will be required once the downsizing program is in place. Include the needs to maintain hardware, software, and the physical plant. Assign these tasks to specialists, form the specialists into a team, and manage the team.

Wrong skills

One conclusion of the 1991 Downsizing/Rightsizing Corporate Computing Conference was that IS personnel require tools for creating distributed and client/server applications. These same employees must also have the skills necessary to use these tools. If they do not have these skills now, they must be given the resources to acquire and use them. Conference delegates noted that mainframe programmers can require up to one year of retraining before they can work competently in object-oriented computing environments.

NEW NEEDS FOR TECHNICAL SKILLS

Yesterday

- Cobol
- Conventional databases
- Computer science degree

Today

- C, CASE, OOP
- SQL and client/server
- Business and technical degrees

Yesterday's technical skills were highly specialized; today, an employee needs more wide-ranging knowledge.

Employees—including both IS professionals and users—need a completely different set of skills than they did as recently as 10 years ago. In the past, employers looked for knowledge of COBOL, mainframe security, and in general, a strong technical background. Now, an IS professional must be more diversified. C and SQL are the languages of choice, and a business degree is a sought-after complement to a technical education.

The so-called people skills have also become more important. In the past, a computer professional was expected to work independently on specific technical tasks. Today's IS employee must be as prepared to work with other people as with technology.

"PEOPLE SKILLS" ARE MORE IMPORTANT

Yesterday

- Independence
- Technical skills
- Ability to follow

Today

- Teamwork
- Communication skills
- Ability to lead

Technical skills are still important, but one of the greatest challenges is to learn human relations techniques as well.

Lag control

As companies standardize on PC and workstation technology, the primary work force skill requirements are shifting to such graphical user interface environments as Microsoft Windows, OS/2, or X Window under Unix. The dominant need for programming experience is in C or the C⁺⁺ object-oriented development language. But many large companies that are downsizing from mainframe environments are staffed with hundreds or thousands of COBOL programmers.

Correcting this lag can be a major challenge to managers. It means they must wait out a substantial learning curve before many of their key people are ready to take on their new roles in society.

Climbing that curve can be daunting for the employees, due to new tools and new terminologies. In many instances, there is no direct correlation to the same tools and terminals on the mainframe side. Now, these experienced hands are going to make their way back to the top. Some of them might have a rough time, particularly those who have committed entire careers to mainframe systems. They're now being thrust into an environment of new systems in which they have no background.

CLOSING THE SKILLS GAP

- Build your own work force
  - —Recruiting
  - —Retraining
- Ease the transition
  - —Form user groups
  - —Encourage self-education

There are several ways to build a skilled work force. The most effective, though not the quickest, is through a long-term strategic plan.

Old employees, new skills

Retraining is one possibility. Giving people the opportunity to learn can be a worthwhile investment. Start early, so you can take some time and do a thorough job. It makes little sense to throw away your employees' talents and experience unless they are simply unable or unwilling to adapt.

One of many ways to ease this transition is to start an in-house user group. In the past, these groups have been something like clubs, but they can become valuable sources of knowledge and morale-building.

Plan round tables and workshops to help employees learn and get their questions answered. Bring in expert speakers to deliver talks. Make sure the experts address the individuals who have the most direct responsibilities for the subject at hand.

Independent learning can help employees. Some companies have instituted loaner programs, where they keep systems on hand for employees to take home with them at nights and on weekends. An alternative is to provide financial aid for professionals who want to buy their own systems.

Retraining, however, is not entirely the answer. The trainees must be willing and able to take on a tough challenge. Some will not readily learn the new material; others might not want to abandon lifetimes of well-honed skills to go back to beginner status again.

Development tools

Automated software development tools can help speed up both the learning and the application development process. Some of these products are geared primarily for users, however, and lack the power a professional expects. Others might create programs faster but lack the peak performance of a good traditionally coded application.

Recruit from outside

Another option is to recruit qualified people from outside. These people are in demand and can be hard to find—harder as the spread of downsizing creates an even greater demand for their services.

Hiring such a person is still no guarantee of success. Sometimes you can be your own worst enemy. There's the tale of a company that landed a skilled C programmer to join a workstation project team. Someone immediately shipped him off to learn COBOL, because that's what the company had always done.

Comb the campuses

Hiring recent graduates allows you to start building your own staff with the type of people you expect to need. The drawback there is that many recent graduates have not been trained in modern programming skills. University courses are not usually geared to many of the kinds of work you expect from their graduates. The schools aren't entirely blameless, but it's not fully their fault, either. They cannot possibly teach every specialty.

A strategic approach

One strategy that can help is to develop a strategic staffing plan. Take inventory of the needs you expect to have, both now and in the future. For each need, develop one or more specific strategies to meet them.

This process can be time-consuming, and the outcome can be frustratingly long-range. It requires the cooperation of IS, user departments and the recruiting staff. But it can be worth both the investment and the wait.

Resistance to change

"Change is an unnatural act, particularly in successful companies; powerful forces are at work to avoid it at all costs," said Michael Porter in a *Harvard Business Review* article.

Resistance to change is an old management bugaboo. Every manager has had to confront it at some time. In fact, resistance to change has itself proven highly resistant to change. Certainly, that has been true of the great changes that accompany downsizing.

Resistance isn't limited to habit-bound IS staff members, though there has been plenty of it there. Users can be stubborn as well. Cheryl Currid suggests that you "look at some users who still lurk in the hallways of corporate America. They are technology-resistant, clutching yellow writing tablets, calculators, and calendars. Their old, tried-and-true methods still work, and they don't want anyone fixing them."

Most often, resistance stems from fear. When IS professionals resist the conversion to smaller systems, it's often because they are afraid of what might happen to them.

Some are paralyzed by procedure. They match up lists by hand, re-key information from hard-copy reports and keep documentation that no one ever reads. It's the "We've always done it this way" syndrome.

You can turn resistance toward a more constructive direction. Try to replace "What's going to happen to me?" with "What's in it for me?" Show reluctant employees how they stand to benefit from the changes in their way of working life. Most employees want to be able to do their jobs better; only a cynical few do not. Show them, then, how the new technology can improve their value to the organization. This change is an opportunity for them to become more productive and better-appreciated employees.

Get involved

Involvement is another important process. People particularly resist change when they feel it is being imposed from the top. That's a natural reaction. They mistrust the change, and the management that is trying to bring it about. They fear the change will benefit the organization, but not them.

Overcome that fear by building a sense of involvement. Within the context of achieving your overall goal, give the affected employees material roles in determining how the change is to take place. Listen to their suggestions, and implement those that are worthwhile. Set up work teams and planning coalitions. Of course, employees given this kind of opening will

RESISTANCE TO CHANGE

How to cope:

- Tap employees' self interest
  —"What's in it for me?"
- Build involvement
  —Form teams
  —Encourage participation

To overcome resistance, give the employee a stake in the change.

act at least partly in self-interest. That's the point. They can make material contributions to their own well-being. When they are able to do that, they begin to claim ownership of the project—to think of it as "ours" instead of "theirs." They trust their own judgment. The plan they have helped create is no longer mysterious and threatening.

Get it together

While building participation and ownership, let key employees from all the involved departments work together on the plan. Get mainframe and PC people together. Get them together with leaders of the user departments. Involving all these people, and getting them together, can accomplish the following:

* It can help each side overcome its unrealistic expectations of the other.
* The collective wisdom of all these highly involved people can't help but produce a better system.

When users resist

When a Chicago-area hospital installed a LAN a few years ago, it observed conventional wisdom and tried a simple application first: a system used to reserve conference rooms. The process had previously been done manually.

It turned out not to be easy at all. Instead of making room reservations from the PCs on their desks, users would continue to walk out to the reception desk to make their reservations in the log book traditionally used for this purpose. A commonly expressed attitude: If I did it that way before, why can't I keep on doing it that way? The hospital found itself having to maintain a dual system, and that brought new problems. Rooms reserved through the log book were not always entered in the computerized system.

People were actively trying to avoid the system, its manager said. Apparently, the technology outstripped the employees' ability to use it. In any event, conference rooms are now again reserved via the paper record.

Meanwhile, a New York consulting firm implemented a networked communication and scheduling program that has helped unify the organization and make it more cohesive. Users found they could share documents created by their word processors, and the system was much more efficient than its predecessor at scheduling appointments and meetings. Many users have found new ways to capitalize on the system.

One of the main keys to success was that users, who formerly had to request information from the MIS staff found they could get it themselves, and get it immediately. They also liked the ease of being able to schedule meetings without repeated exercises in telephone tag.

Changing work habits

New systems change work habits. Sometimes it is for the better, sometimes not. The big difference is whether the employees perceive the change to be an improvement in their working lives. For example, a Boston-based bakery and restaurant chain improved its ability to monitor store operations, giving management the ability to spot excessive costs almost as soon as they happened. Managers also spotted some procedures store managers had not been scrupulously observing.

The employees, however, named the system Big Brother, complaining that they were being excessively monitored.

That complaint might have masked another difficulty; little in this system suggested that it would help employees improve the way they did their own jobs. The dominant emphasis was on monitoring. Employees felt that while they were now being held to higher standards, the system provided no help in meeting them.

Working with others

Yet another problem with people is that they have to work with each other. They don't always do that very well. This is particularly a problem with those IS professionals who tend to be loners. The profession has many who relate better to technology than to people. For them, the appeal of their jobs is that they can work in relative isolation. They interacted mainly with others in their own profession. That's changing as the IS department is increasingly required to address business goals as well as technical ones.

Many of those who have made the transition from mainframe to LAN environments say the most difficult part of the change was, "I had no idea I was going to be directly involved with so many people." People who had become accustomed with dealing with other technical people now have to interact with users and business managers—people they might once have thought of as the "great unwashed."

Not only that, but a downsized environment presents a greater variety of tasks and challenges. There may be an increased support load, simply because there are more PC applications available, and more systems running them. This necessarily increases the need for good interpersonal and communication skills. Not everyone has these, and they often must be developed through training.

Office politics

People play political games. They do so in any corporate enterprise. The larger the enterprise, the more they do it. There are many who feel that the way to the top is not by doing your own job well, but by making a competitor look as though he or she is not doing the job well.

Here, too, IS offers more than the usual level of risk. And it's not just the tension between large-system and PC people. Actually, most IS professionals support the idea of downsizing and look at it as an opportunity to advance and accomplish new things. Some continue to resist. And many would like to participate in the evolution of computing but feel they cannot.

It's not unusual for proponents of change to feel the subtle revenge of their corporate colleagues. Some advocates receive less-than-subtle warnings to keep quiet and go along with the system. Others find themselves shunted out of the mainstream, doing only minor projects. Performance appraisals slip, and the fear begins to develop that should times become worse, the boat-rocker would be among the first to go.

Still another important factor involved in a downsizing project is that information is power. Another project that changes the balance of that power—and downsizing will certainly do that—is fertile ground for political conflicts and turf wars to arise.

The best responses

As with other problems, the best response here is to build a sense of involvement and ownership. When planning a downsizing project, involve as many people as possible, as soon as possible. Their active participation helps them feel that the project can be a vehicle for success and can relieve their fears that it will become someone else's launching pad.

When Financial Guaranty Insurance Co. (FGIC) launched a downsizing project, it became the focal point of serious internal battles. Many of these conflicts were overcome with the help of well-educated programmers. They understood the bond insurance business and recognized how the different parts of the LAN-based system would fit together.

Even so, sometimes executive force was necessary. The programmers had to cope with conflicting demands from different departments, creating tremendous political frictions. One major complaint was that users had to check data generated by the old system before the data could be entered in the new system. The data cleanup was accomplished only under orders from top management.

Try matrix management

Another response many organizations have used is to farm out IS professionals to the user departments. They use a matrix management approach in which a professional has two supervisors: the traditional IS manager and the manager of a user department.

Clive Finkelstein, originator of information engineering (the linking of information systems with business strategy) says he believes the optimum form of corporate organization, at least through the twentieth century, will be a matrix structure.

Typically, he says, a growing company evolves through these organizational forms:

- **Entrepreneurial.** This is the typical start-up organization. It is informal, and everyone reports to the chief executive officer.
- **Bureaucratic.** As the organization grows, the lines of authority become more hardened and formal, with controls designed to promote greater efficiency. All lines of authority still lead to the CEO.
- **Divisional.** Some managers become more knowledgeable about their specialties than does top management. They become division and department heads, with considerable autonomy within their own areas.
- **Coordinated.** The divisions become semi-independent business units or product groups. Contacts between the heads of these groups and the rest of the organization consists mainly of coordinating activities.
- **Matrix.** This is Finkelstein's ultimate organization of the 90s. It is a highly participatory structure that appears to violate the Biblical injunction about trying to serve two masters.

GETTING PEOPLE TOGETHER

- Train in interpersonal skills
- Form task forces
- Try matrix management
  - —One supervisor for technical questions
  - —Another supervisor for user needs

Training and flexible management techniques can help build teamwork.

Matrix management and IS

The organizational chart of a typical matrix alignment might look like a chart with the team leaders listed down one side and the heads of the operating departments listed across the top. An IS professional could be assigned to work in any of the open blocks across from a team leader and under a department head. That person would report both to one of the team leaders listed on the left and to the head of one of the operating departments listed across the top.

For example, an IS professional working in a marketing department still reports to IS. This department continues to be a source of standards, planning, and implementation. The professional might be assigned by IS to work on a particular project. That individual's specific assignment is to work directly with the marketing staff on aspects of the project that involve marketing.

The IS professional remains a professional. At the same time, he or she gains a first-hand picture of what the department needs to better conduct its work. The delegated professional could report, for example, that "engineering isn't happy with the project we've designed for them. They'd like to make these changes."

This approach provides an opportunity for better communication between the two departments, and better understanding of what each can expect of the other.

"Do what you do best"

In any form of organization, no one need be left out by the downsizing movement.

Downsizing expands the opportunities for those who have developed the PC-oriented concepts of access and flexibility. They can continue to move these ideas from their desktop, single-user origins to make valuable contributions to the organization as a whole.

Meanwhile, IS professionals should bring the discipline and professionalism of traditional IS into the new downsized environment. Important concepts like security and data integrity will best be preserved if the people who are dedicated to their preservation will continue their efforts, even as the computing world takes a rapid spin.

As one commentator put it, "This is your chance to do what you do best."

Downsizing products

The following is a representative list of products available for downsizing products available at time of publication.

Network operating systems

LAN MANAGER
Microsoft Corp.
One Microsoft Way
Redmond, WA 98052-6399
(800) 227-6444

NETWARE
Novell, Inc.
122 East 1700 South
Provo, UT 84606
(800) 453-1267

VINES BANYAN SYSTEMS INC.
120 Flanders Rd.
Westboro, MA 01581
(800) 828-2404, (508) 898-1000, (508) 898-1755 (fax)

Windows front ends

ACCESS FOR WINDOWS
Eicon Technology Corp.
2196 32nd Ave.
Montreal, Quebec H8T 3H7 Canada
(514) 631-2592, (514) 631-3092 (fax)

DYNACOMM/ELITE
Future Soft Engineering
1001 S. Dairy Ashford #101
Houston, TX 77077
(713) 496-9400, (713) 496-1090 (fax)

EXTRA FOR WINDOWS
Attachmate Corp.
13231 S.E. 36th St.
Bellevue, WA 98006
(800) 426-6283, (206) 644-4010, (206) 747-9924 (fax)

FOREST & TREES FOR WINDOWS
Channel Computing, Inc.
53 Main St.
Newmarket, NH 03857
(800) 289-0053

I/F BUILDER
Viewpoint Systems
1900 S. Norfolk St. #310
San Mateo, CA 94403
(415) 578-1591

IRMA WORKSTATION FOR WINDOWS
DCA
1000 Alderman Dr.
Alpharetta, GA 30202
(800) 241-4762

LIGHTSHIP
Pilot Executive Software
40 Broad St.
Boston, MA 02109
(617) 350-7035, (617) 350-7118 (fax)

LOTUS 1-2-3
Lotus Development Corp.
55 Cambridge Pkwy.
Cambridge, MA 02142
(617) 577-8500

PARADOX SQL LINK
Borland International
1800 Green Hills Rd.
Scotts Valley, CA 95066
(408) 438-8400

RELAY GOLD FOR WINDOWS
Microcom, Inc.
500 River Ridge Dr.
Norwood, MA 02062
(800) 822-8224

RUMBA
Wall Data, Inc.
17769 N.E. 78th Pl.
Redmond, WA 98052

Internetworking
Interoperability

3COM CORP.
5400 Bayfront Plaza
Santa Clara, CA 95052
(800) 638-3266, (408) 764-5000

BEAME & WHITESIDE SOFTWARE, LTD.
P.O. Box 8130
Dundas, Ontario,
Canada L9H 5E7
(416) 648-6556, (416) 648-6556 (fax)

CAYMAN SYSTEMS, INC.
26 Lansdowne St.
Cambridge, MA 02139
(617) 494-1999, (617) 494-9270 (fax)

FTP SOFTWARE, INC.
26 Princess St.
Wakefield, MA 01880
(617) 246-0900, (617) 246-0901 (fax)

INFORMATION PRESENTATION TECHNOLOGIES, INC.
555 Chorro St., Ste. C
San Luis Obispo, CA 93401
(800) 233-9993, (805) 541-3000, (805) 541-3037 (fax)

INTERCON SYSTEMS CORP.
950 Merndon Pkwy., Ste. 420
Herndon, VA 22070
(703) 709-9890, (703) 709-9896 (fax)

LOCUS COMPUTING CORP.
9800 La Cienega Blvd.
Inglewood, CA 90301
(800) 955-6287, (213) 670-6500, (213) 670-2980 (fax)

NETWORK RESEARCH CORP.
2380 North Rose Ave.
Oxnard, CA 93030
(800) 541-9508, (805) 485-2700

NOVELL, INC.
122 East 1700 South
Provo, UT 84606
(800) 453-1267, (801) 429-5900

SHIVA CORP.
1 Cambridge Center
Cambridge, MA 02142
(800) 458-3550, (617) 252-6300, (617) 252-6852 (fax)

SUN MICROSYSTEMS, INC.
2 Federal St.
Billerica, MA 01821
(800) 872-4786, (508) 667-0010

WOLLONGONG GROUP, INC.
1129 San Antonio Rd.
Palo Alto, CA 94303
(800) 872-8649, (800) 962-8649, (415) 962-7140 (in California)

Bridges

3COM CORP.
3165 Kifer Rd.
Santa Clara, CA 95052-8145
(408) 562-6400

ADVANCED COMPUTER COMMUNICATIONS
720 Santa Barbara St.
Santa Barbara, CA 93101
(805) 963-9431

BICC DATA NETWORKS
1800 W. Park Dr.
Westborough, MA 01581
(508) 898-2422

CISCO SYSTEMS, INC.
1350 Willow Rd.
Menlo Park, CA 94025
(415) 326-1941

CROSSCOMM CORP.
133 E. Main St.
Marlboro, MA 01752
(508) 481-4060

DIGITAL EQUIPMENT CORP. (DEC)
146 Main St.
Maynard, MA 01754-2571
(508) 493-5111

GATEWAY COMMUNICATIONS, INC.
2941 Alton Ave.
Irvine, CA 92714
(714) 553-1555

HALLEY SYSTEMS, INC.
2730 Orchard Pkwy.
San Jose, CA 95134
(408) 432-2600

IBM
Old Orchard Rd.
Armonk, NY 10504
(914) 765-1900

INFOTRON SYSTEMS CORP.
9 N. Olney Ave.
Cherry Hill, NJ 08003
(609) 424-9400

MICROCOM CORP.
500 River Ridge Dr.
Norwood, MA 02062
(617) 762-9310

MICROWAVE BYPASS
25 Braintree Hill Office Park
Braintree, MA 02184
(617) 843-8260

NETWORK APPLICATION TECHNOLOGY
21040 Homestead Rd.
Cupertino, CA 95014
(408) 733-4530

NETWORK PRODUCTS CORP.
1111 S. Arroyo Pkwy., Ste. 450
Pasadena, CA 91105
(818) 441-6504

NOVELL, INC., COMM. DIVISION
890 Ross Dr.
Sunnyvale, CA 94089
(415) 969-1999

RACAL INTERLAN CORP.
155 Swanson Rd.
Boxborough, MA 01719
(508) 263-9929

RAD DATA COMMUNICATIONS, INC.
151 W. Passaic St.
Rochelle Park, NJ 07662
(201) 568-1466

RETIX
2644 30th St.
Santa Monica, CA 90405
(213) 399-2200

TRW INFORMATION NETWORKS
23800 Hawthorne Blvd.
Torrance, CA 90505
(213) 373-9161

UNGERMANN-BASS, INC.
2560 Mission College Blvd.
Santa Clara, CA 95050
(408) 496-0111

VITALINK
6607 Kaiser Dr.
Fremont, CA 94555
(415) 794-1100

WELLFLEET COMMUNICATIONS
12 DeAngelo Dr.
Bedford, MA 01730
(617) 275-2400

Routers

3COM CORP.
3165 Kifer Rd.
Santa Clara, CA 95052-8145
(408) 562-6400

ADVANCED COMPUTER COMMUNICATIONS
720 Santa Barbara St.
Santa Barbara, CA 93101
(805) 963-9431

BANYAN SYSTEMS
115 Flanders Rd.
Westborough, MA 01581
(508) 898-1000

CISCO SYSTEMS, INC.
1350 Willow Rd.
Menlo Park, CA 94025
(415) 326-1941

DIGITAL EQUIPMENT CORP. (DEC)
146 Main St.
Maynard, MA 01754-2571
(508) 493-5111

EICON TECHNOLOGY CORP.
2196 32nd Ave.
Lachine, Quebec Canada H8T 3H7
(541) 631-2592

IBM
Old Orchard Rd.
Armonk, NY 10504
(914) 765-1900

NOVELL, INC. COMM. DIVISION
890 Ross Dr.
Sunnyvale, CA 94089
(415) 969-1999

PROTEON, INC.
Two Technology Dr.
Westborough, MA 01581
(508) 898-2800

RAD DATA COMMUNICATIONS, INC.
151 W. Passaic St.
Rochelle Park, NJ 07662
(201) 568-1466

TRW INFORMATION NETWORKS
23800 Hawthorne Blvd.
Torrance, CA 90505
(213) 373-9161

VITALINK
6607 Kaiser Dr.
Fremont, CA 94555
(415) 794-1100

WELLFLEET COMMUNICATIONS
12 DeAngelo Dr.
Bedford, MA 01730
(617) 275-2400

Gateways

3COM CORP.
3165 Kifer Rd.
Santa Clara, CA 95052-8145
(408) 562-6400

ADVANCED COMPUTER COMMUNICATIONS
720 Santa Barbara St.
Santa Barbara, CA 93101
(805) 963-9431

AST RESEARCH, INC.
2121 Alton Ave.
Irvine, CA 92714
(714) 863-1333

ATTACHMATE CORP.
13231 SE 36th St.
Bellevue, WA 98006
(206) 644-4010

BANYAN SYSTEMS
115 Flanders Rd.
Westborough, MA 01581
(508) 898-1000

CISCO SYSTEMS, INC.
1350 Willow Rd.
Menlo Park, CA 94025
(415) 326-1941

CROSSCOMM CORP.
133 E. Main St.
Marlboro, MA 01752
(508) 481-4060

DIGITAL COMMUNICATIONS ASSOCIATES (DCA)
1000 Alderman Dr.
Alpharetta, GA 30201
(404) 442-4000

DIGITAL EQUIPMENT CORP. (DEC)
146 Main St.
Maynard, MA 01754-2571
(508) 493-5111

EICON TECHNOLOGY CORP.
2196 32nd Ave.
Lachine, Quebec Canada H8T 3H7
(541) 631-2592

GATEWAY COMMUNICATIONS, INC.
2941 Alton Ave.
Irvine, CA 92714
(714) 553-1555

IBM
Old Orchard Rd.
Armonk, NY 10504
(914) 765-1900

ICOT CORP.
3801 Zanker Rd.
San Jose, CA 95150-5143
(800) 227-8068

IDEASSOCIATES INC.
29 Dunham Rd.
Billerica, MA 01821
(508) 663-6878

INFOTRON SYSTEMS CORP.
9 N. Olney Ave.
Cherry Hill, NJ 08003
(609) 424-9400

J&L COMMUNICATIONS
9238 Deering Ave.
Chatsworth, CA 91311
(818) 709-1778

NETWORK PRODUCTS CORP.
1111 S. Arroyo Pkwy., Ste. 450
Pasadena, CA 91105
(818) 441-6504

NETWORK SOFTWARE ASSOCIATES
39 Argonaut
Laguna Hills, CA 92656
(714) 768-4013

NOVELL, INC., COMM. DIVISION
890 Ross Dr.
Sunnyvale, CA 94089
(415) 969-1999

RABBIT SOFTWARE CORP.
Great Valley Corporate Center
7 Great Valley Pkwy. E.
Malvern, PA 19355
(800) 722-2482

RACAL INTERLAN CORP.
155 Swanson Rd.
Boxborough, MA 01719
(508) 263-9929

RETIX
2644 30th St.
Santa Monica, CA 90405
(213) 399-2200

THE SANTA CRUZ OPERATION (SCO)
400 Encinal St.
Santa Cruz, CA 95061
(408) 425-7222

TRW INFORMATION NETWORKS
23800 Hawthorne Blvd.
Torrance, CA 90505
(213) 373-9161

UNGERMANN-BASS, INC.
2560 Mission College Blvd.
Santa Clara, CA 95050
(408) 496-0111

WOLLONGONG
1129 San Antonio Rd.
Palo Alto, CA 94303
(415) 962-7100

TCP/IP

3COM TCP WITH DPA
3COM Corp.
(408) 764-5000

CHAMELEON
Netmanage, Inc.
(408) 257-6004

EMBEDDED TCP/IP
Venturcom, Inc.
(617) 661-1230

FUSION FOR DOS
Network Research Corp.
(805) 485-2700

LAN WORKPLACE FOR DOS, MACINTOSH, AND OS/2
Novell, Inc.
(801) 429-7000, (800) 638-9273

NET/ONE TCP
Ungermann-Bass Inc.
(408) 496-0111, (800) 873-6381

NEWT-SDK
Netmanage, Inc.
(408) 257-6004

PATHWAY ACCESS FOR DOS, MACINTOSH
Wollongong Group
(415) 962-7100

PC/NFS
Sun Microsystems, Sunconnect Division
(800) 872-4786

RPC-SDK
Netmanage, Inc.
(408) 257-6004

SimPC
Simware, Inc.
(613) 727-1779

Smarterm 340
Persoft, Inc.
(608) 273-3000

TCP Connection
Walker, Richer & Quinn
(206) 324-0407

TCP/IP
Venturcom, Inc.
(617) 661-1230

Client/server

Server 290
Parallan Computer
(415) 960-0288

Development environments

Access SQL
Software Products International
9920 Pacific Heights Blvd.
San Diego, CA 92121
(619) 450-1526

ATxtract
Panttaja Consulting Group, Inc.
103 Plaza St.
Healdsburg, CA 95448
(707) 433-2629

Bigtec SQL Object
Bigtec
P.O. Box 13242
Reading, PA 19612-3242
(215) 478-9660

CHOREOGRAPHER
GUIdance Technologies
800 Vinial St.
Pittsburgh, PA 15212
(412) 231-1300

DATAEASE SQL
DataEase International, Inc.
7 Cambridge Dr.
Trumbull, CT 06611
(203) 374-8000

DBASE IV SERVER EDITION FOR DOS
Ashton-Tate Corp.
20101 Hamilton Ave.
Torrance, CA 90502
(213) 329-9989

DEDE (DATABASE ENTITY DEVELOPMENT ENVIRONMENT)
Bigtec
P.O. Box 13242
Reading, PA 19612-3242
(215) 478-9660

EASYTRIEVE PLUS
Pansophic Systems, Inc.
2400 Cabot Dr.
Lisle, IL 60532
(708) 505-6000

ENFIN/2
Enfin Software
6920 Miramar Rd., Ste. 307
San Diego, CA 92121
(619) 549-6606

ERWIN/ERX
LOgic WOrkS, Inc.
601 Ewing St., Ste. B7
Princeton, NJ 08540
(609) 924-0029

ERWIN/SQL
LOgic WOrkS, Inc.
601 Ewing St., Ste. B7
Princeton, NJ 08540
(609) 924-0029

GURU VERSION 3.0
Micro Data Base Systems, Inc.
Two Executive Dr.
Lafayette, IN 47903
(800) 344-5832

NEVISYS
Nevis Technologies, Inc.
300 Corporate Pointe
Culver City, CA 90230
(213) 338-0257

NOMAD
MUST Software Internatonal
101 Merritt, #7
Norwalk, CT 06856
(203) 845-5000

OMNIS 5
Blyth Software
1065 E. Hillsdale Blvd., Ste. 300
Foster City, CA 94404
(415) 571-0222

POWERBUILDER
Powersoft Corp.
70 Blanchard Rd.
Burlington, MA 01803
(617) 229-2200

Q+E DATABASE LIBRARY
Pioneer Software
5540 Centerview Dr., Ste. 324
Raleigh, NC 27606
(919) 859-2220

QUICKSILVER/SQL
Wordtech Systems, Inc.
21 Altarinda Rd.
Orinda, CA 94563
(415) 254-0900

SQL OBJECT LIBRARY FOR OBJECT/1
Vanguard Business Solutions, Inc.
2401 Marinship, Ste. 290
Sausalito, CA 94965
(415) 331-3883

SQL TOOLKIT
SQL Solutions
New England Executive Park
Burlington, MA 01803
(617) 270-4150

SQLWINDOWS DEVELOPER'S SYSTEM
Gupta Technologies, Inc.
1040 Marsh Rd.
Menlo Park, CA 94025
(415) 321-5471

SQLWINDOWS FOR SQL SERVER
Client-Server Starter System
Gupta Technologies, Inc.
1040 Marsh Rd.
Menlo Park, CA 94025
(415) 321-5471

SUPERBASE 4 FOR WINDOWS
Precision Software, Inc.
8404 Sterling St.
Irving, TX 75063
(214) 929-4888

THE SQLFILE SYSTEM
Vinzant, Inc.
4 Skyline Dr.
Portage, IN 46368
(219) 763-3881

Development tools

JAM/DBI
JYACC
116 John St.
New York, NY 10038
(212) 267-7722

KNOWLEDGEMAN VERSION 3.0
Micro Data Base Systems, Inc.
Two Executive Dr.
Lafayette, IN 47903
(800) 344-5832

OBJECT/1
Micro Data Base Systems, Inc.
Two Executive Dr.
Lafayette, IN 47903
(800) 344-5832

OBJECTVIEW
Matesys Corporation N.A.
900 Larkspur Landing Cr., Ste. 175
Larkspur, CA 94939
(415) 925-2900

PC/FOCUS SQL SERVER INTERFACE
Information Builders
1250 Broadway
New York, NY 10001
(212) 736-4433

SQL SERVER TOOLKIT FOR PRESENTATION MANAGER
DataWiz International
1291 E. Hillsdale Blvd., Ste. 210
Foster City, CA 94404
(415) 571-1300

SQL SERVER TOOLKIT FOR WINDOWS
DataWiz International
1291 E. Hillsdale Blvd., Ste. 210
Foster City, CA 94404
(415) 571-1300

SQLFILE FOR WINDOWS
Vinzant, Inc.
4 Skyline Dr.
Portage, IN 46368
(219) 763-3881

VISUAL BASIC
Microsoft Corp.
One Microsoft Way
Redmond, WA 98052-6399
(800) 227-4679

Server hardware
Superservers

MULTIACCESS SERIES 3000
Advanced Logic Research
(714) 581-6770, (800) 289-7697

NCR 3445, 3450, 3550
NCR Corp.
(800) 225-5627, (513) 445-5000

NF100, NF200, NF300, NF400
Netframe Systems
(408) 944-0600

OMNISYSTEM
Northgate Computer Systems
(612) 943-8181

POWERFRAME
Tricord Systems
(612) 557-9005

POWERPRO
Advanced Logic Research
(714) 581-6770, (800) 289-7697

SERVER 290
Parallan Computer
(415) 960-0288

STARSERVER E
AT&T Computer Systems
(800) 247-1212

SYSTEMPRO
Compaq Computer Corp.
(713) 370-0670

Midrange systems

AT&T COMPUTER SYSTEMS
(800) 247-1212

BULL HN INFORMATION SYSTEMS
(508) 294-6000

CONCURRENT COMPUTER CORP.
(908) 758-7000

CONTROL DATA CORP.
(612) 853-5445

DATA GENERAL CORP.
(509) 366-8911, (800) 328-2436

DATAPOINT CORP.
(800) 733-1500, ext. 7884

ENCORE COMPUTER CORP.
(305) 587-2900

IBM
(800) 426-2468

MAI SYSTEMS CORP.
(714) 730-5100

MIPS COMPUTER SYSTEMS
(408) 720-1700

MODCOMP INC.
(305) 974-1380

NCR CORP.
(513) 445-5000

PRIME COMPUTER INC.
(508) 620-2800

PYRAMID TECHNOLOGY CORP.
(508) 620-2800

SEQUENT COMPUTER SYSTEMS
(800) 854-0428

SEQUOIA SYSTEMS
(508) 480-0800

SIEMENS NIXDORF INFORMATION SYSTEMS
(617) 273-0480

STRATUS COMPUTER
(508) 460-2000

TANDEM COMPUTERS
(408) 285-6000

UNISYS CORP.
(215) 986-4011

Bibliography

Ambrosio, Johanna. "Film company rolls along without mainframe; with a little ingenuity, Courtaulds successfully navigates the transition to Unix system." *Computerworld*, July 22, 1991, p. 31. Courtaulds Performance Films pulled the plug on its mainframe, ditched all its applications and switched to a Unix computer.

——————. "An architectural overview of SQL Server on Netware." *LAN Times*, July 8, 1991, p. 45.

Anthes, Gary H. "A step beyond a database." *Computerworld*, March 4, 1991, "Johns Hopkins' networked databases benefit genetic research.

——————. "Newspaper takes step into the LAN age." *Computerworld*, May 20, 1991, p. 1. On election night at the *Washington Post*, the computer system used by editors and reporters to put together the morning edition went down for two hours.

Arnold, Geoff, "Opening up to open systems computing." *LAN Times*, July 8, 1991, p. 53. Powerful new "open systems" such as Unix workstations are being added to computing resources at a rapid rate, creating yet another category of system. The bigger issue is making use of existing resources—like DOS PCs—within today's heterogeneous networks.

Arrington, Joseph J. "Integrating LANs and Mainframes." *LAN Times*, May 20, 1991, p. 79.

Bandrowski, Paul U. "Downsizing decisions." *Computerworld*, March 11, 1991, p. S1. Downsizing is much more than the use of micros or minicomputers in an effort to reduce costs. It actually constitutes a major modification in business philosophy and the way a corporation uses the vast amount of data at its disposal.

Bender, Eric. "Windows tames the wild mainframe." *PC World*, March 1991, p. 176. Windows packages promise to bring ease of use, consistency, memory management, and hot links between applications to PC front ends for mainframe software.

Berst, Jesse. "The true cost of a GUI." *Computerworld*, October 21, 1991, p. 64. Self-directed IS groups can collapse management layers and increase staff effectiveness, but they can also rock the boat if not eased in correctly.

Boatner, R. Dennis. "LAN backup software." *PC Magazine*, January 29, 1991, p. 273. Flexible, full-featured software for network operations is in demand where system time is too precious to waste, and files too important to lose.

Booker, Ellis. "Frame relay fire ignites." *Computerworld*, September 30, 1991, p. 1. The conference was dominated by talk about frame relay, promising users a cheaper way of interconnecting LANs over WANs.

————————. "Graphic interfaces need artful programmers." *Computerworld*, April 19, 1991, p. 41. GUI technologies, which many believe are the future core of user computing, are putting new demands on software developers. Those developers must now create systems and interfaces as aesthetically pleasing as they are functional.

————————. "New service a welcome guest at Hyatt." *Computerworld*, July 15, 1991, p. 51. Hyatt Hotels Corp. completed the most ambitious step in its migration to Unix: replacing its central IBM mainframe-based reservation system with a relational database management system on multiple Unix processors.

Bozman, Jean S. "JPL's downsizing initiative raises data integrity issues." *Computerworld*, July 22, 1991, p. 29. Downsizing has taken hold here at the Jet Propulsion Laboratories (JPL), an earthly outpost for interplanetary communication that historically has handled most of its data processing on mainframes.

Breidenbach, Susan. "Expo debuts dBASE IV server edition for SQL after delays." *LAN Times*, August 5, 1991, p. 5. Ashton-Tate Corp. was trying to bring dBASE programmers back to the fold with a new version of dBASE IV that doubles as a front end to the Microsoft/Sybase SQL Server.

————————. "Frame Relay, SMDS, Accelerate WANs." *LAN Times*, October 21, 1991, p. 58. While it is a packet-switching technology like its aging X.25 predecessor, Frame Relay offers higher bandwidth and quicker response times.

————————. "OS makers meeting 'smaller' demands." *LAN Times*, August 19, 1991, p. 11. The recent rash of peer-to-peer network announcements is a strong indication that the LAN industry is looking increasingly to the nation's small- and medium-sized businesses to make up the next big wave of networking.

Butler, Martin and Robin Bloor. "Distributed database." *DBMS*, September 1991, p. 16. The primary problem for network administration is not how to set up LANs but how to interconnect them.

———————. "SQL's clouded future." *DBMS*, August 1991, p. 17. SQL promotes interoperability between software products, and as such, the level of support for it is encouraging and healthy for the industry. However, SQL is not without its problems, and potential users of SQL should be aware of them.

Castrucci, Steve. "Office systems migrate, shrink, and become cost-effective." *Computing Canada*, January 17, 1991, p. 18. The three main reasons for "migrating" an office system to a smaller computer are improved control over the system, cost savings for the organization, and the creation of a distributed, cooperative processing computing platform.

Chivvis, Andrei M. "FGIC: A case study in success." *LAN Times*, May 20, 1991, p. 78. FGIC had to find a way to access and turn around information in increasingly short periods in order to remain competitive.

Circa, Joe. "Downsizing doesn't mean the death of the mainframe." *Computing Canada*, January 3, 1991, p. 8. The issue is not whether the mainframe will survive, but how it can best be incorporated into an overall enterprise strategy. A key role for the mainframe will be as a corporate data repository.

Clark, Frederick P. "Strength in numbers: Networking several smaller AS/400s offers a cost-effective way to get the power of a big machine at a cheaper price." *Computerworld*, October 14, 1991, p. 93.

Comaford, Christine. "Don't say the D word." *Computerworld*, October 21, 1991, p. 94. Old pros aren't always thrilled at the opportunity to become young novices again. Change can be very threatening. Comaford enumerates several suggested methods to try.

———————. "Graphical user interfaces: Keep them sleek and simple." *Computerworld*, April 22, 1991, p. 37.

Connor, Deni. "LAN Workplace for DOS widens access to protocols." *LAN Times*, October 21, 1991, p. 44. The interoperability pieces are starting to fall into place with Novell's NetWare.

Coursey, David. "Frame relay bypasses WAN bottlenecks." *InfoWorld*, April 8, 1991, p. S1. Frame relay, an emerging international networking standard, gives witness to the virtue of simplicity, resulting in a protocol well suited for handling large amounts of "bursty" data.

Cox, Tom. "Peer-to-peer computing." *Oracle Magazine*, Spring 1991, p. 43. There are at least four different areas of computing that are correctly identified by the phrase *client-server*. The computing areas that use this architecture include file sharing, database serving, computation engine sharing, and the X Window System display.

CrossComm Corp., "Building enterprise networks: The fundamentals of internetworking," Special Report, 1991. The basic building block of a corporate internetwork is the local area network (LAN). An internetwork is a network of LANs.

Currid, Cheryl and Jeffrey Mason. "SQL support levels vary for six front ends." *PC Week*, November 12, 1990, p. 155. Client/server operates differently on multi-user PC databases than do current-generation PC databases. Client/server combinations split the tasks of database applications.

_____. "'NATO' won't help companies shrink mainframes." *PC Week*, March 25, 1991, p. 68. Are you trying to shrink the mainframe? Make sure you aren't guilty of NATO: No Action, Talk Only. While pundits pontificate on the topic, I've come up with my own 10-step plan of action.

_____. "Computer support staffs lead organizational change." *PC Week*, May 14, 1990, p. 139. Change is a dirty word in many sectors of corporate America, and nobody knows that better than PC managers.

_____. "Downsizing can evoke shock, disbelief, and anger." *PC Week*, September 10, 1990, p, 147. The consensus among the speakers: Get ready—downsizing is going to happen. Be careful, watch what you're doing, but do it. Audience reaction was mixed. There was shock, disbelief, anger, and denial.

_____. "Getting simple things right paves way for downsizing." *PC Week*, April 23, 1990, p. 115. How are smart companies dealing with downsizing? The authors provide a few guidelines.

_____. "The time for LAN application downsizing is now." *PC Week*, January 14, 1991, p. 72. If my radar is tuned to the right frequency, one of the hottest concepts will be downsizing computer applications. The signals are loud and clear: Corporate computing platforms will (and should) be challenged.

_____. Today's PC support staffs aren't ready for downsizing." *PC Week*, April 16, 1990, p. 171. But once you've gotten over the technology hurdle, the bigger hurdle will remain: people. Companies haven't built up the necessary human infrastructure to support LANs correctly. All too often, microcomputers have been looked upon as toys.

Cusack, Sally. "Insuring success with patience." *Computerworld*, August 5, 1991, p. 45. Although the firm has smoothly completed the transformation of 50 of its larger offices from minicomputers to PC LAN platforms, it has decided to take a break. The biggest challenge is to determine how best to manage remote computing.

Daly, James. "Complexity lurks for Windows programmers." *Computerworld*, March 18, 1991, p. 16. Windows is the best thing yet to come along for PC users, but if you employ it improperly, it only winds up creating a new layer of fluff and static.

Darling, Charles B. "Waiting for distributed database." *DBMS*, September 1991, p. 46. A geographic information system makes use of elements of distributed database.

Dauber, Steven, "Finding Fault." *Byte*, March 1991, p. 207. As networks become more widespread and important, fault management and performance monitoring become business necessities.

DePompa, Barbara. "Choosing a computing platform requires careful study." *MIS Week*, May 28, 1990, p. 30. Although the decision to buy networked microcomputers, a minicomputer, or a mainframe system is based on far more than the merits of these technologies, you should know the advantages and disadvantages of each before you buy.

Derfler, Frank J., Jr., and Kimberly J. Maxwell. "The media move the message." *PC Magazine*, September 10, 1991, p. 351. Finding, selecting, buying, and installing the communication links between LAN segments is often a challenging proposition.

——————————, and Steve Rigney. "Smart links between LAN segments." *PC Magazine*, September 10, 1991, p. 121. When you need to bridge the gap between two LANs, the range of choices spans everything from E-mail gateways to bulletin board systems to access servers. The real heart of LAN-to-LAN connectivity is perhaps found in bridges and routers.

Derfler, Frank. *PC Magazine guide to connectivity*. Emeryville, CA: Ziff Davis, 1991.

DiDio, Laura. "Sales are soaring for new LAN interoperability products." *LAN Times*, October 7, 1991, p. 26. It's hardly a secret that in 1991, internetworking and interoperability are the hottest-selling devices and most talked-about topics in the LAN industry.

——————————. "SQL access group demos interoperability as reality." *LAN Times*, August 5, 1991. The SQL Access Group's ability to stage a successful interoperability demo with a multitude of divergent workstations and database servers interoperating in real time with no apparent problems is a milestone for the LAN industry.

Duncan, Judy. "Front ends; *InfoWorld* test drives four software programs for tapping into database servers." *InfoWorld*, March 25, 1991, p. 56. Now, after years of fanfare and promises, the client/server model of computing is finally becoming a tangible solution.

Duncan, Ray. "Actor: A development environment for Windows applications." *PC Magazine*, March 26, 1991, p. 369. A full-fledged object-oriented language that lends itself well to application development, Actor nonetheless has some severe limitations.

Ferris, David. "Multiprocessing: The new LAN architecture." *LAN Times*, June 3, 1991, p. 56.

_____. Security and PC networks: Old problems, new cures."
LAN Times, August 5, 1991, p. 33. Computer security is a recognized
issue with mainframe-based systems, but it's new to the world of PC
networking. Many of the problems are similar, and some—such as
viruses and software licensing—demand new solutions.

Fetterolf, Peter. "Connectivity: The sum of its parts." *Byte*, November
1991, p. 197. We are making headway connecting the worlds of wide
area networks (WANs), LANs, and metropolitan area networks
(MANs). Bridges, multi-protocol routers, and other devices are the
glue that is finally making the promise of network connectivity come
true.

Finkelstein, Richard and Colin White. "The pluses and minuses of going
distributed." *Computerworld*, June 3, 1991, p. 101. Most organizations are focusing their attention on client/server and cooperative processing. Both these distributed computing technologies offer several
pluses, but these potential benefits come with unresolved questions.

Finkelstein, Richard. "Four rules for downsizing databases." *Data Based
Advisor*, April 1991, p. 67. Aside from its benefits, downsizing also
has its costs and potential traps that you'll have to understand before
undertaking any major project. The author gives some rules for avoiding the associated risks.

_____. "SQL database servers run the gamut." *LAN Times*,
June 17, 1991, p. 65. The popularity of OS/2 and Unix database servers continues to grow. Database servers offer greater price/perfor-
mance, more scalability to various platforms, greater productivity, and
greater support for distribution of data.

Fisher, Sharon. "A working definition." *Computerworld*, October 7, 1991,
p. 98. As the name implies, TCP/IP stands for two separate protocols.

_____. "Data security experts say errors are greatest threat."
InfoWorld, September 9, 1991, p. S74. When it comes to computer
security, many corporations focus on protecting themselves from outsiders rather than insiders. But more often than not, crimes are inside
jobs.

_____. "Dueling protocols." *Byte*, March 1991, p. 183. One
of the hottest topics in networking today is network management.
Much of the attention in managing heterogeneous networks has
focused on two families of network management protocols.

_____. "Five ways networks pay off." *PC World*, March 1991,
p. 193. Organizations of all sizes are installing networks at an amazing
rate, anticipating enormous payoffs. Networks enable automation of
routine tasks, group data analysis, staying close to your customers, and
enterprise-wide access to data.

_____. "New Windows on corporate data." *PC World*, August
1991, p. 189. PCs will run an application developed with SQL Win-

dows. It allows executives to use a Windows front end to query an Oracle database on the VAX.

—————————. "Parts for assembly." *Computerworld*, October 7, 1991, p. 99. To connect a PC network to an enterprise network using TCP/IP, several pieces are required.

—————————. "Superman? No, superserver." *Computerworld*, May 6, 1991, p. 73. LAN server vendors are touting power and speed, but buyers need to decide how much is actually too much.

—————————. "TCP/IP." *Computerworld*, October 7, 1991, p. 97. TCP/IP is not for everyone, especially now that personal computers have entered the scene. Many corporations are now looking at using this protocol to link their PC LANs into the rest of the enterprise and to hosts from the likes of IBM and Digital Equipment Corp.

—————————. "Unix, DOS, and OS/2: There is no simple answer." *LAN Times*, October 7, 1991, p. 145. The problem is deciding which PC operating system—DOS, OS/2, or Unix—is the best one on which to base your network.

Fitzgerald, Michael. "Aetna links laptops and LANs for field engineers." *Computerworld*, August 12, 1991, p. 56. When Aetna Life and Casualty Co. downsized to LANs through much of its operation, it decided to give its field engineers laptop computers that linked into the LANs.

Flynn, Laurie. "For most managers, Windows networking is still an oxymoron." *InfoWorld*, August 26, 1991, p. 35. Hearing that networking Windows was still such a sore subject not only among industry luminaries, but an audience of business users, was unnerving.

Foshay, Laird. "Client/server computing: A state of mind." *Personal Workstation*, March 1991, p. 80. Increased productivity depends on a broad, clear vision of the role of computing in our lives.

Foster, Ed. "Payroll Downsizing." *InfoWorld*, March 11, 1991, p. S3. The great attraction is the greater flexibility it will provide. Another area where the PC LAN solution appeals to users—at least in comparison to the mainframe system—is security.

—————————. "WANs: Are they too big and too slow to play with your LANs?" *InfoWorld*, April 8, 1991, p. S1. WANs such as IBM's System Network Architecture (SNA) have been around a comparatively long time, so they are likely to seem rather old and slow to those used to being on the cutting edge.

Furger, Roberta. "The ten deadly network sins." *PC World*, March 1991, p. 201. Not surprisingly, most of the troubles organizations encounter come down to unrealistic expectations about the commitment required in planning, installing, and managing the net.

Germann, Christopher. "WANs: Conditions Count." *LAN Times 1991–1992 Buyers Guide*, p. 10. Mainframes and minis are not going to be shelved for LANs. Instead, important developments will center around internetworking.

Gibson, Steve. "Developing software for the Windows API is no simple task." *InfoWorld*, June 10, 1991, p. 34. The Windows "difficulty dilemma" arises from the fact that the development and debugging tools we've had to work with have been inadequate for the task of managing the weirdness of Windows programming.

Gillespie, Kelly. "Secrets of Novell's NetWare requestor and Microsoft's SQL server." *Data Based Advisor*, July 1991, p. 92. Many networks use Novell's NetWare and want to run Microsoft's OS/2-based SQL Server. One solution is to use Novell's NetWare Requestor for OS/2.

Glass, Brett. "Database Tower of Babel: Portable SQL still a dream." *InfoWorld*, March 11, 1991, p. S14. Database vendors frequently make inflated claims about the portability of database applications written in Structured Query Language, or SQL. Alas, while this "SQL Myth" might be so in an ideal world, it has little to do with reality.

_____. "Windows 3.0 and Networks." *Byte*, April 1991, p. 343. What you don't know about Windows 3.0 and LANs can get you into a lot of trouble. The author lists mistakes to avoid.

Gow, Kathleen A. "No thanks, I can do it by myself." *Computerworld*, May 20, 1991, p. 98. New tools and utilities are helping to turn passive end users into PC adventurers.

Greenstein, Irwin, "Wideband for the 1990s." *Networking Management*, March 1991, p. 70. Frame relay and wideband SMDS are gaining popularity with the spread of distributed processing and multimedia communications. Driving frame relay and SMDS is the need for fast, dynamic bandwidth for bursty and intermittent applications.

Griendling, Paul. "The bright side of WANs." *California Lawyer*, December 1991, p. 64. With a wide area network, every workstation in the firm has access to documents.

Hammons, Jim. "Teaching minis new tricks." *Computerworld*, June 10, 1991, p. 63. Necessary changes lie ahead, but midrange machines are proving they can be right for server jobs.

Hawkins, John L. "Rightsizing. (Microsoft's Corp.'s approach to downsizing)." *Data Based Advisor*, April 1991, p. 10. Why can't Microsoft and IBM jointly pick a path and follow it? Two reasons: a changing marketplace and divergent goals.

Hendricks, Mark. "Visual tools aid Windows program developers." *PC World*, March 1991, p. 78.

Hildebrand, Carol. "Managing the aftermath." *Computerworld*, August 5, 1991, p. 58. The PC has made the world a different place for IS departments. From programming to organization to vendor relations, here's a look at its dramatic impact.

Holmes, Bill. "Going down (downsizing from IBM System/36 minicomputers to microcomputers)," *IBM System User*, March 1990, p. 33. Perhaps surprisingly, the best solution for the S/36 user may be to downsize his RPG systems to a PC—or a network of PCs.

Hubley, Mary. "Distributed open environments." *Byte*, November 1991, p. 229. Open Software Foundation and Unix International pave the way toward true interoperability.

Hylas, Robert E., Bruce Gordon, and Glenn R. Dinetz. "The upside of downsized systems." *Best's Review, Property/Casualty Insurance*, December 1989, p. 78.

"Installing SQL server on an existing NetWare network," *Microsoft Technical Note*, January 1991. In some cases it may be necessary to install the entire LAN environment—the NetWare file server, the NetWare Requester, DOS and OS/2 clients, and SQL server. In other cases, SQL server will be installed on an existing NetWare network.

International Data Corp. "Interoperability: Cornerstone of open systems." *Computerworld*, October 7, 1991. Interoperability and open systems are terms commonly and loosely used in conversations about computing. The emergence of open systems depends on a new generation of sophisticated users seeking solutions to their application requirements.

Janson, Jennifer L. "Smaller hardware can mean safer data, users say." *PC Week*, September 10, 1990, p. 148. MIS managers seem to agree that data is more secure on LANs than on other networks, with benefits ranging from better data backup and data control to increased reliability of data over time.

_____. "Survey or no survey, some MIS staff fear 'downsizing' will mean 'layoff.'" *PC Week*, September 10, 1990, p. 147. Neither a *PC Week* survey nor industry analysts foresee many management information systems (MIS) staff members hitting the unemployment line because of downsizing to smaller systems.

Juneau, Lucie. "End-user liberation forces change in IS mindset." *Computerworld*, August, 5, 1991, p. 59. Many users have learned not just computer jargon but also how to program applications and make hardware and software selections.

_____. "The trials, tribulations, and triumphs of TCP/IP." *Computerworld*, October 7, 1991, p. 103. Despite compatibility snags and implementation glitches, users say TCP/IP is worth it.

Kac, Walter. "An opinion on OS/2." *LAN Times*, October 7, 1991, p. 151. Today's operating environment demands a very high level of concurrency.

King, Julia. "Linking LANs: Payoffs, pitfalls, pathways." *Computerworld*, April 11, 1991, p. 67. First came turf wars with information systems personnel, who resisted the idea of spreading around centralized computing assets. Next came the lengthy process of choosing a network operating system.

_____. "Still up in the air." *Computerworld*, May 27, 1991, p. 71. Despite vendors' claims to the contrary, integrated network management does not exist today. No single system can manage the entire sprawl of interconnected, multi-vendor, multi-technology LANs many companies are contending with.

Kosiur, Dave. "Macintosh: The universal client?" *InfoWorld*, August 5, 1991, p. S1. The trend toward heterogeneous networks and multiple computing platforms makes it harder for customers to settle on only one computer as the perfect client. Apple Computer would like the Macintosh to step into this morass as the ideal universal client.

LaPlant, Alice. "Downsizing difficulty." *InfoWorld*, March 11, 1991, p. S6. At Western General Services, a Chicago-based insurance company, officials made the decision to move one of their main applications to LAN-based applications. Though it was ultimately successful, it was not accomplished without some mistakes being made.

_____. "Downsizing with superservers: Experts urge caution." *InfoWorld*, March 11, 1991, p. S11. The superserver is becoming a key strategic tool in the eyes of many corporate IS managers. But those on the cutting edge of this technology warn that it can be dangerously sharp.

_____. "Guarding their turf." *InfoWorld*, September 9, 1991, p. S59. The move to corporate-wide networking is causing IS managers to focus on security. LANs are more vulnerable to security risks than their larger system components.

_____. "Leaving MIS standards behind." *PC World*, November 1991, p. 71. Standards are the mainstay of most MIS departments, but if the PC users in your department are confined to particular programs, they may feel limited when more attractive alternatives beckon.

_____. "The tamperproof office." *PC World*, July 1991, p. 238. Guarding against security threats requires a strategy that involves all levels of users and management. Here's how one company protects its most important asset—data.

Lauriston, Robert. "Can you do better than NetWare?" *PC World*, March 1991, p. 157. NetWare 286 has ruled the roost for years, but networks have grown. The author tested Microsoft LAN Manager, Banyan Vines, and Novell's own NetWare 386 and tells whether they offer enough speed and reliability for today's demanding LANs.

Letson, Russell. "OLTP migrates to PC LANs." *Systems Integration*, May 1990, p. 40. On-line transaction processing (OLTP) has not traditionally been considered a job for the personal computer (PC) local area network (LAN) area, although nothing in the basic idea of a transaction exceeds the capacity of a DOS-based PC.

Liebing, Edward. "A to Z: Networking basics." *LAN Times 1991–92 Buyers Guide*, p. 14. The best place to start is with good initial planning and laying out what you expect to accomplish.

Lifton, Ron. "Selecting Bridges, Routers." *LAN Times*, October 7, 1991,

p. 99. In order to make intelligent buying decisions, network administrators must decipher the type of technology the manufacturer is offering, evaluate the features and benefits of each product under consideration, and investigate the manufacturer's position in the industry.

Lindquist, Christopher. "Sara Lee adds PC tools to DB2 mix." *Computerworld*, September 16, 1991, p. 24. Moving from a mainframe to PC-based application development was not a step to be taken lightly. Many of the programmers were not PC-literate, and cultural differences had to be considered.

Maglitta, Joseph. "IS dilemma: How to measure your return on investment." *Computerworld*, April 29, 1991, p. 83. Are we getting the value for our IS investment? Nobody can really tell.

Mandell, Mel. "Subaru project aiming to put the right car in the right place. Unisys databases ensure that customers get what they want." *Computerworld*, June 3, 1991, p. 100.

Manson, Carl and J. Scott Haugdahl. "Dynamic and Distributed." *Byte*, March 1991, p. 167. Unless you want a system manager at each distributed site, you need automated network management tools.

Mardesich, Jodi, "Meeting halfway." *InfoWorld*, April 22, 1991, p. 48. The Mac and the PC may finally be on course, but the work isn't over yet.

───────────────. "Novell Consolidates 286 Line with Netware 2.2." *InfoWorld*, February 25, 1991, p. 1.

───────────────. "Windows front ends tame mainframe data access." *InfoWorld*, May 20, 1991, p. S75. Information systems managers are attempting to ease the process of accessing important data by using Windows as a front end to the host.

McCusker, Tom. "Classic mainframe software moves to PCs." *Datamation*, February 1, 1991, p. 50. Longtime IBM mainframe users have strong loyalties to some of the utilities they've been using for the past 20 years. Two of their favorites will soon be available on PCs running Windows 3.0 and OS/2 Presentation Manager.

Molloy, Maureen. "Downsizing to LANs not easy, users say." *Network World*, July 8, 1991, p. 21. Few users have downsized key applications because the implementation process is costly and complex. Many lack the expertise and technical tools necessary, and resistance from both internal MIS personnel and end users is common.

Nance, Barry. "Interoperability today." *Byte*, November 1991, p. 187. The OSI stack provides a blueprint for interoperability and shows that our reach still exceeds our grasp. While interconnecting different systems at the lower levels of the model, getting applications to work together seamlessly across a heterogeneous network is not yet feasible.

───────────────. "Managing Big Blue." *Byte*, March 1991, p.

197. IBM provides some serious network management tools for serious networks.

Nash, Jim. "Downsizing focus shifts to impact IS function." *Computerworld*, September 16, 1991, p. 4. Where top-down management is occurring, systems personnel said, downsizing is orderly and healthy. Some others doubt that the model is practical for their outfits. Sometimes, the PC ethic—don't wait for IS—is the most acceptable method.

_____. "NetWare update has users cheering." *Computerworld*, March 25, 1991, p. 8. Novell Inc.'s replacement of NetWare 286 with NetWare Version 2.2 last week drew applause from network managers.

_____. "Niagara Mohawk looks to tap the power of networking." *Computerworld*, February 25, 1991, p. 52. Enticed by the possibility of increasing database access by as much as 25%, Niagara Mohawk Power Corp. is moving some of its employees off the mainframe and onto PC LANs.

Netware joins the TCP/IC crowd." *InfoWorld*, September 7, 1991, p. 46. A recent convert to TCP/IP, Novell Inc., with a 65% share of the PC LAN market, this year began shipping its advanced network operating system, NetWare 3.11, bundled with TCP/IP server software.

Norman, Carol A. and Robert A. Zawacki. "Teamwork takes work." *Computerworld*, April 1, 1991, p. 77. Self-directed IS groups can collapse management layers and increase staff effectiveness, but they can also rock the boat if not eased in correctly.

Novell, Inc., NetWare 3.11 product brochure. NetWare 3.11 is a sophisticated network operating system that integrates diverse computing resources—from PCs and Unix workstations to Apple Macintoshes and mainframes—into a single, enterprise-wide system.

_____. NetWare Name Service product brochure. NetWare Name Service (NNS) is a naming service that lets NetWare users access resources of multiple servers with a single log-in. Simplifies network administration; gives users access to network resources; supports NetWare security.

_____. NetWare SQL product brochure. With NetWare SQL, you can choose a spreadsheet program, accounting package, fourth-generation programming language (4GL), database manager, and application program generator, all sharing a common database with other users, using other front-ends.

_____. Remote Management Facility (RMF) Version 1.0 product brochure.

O'Brien, Timothy. "IS workers meet, share notes on difficulty, viability of downsizing." *Network World*, July 29, 1991, p. 3. IS employees must also have the experience to use the tools or be given the resources to acquire the skills necessary to use them. Mainframe programmers can require up to one year of retraining.

Pascal, Fabian. "SQL in perspective." *InfoWorld*, July 8, 1991, p. S48. Viewed in the proper perspective, SQL is much better than what we had, but worse than what it should and could have been. Unfortunately, there are some entrenched misconceptions about both positive aspects and flaws.

Pastore, Richard. "Beyond the beginner's slope." *Computerworld*, May 20, 1991, p. 96. In the personal computer environment, developments in hardware and peripherals, operating systems software applications, communications, and connectivity continue to open doors for new kinds of PC uses and users.

Plotkin, Steve. "Determining management issues is vital." *LAN Times*, October 7, 1991, p. 45. As LANs grow and change, a constant goal of MIS and Information Center management is to isolate the critical success factors and vital issues that need attention. One challenge is to focus on significant mission issues while deflecting technical trivia.

Porter, Blair. "Offloading development to the PC pays off for CGI." *Computing Canada*, September 27, 1990, p. 47. Processing one million database transactions daily in a multi-user, database server environment, a major Canadian consultancy is using a PC database management system to prototype, develop, and test mainframe applications.

"Product highlights." *Computerworld*, October 7, 1991, p. 98. In the increasingly crowded TCP/IP software marketplace, personal computer software vendors are being forced to differentiate their products. Here's a sampling of where some vendors claim to stand out.

Radding, Alan. "Linking databases: Many paths." *Computerworld*, June 3, 1991, p. 93. Users don't care where data resides, or whether it's scattered among mainframes, minicomputers, personal computers, or local area networks. They just want transparent, real-time, online access and update capabilities—now!

Rose, Marshall. "Making the transition from TCP/IP to OSI." *Computerworld*, October 7, 1991, p. 99. It's questionable when—and if— OSI will achieve dominance over TCP/IP, but it's still a good idea to plan for coexistence or an eventual transition.

Ryan, Alan J. "Cigna re-engineers itself." *Computerworld*, July 8, 1991, p. 79. What does a reinsurance firm get when it replaces 85% of its systems and organizes itself along team lines? Annual savings of $1.5 million and quick delivery of information to line staff.

Ryan, Bob. "On the fast track." *Byte*, November 1991, p. 361. If you need to interconnect your company's LANs, you need to look at frame relay services.

Sautter, William. "Improving LAN Performance." *Oracle* Magazine, Fall 1991, p. 78. Over the past year, two trends have emerged that are garnering significant attention in the computer industry: the need to increase local area network (LAN) performance and the desire to rightsize applications from minicomputers and mainframes to PC-based LANs.

Scheier, Robert L. "Destroying the myths about downsizing." *PC Week*, September 10, 1990, p. 87. Down-and-dirty cost-cutting is not the major reason companies move applications from mainframes or minis to PC LANs. The greater motivation is to give users the data they need, when they need it, in a form they can use.

_____. "Effectiveness, not dollars, drives downsizing." *PC Week*, September 10, 1990, p. 147. Analysts and portfolio managers get more information, more quickly, from their PC/LAN than they could from a minicomputer or mainframe.

_____. "FGIC gets more bang for the buck by downsizing; builds a better system, saves $4 million a year." *PC Week*, March 25, 1991, p. 16. Developing and enhancing applications on a LAN is the only way the New York-based bond insurer can eliminate the generation gap between its applications and its business processes.

_____. "Local area networks pull end run on the mainframe." *PC Week*, September 10, 1990, p. 1. PC LANs increasingly are becoming the platform of choice for running mission-critical applications. But the move to PC LANs isn't entirely at the expense of the "glass house" mainframes or the staffs that support them.

_____. "Networks replace stand-alone PCs, but users come out ahead." *PC Week*, October 1, 1990, p. 131. Users are happier than ever because they are now linked to a network that serves up standard versions of popular applications, more disk space than was provided by their stand-alone PCs, and mainframe connectivity in a window environment.

Schussel, George. "Distributed DBMS decisions." *Computerworld*, May 6, 1991, p. 81. Will you go with a client/server DBMS or a true distributed DBMS?

Schute, Phil. "Client/Server workstation computing." Seminar, Wave Technologies. Downsizing and the graphical environment are, to some degree, causing us to rethink our strategies of how our networks are laid out.

Scott, Karyl. "Parlez-vous TCP/IP?" *InfoWorld*, October 7, 1991, p. 45. Internetworks, once the exclusive preserve of government and university researchers armed with sophisticated Unix workstations and supercomputers, are now widespread. And the main reason is the TCP/IP protocol suite.

Scott, Mary E. "A downside to downsizing." *ComputerWorld*, September

30, 1991, p. 62. Are you frustrated by the skills gap—or gulf—that's stalling your company's ability to leverage new technology fully? There's no quick or easy fix to having a mismatched technical skills base

Senne, Lynn. "Strategies for handling today's vast LANs." *LAN Times*, October 7, 1991, p. 123. Enterprise networking is getting vast and complex. In addition to the original shared-resources concept of a LAN, we now see many new paradigms emerging: distributed computing, workgroup/collaborative computing, and enterprise computing.

Shafer, Les. "Connecting Unix and DOS." *LAN Times*, October 7, 1991, p. 154. Unix is a protected OS offering better performance and greater capacities than DOS and is available on a range of systems.

Shah, Kumar. "Interconnectivity services in the corporate network." *LAN Times*, August 19, 1991, p. 53. Corporate MIS managers must select from a broad range of internetworking tools that support their SNA, DECnet, TCP/IP, and OSI networks.

Shaw, Carrel. "PC vendors move into position as end-users downsize." *Computing Canada*, January 17, 1991, p. 19. In most downsized organizations PCs will be the hardware of choice. And PC vendors including Compaq, Inc., Sun Microsystems, Inc., and Dell Computer Corp. will be competing to provide the most appropriate solutions to meet client needs.

Shirk, Gary. "Building a Superserver." *LAN Times*, June 3, 1991, p. 61. Processing on a file server is I/O intensive. The applications server gives the CPU much more work. Today, the most obvious need for multiple CPUs is in database management applications.

Sloman, Jeffrey. "Control Central." *Byte*, March 1991, p. 175. Tools, techniques and advice for managing centralized network services.

Smalley, Eric. "Costs are declining for TCP/IP on PC LANs." *Computerworld*, October 7, 1991, p. 102. Changes in the last few years have made it more affordable to bring TCP/IP to the personal computer local area network environment.

Stallings, William. *The business guide to local area networks*. Carmel, IN: Howard W. Sams & Co., 1990.

Stanley, Floyd. "Making the move: Creating a downsizing plan." Seminar, Wave Technologies. This is an opportunity to do what you do best. Do what you've always been doing, just on a different platform.

Stephenson, Peter. "LAN bridges: Connecting your LAN to a world of information." *Government Computer News*, August 15, 1988, p. 63. Each type of internet has its own set of communications parameters. Solutions often include specialized hardware as well as software to drive it. The solutions are by no means obvious.

——————————. "Mixing and Matching LANs." *Byte*, March 1991, p.

157. The primary problem for network administration is not how to set up LANs but how to interconnect them.

Sullivan-Trainor, Michael. "Everything's relational." *Computerworld*, February 25, 1991, p. 69.

Syed, Rehan and Sam S. Gill. "A CASE for Rightsizing Applications." *Oracle Magazine*, Fall 1991, p. 82.

"Taming the Mac's network albatrosses." *LAN Times, 1991–92 Buyers Guide*, p. 11. How do you internetwork the Mac so it works?

Taylor, Allen G. "How vendors have and have not met criticism." *Computerworld*, February 25, 1991, p. 73.

_____. "The next standard for SQL and what it will mean to you." *Computerworld*, February 25, 1991, p. 72.

Tomlinson, Gary B. "Redefining interoperability in the 90s." *LAN Times*, August 19, 1991, p. 50. A completely new approach to network computing was taken in the early eighties. This concept has evolved into the modern network operating systems, but are now becoming more commonplace on enterprise-wide internetworks of LANs and WANs.

Trutna, Rick. "SQL: An idea whose time has come." *LAN Times*, June 17, 1991, p. 64. In the information age, a company's database is one of its most valuable assets. As downsizing becomes a business reality, users will need to access this database through their PC LANs.

Udell, John, Tom Thompson, and Tom Yager. "Mix 'n' match LAN." *Byte*, November 1991, p. 272. The business computing landscape today is like a loose federation of republics; Macs in the marketing department, Unix workstations in engineering, PCs for general business. The challenge is to unite these republics without compromising their individuality.

Ullman, Ellen. "You can't run on everything." *Byte*, November, 1991, p. 255. How to choose a portability tool kit or decide on a long-term portability strategy. Ideally, you should be able to write portable applications, but you might find it more practical to rewrite the software for specific applications. Portability is a goal, not an edict.

Vaughan-Nichols, Steven J. "Transparent data exchange." *Byte*, November 1991, p. 211. Data transparency refers to being able to use data residing on different types of systems connected by a network. We have made progress in transferring the data between systems, but mere access to files located on systems with different architectures isn't enough.

Vinzant, David R. "Running Oracle server for OS/2 on NetWare." *Oracle News*, March 1991, p. 5. As database servers go, the Oracle server for OS/2 comes with reasonably good instructions for installing it on Novell networks.

_____. "Getting started with your own data." *Oracle News*, June 1991, p. 6. So you've decided to try using an Oracle Server for your database needs. But one big question still looms in your head: How will it behave with our data?

Wexler, Joanie M. "Growth of networks nurtured at EPA." *Computerworld*, June 3, 1991, p. 59. People are shifting mainframe applications to LANs because of the diversity of what people are doing and because it's cheaper to add computing power to LANs.

—————————. "Hospital Consolidates LANs." *Computerworld*, September 16, 1991, p. 81. A major integration effort is underway at a large hospital, where the foundation is in place for an organization-wide network aimed at blending an assortment of local area networks and computers that have sprung up.

—————————. "PC users gain part-time X terminal capabilities." *Computerworld*, March 4, 1991, p. 45. The infiltration of X Window System–based networks into corporate computing does not necessarily mean companies must swap out their PCs for X terminals or full-blown Unix workstations.

—————————. "Hub routing modules address growing networks." *Computerworld*, July 8, 1991, p. 50. Routing is intended to make efficient use of the network by sending data over the most available and direct route between nodes. It also allows the partitioning of networks for tighter access control by eliminating the "broadcast" nature of bridges.

Winship, Sally. "Buyers applaud rapid application development SQL front ends provide." *PC Week*, November 12, 1990, p. 155. While Structural Query Language (SQL) front ends afford developers a number of benefits, paramount among them is the ability to develop complex applications quickly.

Zachmann, William F. *Upsizing: The other half of the equation."* *PC Magazine*, December 11, 1990, p. 95. Upon further reflection I've realized that downsizing, important as it may be, is only part of the picture. Another, equally important aspect is what I've chosen to label "upsizing."

Zornes, Aaron. "Relational DBMS: Making peace with the past." *Computerworld*, February 25, 1991, p. 65. The walls that separate non-relational and relational database management systems are gradually starting to crumble.

Index